D0715147

Malalai Joya was four days old when the Soviet Union invaded Afghanistan. Following a childhood spent in refugee camps in Iran and Pakistan, she returned to Taliban-ruled Afghanistan in the late 1990s, where she worked for underground organisations promoting the cause of women. At the historic Loya Jirga assembly in 2003 where Afghanistan's new constitution was debated, she made world headlines. In 2005, at the age of twenty-seven, she was the youngest person to be elected to the new Parliament. Since then, she has survived numerous assassination attempts and continued to press the cause of those who elected her. She received the International Human Rights in Film Award at Berlin in 2007, was awarded the Anna Politkovskaya Award in 2008, and named on *Time* magazine's list of the world's 100 most influential people in 2010.

Visit her website: www.malalaijoya.com

RAISING MY VOICE

THE EXTRAORDINARY STORY
OF THE AFGHAN WOMAN WHO
DARES TO SPEAK OUT

MALALAI JOYA
WITH
DERRICK O'KEEFE

RIDER

London · Sydney · Auckland · Johannesburg

3 5 7 9 10 8 6 4

First Published in 2009 by Rider, an imprint of Ebury Publishing
This edition published by Rider in 2010
A Random House Group Company

Copyright © 2009 Malalai Joya

Malalai Joya has asserted her right to be identified as the author of this Work
in accordance with the Copyright, Designs and Patents Act 1988

All rights reserved. No part of this publication may be reproduced, stored in a
retrieval system, or transmitted in any form or by any means, electronic,
mechanical, photocopying, recording or otherwise, without the prior
permission of the copyright owner

The Random House Group Limited Reg. No. 954009

Addresses for companies within the Random House Group can be found at
www.randomhouse.co.uk

A CIP catalogue record for this book is available from the British Library

Penguin Random House is committed to a sustainable future for
our business, our readers and our planet. This book is made from
Forest Stewardship Council® certified paper.

Printed and bound in Great Britain by Clays Ltd, Elcograf S.p.A.

ISBN 9781846041501

Copies are available at special rates for bulk orders. Contact the sales
development team on 020 7840 8487 for more information

To buy books by your favourite authors and register for offers visit
www.randomhouse.co.uk

Verses quoted on page 37 are from the song 'In Praise of Fighting' from *The Mother*
(1930) by Bertolt Brecht and from the poem 'In Praise of Learning' by Bertolt Brecht
in *Selected Poems of Bertolt Brecht*, translation and introduction by H R Hays, NY:
Grove Press, London: Evergreen Press. Copyright 1949. First Grove edition 1959.
Whilst every effort has been made to trace all copyright holders, if any have been
inadvertently overlooked the author and publisher will be pleased to make the
necessary arrangement at the first opportunity.

CONTENTS

ACKNOWLEDGEMENTS

I would like to acknowledge friends, family and supporters for their invaluable assistance in bringing this book to fruition. Derrick O'Keefe is one of my supporters who encouraged me to share my story. I was finally willing to take this step because I trusted him to be my co-writer and was sure that he would treat not only my story, but that of my country and its people, with respect. I am deeply grateful for the countless hours he devoted to this project.

The Defence Committee for Malalai Joya – made up of dedicated volunteers both inside and outside Afghanistan – provided invaluable help to the project, including research and translation.

This book would not have been possible without the efforts of Mable Elmore, Hakeem Naim and Neda Raheen, Gina Whitfield, Sonali Kolhaktar, James Ingalls, and Catherine O'Keefe, all of whom generously shared their time, skills and labour.

Special thanks as well to Maryanne Vollers for taking on a formidable editing task on a tight deadline, and to Hilary McMahon and Natasha Daneman for bringing this book to a wide audience in a number of countries.

Malalai Joya

LIST OF ILLUSTRATIONS

Map on Page X
Afghanistan and its neighbours

Plate Section
With the exception of image 19, which is copyright Jenny Matthews, all photographs are the copyright of the Defence Committee for Malalai Joya.

1. Malalai Joya as a little girl.
2. Malalai's historic speech on 17 December 2003 at the Loya Jirga in Kabul.
3. Speaking at a rally back in Farah.
4. Malalai Joya's maiden speech during the first session of Parliament in December 2005.
5. During a question and answer period in April 2006.
6. Sayyaf, the MP from Paghman who violently opposed Malalai Joya's comments in April 2006.
7. The former jihadi commander Alam Khan Azadi.
8. A heated television debate in 2007 with Jabar Shelgari, an ally of Sayyaf's.
9. On 7 May 2006, Malalai Joya was physically attacked in Parliament.
10. Malalai and her bodyguards, waiting for the building to empty after the May 2006 attack.
11. Malalai Joya speaking at a mosque in Farah.
12. Malalai talking to girls in Farah.
13. Malalai Joya with children at the orphanage in Farah.
14. Malalai meets the bereaved father of two children killed in Takhar.

15. Afghan women protest against Malalai Joya's suspension from Parliament in May 2007.
16. Women march to the United Nations' office in Jalalabad to demand Malalai's reinstatement.
17. Protestors in New York on 21 June 2007.
18. Malalai Joya addressing the European Parliament in 2008.
19. Malalai was awarded the prestigious Anna Politkovskaya Award in 2008 (© Jenny Matthews).

*To the Bashiras, Rahellas, Bibi Guls, Pukhtanas
and all my oppressed people whose sighs, tears
and sorrows nobody sees*

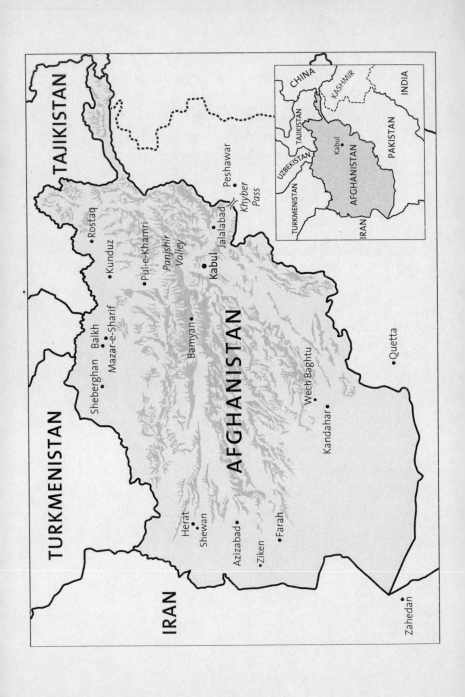

INTRODUCTION

DUST IN THE EYES
OF THE WORLD

I COME FROM A LAND OF TRAGEDY called Afghanistan. My life has taken some unusual turns, but in many ways my story is the story of a generation. For the thirty years I have been alive, my country has suffered from the constant scourge of war. Most Afghans my age and younger have known only bloodshed, displacement and occupation. When I was a baby in my mother's arms, the Soviet Union invaded my country. When I was four years old, my family and I were forced to live as refugees in Iran and then Pakistan. Millions of Afghans were killed or exiled, like my family, during the battle-torn 1980s. When the Russians finally left, and their puppet regime was overthrown, we faced a vicious civil war between fundamentalist warlords, followed by the rule of the depraved and medieval Taliban.

After the tragic day of 11 September 2001, many in Afghanistan thought that – with the overthrow of the Taliban – they might finally see some light, some justice and progress. But it was not to be. The Afghan people have been betrayed once again by those who are claiming to help them. More than seven years after the invasion by America and its allies, we are still faced with foreign occupation and an American-backed government filled with warlords who are just like the Taliban. Instead of putting these ruthless murderers on trial for war crimes, the United States and its allies placed them in positions of power, where they continue to terrorise ordinary Afghans.

You may be shocked to hear this, because the truth about Afghanistan has been hidden behind a smokescreen of words and images carefully crafted by the United States and its NATO allies and repeated without question by the Western media.

You may have been led to believe that once the Taliban was driven from power, justice returned to my country. Afghan women like me, voting and running for office, have been held up as proof that the United States has brought democracy and women's rights to Afghanistan.

But it is all a lie, dust in the eyes of the world.

I am the youngest Member of the Afghan Parliament, but I have been banished from my seat and threatened with death because I speak the truth about the warlords and criminals in the puppet government of Hamid Karzai. I have already survived at least five assassination attempts and uncounted plots against me. Because of this, I am forced to live like a fugitive within my own country. A trusted uncle heads my detail of bodyguards, and we move to different houses every night to stay a step ahead of my enemies.

To hide my identity, I must travel under the cover of the heavy cloth burqa, which to me is a symbol of women's oppression, like a shroud for the living. Even during the dark days of the Taliban I could at least go outside under the burqa to teach girls in secret classes. But today I don't feel safe under my burqa, even with armed guards to escort me. My visitors are searched for weapons, and even the flowers at my wedding had to be checked for bombs. I cannot tell you my family's name, or the name of my husband, because it would place them in terrible danger. And for this reason, I have changed several other names in this book.

I call myself Joya – an alias I adopted during the time of the Taliban when I worked as an underground activist. The name Joya has great significance in my country. Sarwar Joya was an

Afghan writer, poet, and constitutionalist who struggled against injustice during the early twentieth century. He spent nearly twenty-four years of his life in jails, and was finally killed because he would not compromise his democratic principles.

I know that because I refuse to compromise my opposition to the warlords and fundamentalists or soften my speeches denouncing them, then I, too, may join Joya in the long list of Afghans who have died for freedom. But you cannot compromise the truth. And I am not afraid of an early death if it advances the cause of justice. Even the grave cannot silence my voice, because there are others who would carry on after me.

The sad fact is that, in Afghanistan, killing a woman is like killing a bird. The United States has tried to justify its occupation with rhetoric about 'liberating' Afghan women, but we remain caged in our country, without access to justice and still ruled by women-hating criminals. Fundamentalists still preach that 'a woman should be in her house or in the grave'. In most places it is still not safe for a woman to appear in public uncovered, or to walk on the street without a male relative. Girls are still sold into marriage. Rape goes unpunished every day.

For both men and women in Afghanistan, our lives are short and often wracked by violence, loss and anguish. The life expectancy here is less than forty-five years – an age that in the West is called 'middle age'. We live in desperate poverty. A staggering 70 per cent of Afghans survive on less than two dollars per day. And it is estimated that over half of Afghan men and 80 per cent of women are illiterate. In the past few years, hundreds of women have committed self-immolation – literally burned themselves to death – to escape their miseries.

This is the history I have lived through, and this is the tragic situation today that with many others I am working to change. I am no better than any of my suffering people. Fate and history have made me in some ways a 'voice of the voiceless', the many thousands and millions of Afghans who have endured decades of war and injustice.

For years, my supporters have urged me to write a book about my life. I have always resisted because I do not feel comfortable writing about myself. I feel that my story, on its own, is not important. But finally my friends persuaded me to go ahead with this book as a way to talk about the plight of the Afghan people from the perspective of a member of my country's war generation. I agreed to use my personal experiences as a way to tell the political history of Afghanistan, focusing on the past three decades of oppressive misrule. The story of the dangerous campaign I ran to represent the poor people of my province; the physical and verbal attacks I endured as a Member of Parliament; and the devious, illegal plot to banish me from my elected post – all of it illuminates the corruption and injustice that prevents Afghanistan from becoming a true democracy. In this way it is not just my story, but the story of my struggling people.

Many books were written about Afghanistan after the 9/11 tragedy, but only a few of them offer a complete and realistic picture of Afghanistan's past. Most of them describe in depth the cruelties and injustices of the Taliban regime, but usually ignore or try to hide one of the darkest periods of our history: the rule of the fundamentalist mujahideen between 1992 and 1996. I hope this book will draw attention to the atrocities committed by these warlords who now dominate the Karzai regime.

I also hope this book will correct the tremendous amount of misinformation being spread about Afghanistan. Afghans are sometimes represented in the media as a backward people, nothing more than terrorists, criminals and henchmen. This false image is extremely dangerous for the future of both my country and the West. The truth is that Afghans are brave and freedom-loving people with a rich culture and a proud history. We are capable of defending our independence, governing ourselves and determining our own future.

But Afghanistan has long been used as a deadly playground in the 'Great Game' between superpowers, from the British Empire to the Soviet Empire, and now the Americans and their allies. They have tried to rule Afghanistan by dividing it. They have given money and power to thugs and fundamentalists and warlords who have driven our people into terrible misery. We do not want to be misused and misrepresented to the world. We need security and a helping hand of friends around the world, but not this endless US-led 'war on terror', which is in fact a war against the Afghan people. The Afghan people are not terrorists; we are the victims of terrorism. Today the soil of Afghanistan is full of landmines, bullets and bombs – when what we really need is an invasion of hospitals, clinics and schools for boys and girls.

I was also reluctant to write this memoir because I'd always thought that books should first be written about the many democratic activists who have been martyred, the secret heroes and heroines of Afghanistan's history. I feel the same way about some of the awards that I have received from international human rights groups in recent years. The ones who came before me are more deserving. It is an honour to be recognised, but I only wish that all the love and support I have been shown could be given to the orphans and widows of Afghanistan. For me, the awards and honours belong to all my people, and each distinction I receive only adds to my sense of responsibility to our common struggle. For this reason, all of my earnings from this book will go towards supporting urgently needed humanitarian projects in Afghanistan, aimed at changing lives for the better.

As I write these words, the situation in Afghanistan is getting progressively worse. And not just for women, but for all Afghans. We are caught between two enemies – the Taliban on one side and the US/NATO forces and their warlord friends on the other. And the dark-minded forces in our country are gaining power with every Coalition air strike that kills civilians, with every corrupt government official who grows fat on bribes and thievery, and with every criminal who escapes justice.

During his election campaign, the new President of the United States, Barack Obama, spoke of sending tens of thousands more foreign troops to Afghanistan, but he did not speak out against the twin plagues of corruption and warlordism that are destroying my country. I know that Obama's election has brought great hopes to peace-loving people in the United States. But for Afghans, Obama's military build-up will only bring more suffering and death to innocent civilians, while it may not even weaken the Taliban and al-Qaeda. I hope that the lessons in this book will reach President Obama and his policymakers in Washington, and warn them that the people of Afghanistan reject their brutal occupation and their support of the warlords and drug-lords.

In Afghanistan, democratically minded people have been struggling for human and women's rights for decades. Our history proves that these values cannot be imposed by foreign troops. As I never tire of telling my audiences, no nation can donate liberation to another nation. These values must be fought for and won by the people themselves. They can only grow and flourish when they are planted by the people in their own soil and watered by their own blood and tears.

In Afghanistan, we have a saying that is very dear to my heart: 'The truth is like the sun: when it comes up nobody can block it out or hide it.' I hope that this book and my story will, in a small way, help that sun to keep shining and inspire you, wherever you might be reading this, to work for peace, justice and democracy.

Malalai Joya

CHAPTER 1

THE ROAD
FROM FARAH

I WAS BORN IN THE SMALL VILLAGE of Ziken in the mountainous Anardara district of western Afghanistan on 25 April 1978. Three days later a Soviet-backed coup changed the course of our lives for ever. Within a year we were an occupied country, and since then war is all we Afghans have known.

I am the second born of ten children, and the eldest of seven daughters. Although my family has suffered many deprivations, the only commodity that has never been in short supply is love. But we often lived in fear. One of my earliest memories is of clinging to my mother's legs while policemen ransacked our house, looking for my father. They turned the place upside down searching for clues, emptying everything out of our drawers and suitcases and ripping open mattresses and pillows. But my mother did not know where he was either. He had lost a leg while fighting with the mujahideen against the Soviet occupiers. Then he had to flee Afghanistan. My family thought he was living in exile in Iran, but no one had heard from him in many months. Already, the neighbours were calling my mother a widow. My grandfather told her not to give up hope, but truly they did not know whether my father was alive or dead.

Soon after my birth, my family moved to Farah City, in the

province of the same name, which borders on Iran. It is a poor, sparsely populated region, plagued by drought and windstorms. Only half a million people live in the whole province; 50,000 of them in the area around Farah City. These days Farah is mostly out of sight and out of mind of the capital, Kabul, but there was a time when great armies poured through the wide river valley along the road between the ancient cities of Herat and Kandahar. Darius I of Persia once ruled here. The ruins of a mud-brick citadel, known as Infidel's Castle, built by Alexander the Great still stand in Farah, in the shadow of the mountains. Later, Genghis Khan sacked Farah on his march through Afghanistan. More recently, the British Empire tried to swallow Afghanistan, as did the Soviets. And now the Americans and their European allies. Afghanistan has always been on the route of conquerors because of its strategic location at the crossroads of Central Asia, perched between India and Russia, Persia and China. There is a wise saying in Africa: 'When elephants fight, it is the grass that is trampled.' Afghanistan has been that grass, but it never stays trampled for long. A longing for freedom beats in every Afghan's heart, and we have eventually repelled every foreign occupier. This is something the United States government might consider as it rains bombs on our villages in the name of liberating us.

As I have said, I can't tell you the real names of my parents or close relatives. Because of my outspoken politics, it would put my whole family in danger. But I can tell you that my father is an educated man who believes in democracy. He attended post-secondary school and even studied to become a doctor at Kabul University, but his involvement in politics and the persecution that came with the Soviet Union's invasion in 1979 meant that he never got the chance to practise medicine.

My mother, on the other hand, did not have the opportunity to get an education. Her life has not been easy. Both her parents died when she was still young, and so she had to take care of both her own children and some of her younger siblings. She had two older brothers who became the family breadwinners. My maternal grandfather had been an honest and well-respected tribal leader, or Malik, for forty years. The people of Ziken called him the 'stick holder', because he was famous for having beaten someone with his stick after he saw him taking a bribe. Even though tribal heads in Afghanistan are among the richest men, my grandfather was too honest to keep anything for himself. When he died nothing was left for his children, but the surrounding villages helped support my mother and her siblings. When my mother was born, the families arranged for her to marry my father. This custom remains common in the villages of Afghanistan today.

I am often asked by reporters to describe my ethnic background and I always tell them 'I am an Afghan. Tajik, Pashtun, Hazara, Uzbek, Nooristani, Baluch, Pashaee and other ethnic groups are all the same for me.' In Ziken, Pashtuns and Tajiks mixed, intermarried and lived in brotherhood. I prefer not to play into the hands of those who would use religious and tribal differences to divide us. A divided country is easiest for outsiders to control, and that is something I have fought against all my life.

My parents named me Malalai, a popular name in Afghanistan. It was given to me as a tribute to one of the great freedom fighters from our country's history: Malalai of Maiwand. In our schools and in our homes, all Afghan children learn of Malalai's bravery and sacrifice in our struggle for independence against the British Empire. In 1880, during the Second Anglo-Afghan War, she was a very young and patriotic woman who went to the front lines to tend to the wounded during an important battle against British colonial forces at Maiwand, in Kandahar Province. At a key point when the British had gained the upper hand and the Afghan fighters were becoming demoralised, she took over from a fallen flag bearer and led the men back into battle. Malalai encouraged the Afghan fighters with defiant and poetic words:

Young love! If you do not fall in the battle of Maiwand then
By God, someone is saving you as a symbol of shame!

Malalai of Maiwand was struck down soon after, sacrificing her life to inspire the resistance fighters who delivered the British a stunning defeat. Nearly 3,000 Afghans died, but an entire British brigade was destroyed, and this victory was an important landmark in our country's struggle for independence. My parents named me Malalai because my father was a strong supporter of democracy and human rights at a time when these values were also under siege.

Although he would later become the most important influence in my life, in my first years I did not know my father. Because of the political situation in the country, he often had to live apart from us in hiding. Father was part of the politically active generation that came of age during the time known as the 'constitutional period', from 1964 to 1973.

In 1964 King Zahir Shah, under pressure from mass movements, introduced a new constitution that maintained the monarchy's ultimate control but included provisions ensuring women's rights and the creation of an elected parliament. Many new political parties were formed in these years, and the campuses became hotbeds of political activity. Islamic fundamentalists, nationalist reformers and communists were able to organise, up to a point. Even though my father was independent of any political party, he was very active in the democracy and human rights movements, and had been since he began attending university in 1972.

This brief period of relative tolerance ended in 1973, when the king was overthrown by his cousin Mohammed Daoud Khan, who declared himself president and Afghanistan a republic. In 1978, Daoud himself was killed in the coup d'état called the 'Saur' or 'April' Revolution by its Russian-backed leaders in the People's Democratic Party of Afghanistan (PDPA), which had earlier helped him to kick out the king. This coup ushered in the period of direct Soviet intervention in Afghan affairs. The pro-Russian PDPA and its two major factions, Khalq and Parcham, were ruthless in repressing and killing their opponents – as well as each other – in mass purges. Noor Mohammad Taraki, the first Russian puppet was soon killed by Hafizullah Amin, who ruled briefly until 1979. When Soviet troops rolled into Kabul, they killed Amin and installed a more reliable puppet, Babrak Karmal, as ruler of Afghanistan.

While he studied medicine in Kabul during those years, my father became known as a strong supporter of democracy and an opponent of both the monarchy and the Soviet puppets. The authorities knew about my father and his activities.

But his own father did not always realise the extent of his involvement.

One day, when my father was back home in Farah, some government officials came to complain to my grandfather about his son's activities. Grandfather was a very religious man who ran a small pharmacy to support his family. He was a respected elder in our community, very well known in Farah, and his door was open to everyone. On this day, however, he did not like what his visitors told him.

'Your son has been involved in some of the student demonstrations at the university.'

'No, I don't think so. My son only goes to school to study,' Grandfather said.

But the government men explained that in fact my father had been a speaker at a number of protests, and was scheduled to speak again the next day in Farah. They told Grandfather that his son's involvement in the student movement was well known to police intelligence and that he could find himself in jail if he didn't cut out these extra-curricular activities. Grandfather was upset and worried for the safety of my father, ordering him to stay home the next day.

To emphasise how serious he was, Grandfather added that if he went he would not be forgiven, nor let back into the house. In fact, that night, Grandfather even locked the door to my father's room from the outside!

My father, however, was very determined to participate in the demonstration. He stuffed towels and pillows under the bed covers and, with the help of a cousin, snuck out through the bedroom window. Until lunchtime or so, Grandfather just thought he was sleeping in. But when he discovered he had been deceived, he was very angry. He also prayed for my father's safety. For a week my father did not return home, in order to show respect for Grandfather's anger towards him. In the end, he was forgiven and taken back into the house.

My father took many risks during these years, and was jailed for sixteen months in the early 1970s, delaying his medical studies. He finally had to leave school in 1979, when Soviet tanks and troops poured into Afghanistan.

Like many young men my father joined the fight against the invasion. While I was still an infant he began to train with the local mujahideen. Like many such groups that rose up in the villages, they were largely self-organised with limited resources. Uncle Azad,* my mother's brother, also joined the freedom fighters, and he often travelled alongside Father during their clandestine operations in the province.

One night their headquarters in the mountains near our village was attacked by Soviet troops. After days of heavy fighting, the mujahideen ran out of food and ammunition, so they had to retreat. Before they left, the Russian troops destroyed the headquarters and planted anti-personnel mines everywhere, including around the bodies of thirteen slain mujahideen. Father and Uncle Azad took on the grisly mission of retrieving the bodies for their families. Before they could finish the job, Father stepped on one of the landmines. The force of the explosion knocked him uncon-

---

* I have changed this and other names in this book for security reasons

scious, and when he woke up in the field, his left leg had been shattered by the blast, and he was bleeding profusely. Luckily, Uncle Azad was nearby, and he reacted quickly and helped tie a tourniquet to stem the bleeding. In fact, Father was able to give instructions for his own treatment, and this is one of the reasons he survived. After a dangerous thirty-hour journey by car to Iran, Uncle Azad managed to get Father to a hospital. Today, the same uncle who saved my father's life is the head of my security.

To keep Father alive, the doctors had to amputate part of his leg. In fact, they had to operate three times. He was one of hundreds of thousands of Afghans who lost a limb during the long war against the Soviets. A 2005 survey conducted by Handicap International put the number of 'severely disabled' Afghans at up to 867,000 people. And landmines like the one that maimed Father still lie buried in fields throughout the country, injuring children and farmers, continuing their evil work long after their makers have gone home.

As you can imagine, Father's injury was a traumatic and difficult thing for my mother, too. To make matters worse, shortly after he sustained this injury it became too risky for him to live with us at all. The Soviets and their Afghan puppets were killing thousands of opponents during this time. During the brief rule of Hafizullah Amin, the puppet regime itself issued a list of over 12,000 people it said were killed in prisons and blamed Noor Mohammad Taraki for it. My father lost many of his friends and colleagues, and he knew the pro-Soviet forces wanted to do away with him as well. So, sadly, he had to leave our family home and live in exile.

When my father left, his older brother, my Uncle Babak, looked after and provided for our family. Retired, he returned to work as a teacher to support us. Since this happened when I was just an infant, I did not have a clear understanding of our relationship and started calling my uncle 'Baba', which means 'Daddy' in Dari. All my life Uncle Babak has been very close to me and to our whole family. Even though he was not a political person, this uncle was jailed three times and tortured because of my father's activities against the Soviet occupation. The authorities were punishing him because he would not give information on the whereabouts of his brother. Later, my activism caused him to be harassed by some. He had a severe heart condition, which could only have been treated abroad. Uncle Babak died in July 2006. His loss was a tough blow for my whole family. And it still troubles me that I was not in a position to be able to pay for his treatment.

But as much as he loved his brother, Uncle Babak was in many ways very different from Father. My father was unlike most Afghan men his age, and we did not have male domination in our household. My uncle preferred girls to cover their head with a scarf when men came to the house – for my father it didn't matter. One day my uncle bought me a scarf and he asked me to wear it. He also didn't like me to shake hands with males.

As a little girl, I was very close to my paternal grandmother, who also lived in Farah. Most of what I know about her comes from the stories of others. She loved me a lot, and at meals I would often share food from her dish. This was a great treat, because, in our tradition, elderly people always get the best food. Grandmother once told my mother that, after she died, she wanted me to go to her grave, put water on it and shout three times. 'I want to hear her voice,' she said.

In the days when my father was in exile, my grandparents still lived with us. My grandfather remained very active even in old age. As kids, we were told he was over a hundred years old. But you have to understand that in Afghanistan many people's birthdates are not recorded, and there is often some exaggeration of ages. He had a way with words, and loved to talk to new people wherever he went. In a way he was our family's first 'politician'. I like to think that I picked up some of these traits from him.

Grandfather was an extremely hospitable and unselfish man who always put others ahead of himself. I was told as a child a story well known in our family: Grandfather was hosting some friends for lunch, and food was about to be served when he received terrible news – his twelve-year-old son, my father's eldest brother, who had fallen gravely ill, had died. Rather than break the news to his guests right away, Grandfather made sure everyone enjoyed their meal first. It was only after the meal and pleasant conversation was finished that he shared the tragedy, and everyone cried together and comforted each other for the terrible loss. He was well loved in our community.

When government police officers came to search our house and interrogate us about my father's whereabouts, Grandfather would often make them ashamed of their actions. He appealed to their sense of patriotism and pride to make them see that they were serving the wrong master. 'It is a shame that Afghans are fighting and killing Afghans,' he would say.

'Sorry, Grandfather,' the policemen often replied, 'but we are just doing our job.'

On some of these occasions when the authorities came to our home, Grandfather would recite and even improvise poetry, speaking verses that combined religious and political ideas. He had a creative talent for writing and recitation, and he was an excellent communicator.

Once some policemen pleaded *their* case to my grandfather. 'We are good people,' they declared righteously. 'We are just doing what we have to do.'

Grandfather responded right away: 'Yes, you are right. *We* are truly the ones who are bad people. Please forgive us.'

The policemen became so embarrassed that they left.

Another time the police were looking at our display of photos, which featured many of my father's university friends and colleagues who had since been killed or thrown in jail. When one of the policemen pointed at my father's picture and asked harshly 'Where is this man?', my grandfather's response was to recite a very beautiful and patriotic poem.

When he was finished some of the policemen had tears in their eyes, and again they left as quickly as they could.

On some occasions, however, the police were far more brutal. We heard stories of times when the authorities even killed children and babies in their cradles while going through the houses of suspected dissidents.

These years were, as you can imagine, very hard on my mother emotionally. Soon after my father lost his leg, as I have already mentioned, he had to leave Afghanistan entirely. We believed that he had taken refuge in neighbouring Iran, but there were long periods of time when Mother had no news at all from her husband. There was a war raging through our country and we had no means to communicate or even to receive messages.

Mother began to fear the worst. Then, when I was four years old, Uncle Azad, my mother's brother, arrived one day with dramatic news: my father was still alive! Uncle also carried the message that it was time for all of us to leave at once and join him in Iran. Mother could not believe her ears, could not believe that her husband was really alive.

The war with Russia was only getting worse. The bitter conflict showed no sign of ending soon and, by 1982, already tens of thousands of Afghans were pouring out of the country to escape the war and its brutalities. Our family joined this exodus. We packed up what we could carry and left Farah Province and Afghanistan behind us. Uncle Azad, Mother, my older brother and young sister – we all piled into a car for the journey to Iran. We said goodbye to Grandfather. It would be the last time I ever saw him. He stayed behind, never wanting to leave his beloved Farah Province. When he died there in 1987, we were told that hundreds of people came from many faraway villages to pay their final respects.

Like so many Afghans my age, I spent most of my childhood outside the country in refugee camps. Over the course of the war, literally millions of Afghans would be displaced, living mostly in crowded camps in Iran and Pakistan. This toll doesn't include the over 1 million Afghans killed during the decade-long Soviet occupation, which lasted from 1979 to 1989.

During this time, the United States was also involved in Afghanistan. In the name of the legitimate struggle of the mujahideen to liberate our country, the US funded, trained and armed some of the worst extremists in the world – people like Gulbuddin Hekmatyar, Abdul Rab al-Rasul Sayyaf and Osama bin Laden. The latter, of course, was not an Afghan. He was one of the thousands of foreigners that the United States and Pakistan recruited, trained and funded with the collusion of wealthy Saudi Arabian extremists. This intervention helped lead to the eventual downfall of the Soviet Union and contributed to the end of the Cold War, but it left us plagued with well-armed fundamentalists. Even before the Russians were driven out, many of the extremist groups had begun fighting each other and making life terrible for the Afghan people. Ultimately both the superpowers used Afghanistan for their own interests. And for us Afghans, this war brought great destruction from which we have yet to recover. And it sowed the seeds that grew into the ongoing misery we are still dealing with today.

Leaving Afghanistan, we travelled first to the eastern Iranian city of Zahedan. We were careful not to inform many people of our plans, because the authorities were trying to stem the mass emigration the war was causing. At the same time, the United States and its allies, along with Pakistan and Iran, were encouraging the exodus because it was easier for them to recruit mujahideen which they could then arm to fight the Russians. Pakistan and Iran wanted to increase the number of refugees because they brought in money from the UN and other donors. Also, these neighbouring governments could work among the Afghan refugees to recruit them as their agents and create political parties they could control. During these years eight new pro-Iranian parties were formed, and seven such parties were created under the control of the Pakistan intelligence services (ISI).

Cultural similarities made Iran a natural destination for those of us fleeing western Afghanistan. One of the official languages of my home province is Dari, which is a dialect of Persian, the national language of Iran. But once an Afghan crossed the border, it was illegal to live outside the dangerous, crowded refugee camps without government permission. Anti-fundamentalist intellectuals like my father were being targeted and killed at the Zahedan camps, so he was living quietly in town, in a single rented room in a house with friends. And that was where all of us joined him at last.

I don't personally remember the event, but over the years Mother would often tell the story of her reunion with Father in Zahedan. When he first walked into the room it was as if the whole building filled with light. She said it was like witnessing the miracle of his coming back to life right before her eyes.

I was still very young, only four years old, so I did not understand that this man with one leg was my father. At first, I wouldn't let him hug me or give me a kiss. Emotionally I remained closer to the uncle I had taken to calling 'Baba'. I did not yet realise how fortunate I was just to have a father, unlike so many thousands of Afghan children orphaned over the preceding decades of war.

Father worked hard to gain my affection. There was a market nearby, and even an ice cream stand that kept its freezer working with a noisy portable generator. Before a meal I was often sent out to buy some bread from the market and Father would slip me a little bit of extra money so that I could stop on the way back and get myself some ice cream. This was such a treat for me and, to this day, just the thought of ice cream brings back happy memories.

Sometimes my love of ice cream got me into trouble. On one occasion we had guests over for dinner and I was sent out at the last minute to pick up some bread. My instructions were crystal clear: 'Hurry home. Do *not* stop for ice cream.'

But I couldn't help myself. Not only did I stop for ice cream, but I hung around talking to some other kids while I ate. When I got back, everyone was annoyed. I realised I had been a brat but, despite this, Father didn't even yell at me.

And so I gradually came to understand and accept who my

father really was. He told me he first knew that he had won me back when he overheard me singing myself a little song that went, 'My father has only one leg, my father has only one leg ...' It certainly wasn't poetry, but Father was thrilled to hear this odd little ditty of mine.

As new siblings kept arriving in our family, my father became less and less able to support us financially – despite the fact that he was both well educated and a hard worker. There simply weren't enough jobs to go around. Back home in Farah, while we were certainly never rich, we weren't poor either. But now, along with thousands of other displaced Afghan families, we faced very difficult conditions.

The fundamentalist, fascist Iranian government has committed unforgivable crimes against its own people, but Afghan refugees have been – and still are – treated with even more brutality. Every Afghan who has lived in Iran has painful stories to tell.

Afghans, in general, were seen as second-class humans by the Iranian government. We were called 'dirty' by camp guards and forced to do the most difficult jobs for lower wages. The regime of the mullahs in Iran was only friendly to Afghans who were linked to its eight puppet fundamentalist parties. They were later merged into the Wahdat Party – or 'Unity Party' – dedicated to exporting Tehran's brand of political Islam to Afghanistan. Some ministers and many officials in Hamid Karzai's government – such as Karim Khalili, now vice president – come from this party. Given the bloodthirsty behaviour of Wahdat during the civil war years of 1992 to 1996 and otherwise, these men must be held to account.

These groups had free rein in the camps to forcibly recruit refugees and terrorise and kill their opponents. That's why it was actually safer for us to live in Zahedan and risk getting picked up by the police and sent to one of the dreaded detention centres. Like concentration camps, they were designed to humiliate Afghans and break their national pride. Detainees faced torture, deportation or worse. Some of the famous detention/deportation centres were 'Tal-e-Sea', 'Askar Abad', and 'Safaid Sang'. The low point of the systemic abuse of Afghan refugees in Iran came in 1998, with the little-known massacre at Safaid Sang (White Rock, in Dari). After detainees revolted against their conditions and tried to escape, more than 600 were shot down and killed; some were strafed by machine-gun fire from helicopters.

We lived as exiles in Iran for four years. After one year of uneasy but relatively comfortable conditions in Zahedan, for economic reasons we were soon forced to move hundreds of miles north into less hospitable lodgings at the Khunuk Buzghala camp. At the time, about 85,000 Afghans were squeezed into filthy, over-crowded camps in the desert frontier of the Birjand district. The rest of the world knows this region for its beautiful Persian carpets and its history as a waypoint along the famous Silk Road; we knew it as a place where we were neglected and forgotten, where we baked in the heat of the day and shivered at night.

The houses in the camps were hastily thrown-together mud and brick structures lined up along open sewers. Most of the dwellings didn't have proper doors, and night could be a fearful time. There were some horrific incidents when foxes, wolves and other wild animals crept inside to attack and kill infants and young children while they slept. I will never forget Mother instructing us how to scream for help if we woke up to find an animal in our hut. She even had a special string attached to my newborn sister that would wake her if her baby was disturbed.

Even worse than these dangers and deprivations, however, was the fact that there were no schools in these camps. Afghan children were not allowed to attend Iranian schools, and were prevented from setting up their own education system. This was unacceptable to my family and especially to my father, who believed so strongly in the value of education, for young girls also. I was now seven years old and it was past time for me to begin school. So Mother and Father packed all of us up and we said goodbye to Iran.

CHAPTER 2

GROWING UP
IN PAKISTAN

*T*HE TRIP TO PAKISTAN from Iran took two days, travelling on large old passenger buses. I was very young, and slept most of the way – I didn't know what a treacherous route it was, plagued by thieves and bandits. My family and other Afghan refugees also had to fear the Iranian police, who could have sent us to the notorious detention centres.

Our family settled in Quetta, which is the capital city of Balochistan, a mountainous region in western Pakistan just across the border from the Afghan province of Kandahar. Known as the 'Fruit Garden of Pakistan', Quetta sits almost a mile above sea level and is surrounded by imposing mountain peaks with dramatic names like Murdar and Takatoo. Quetta is a good-sized metropolis, although certainly not immense by Pakistani standards, and its population was probably less than half a million when we were living there. This time we didn't live in a refugee camp. Instead we rented a cheap little house and my father worked at a series of odd jobs. In those years, most Afghan refugees in Pakistan were either in Quetta or Peshawar, and the former was safer for democratically minded activists like my father.

Soon after our arrival in Pakistan I went to school for the very first time. One of the reasons my family chose Quetta was because it had a school with a good reputation among democracy activists. Watan School was the only school for Afghan refugees in that area that girls could attend. The school had both boys' and girls' branches attended by hundreds of children. It was run with finance and support from an underground organisation called the Revolutionary Association of the Women of Afghanistan (RAWA), which was started in the late 1970s both to advocate for women's rights and to help in the struggle against the Soviet occupation of Afghanistan.

This was a boarding school – there was no option to attend as a day student, so it meant that I was separated from my family for long periods of time. It was difficult for both me and my parents, but they believed it was important that I get the best education possible. I remember crying when my parents dropped me off for my first day of school. I was only seven years old and it was sad and frightening to be separated from Mother and Father and all my brothers and sisters. I was also worried about my hair, of all things. At the time, I was extremely fond of the long, thick hair that flowed down my back, and I insisted that my mother ask the teachers to promise that they would look after it.

Once I settled in I really enjoyed my classes. I loved reading and writing right from the beginning, especially poems and proverbs. I would memorise my favourites and recite them aloud. Although this school was supported by a political organisation, all of the teachers believed in letting children have their childhood. We did our lessons in all the usual academic subjects, but we were also given time to play and just be kids.

For the most part, the teachers tried not to burden such small children with worries about the political troubles back in Afghanistan. But they did teach us some basic facts about a woman named Meena, the brave founder of RAWA, who had left university in Kabul to devote herself to social activism.

One day our teacher brought us down to the main hall for a special assembly. We were all very excited and wondered what the big occasion might be. Then, much to my amazement, my teacher introduced a guest speaker, and it was Meena herself. I couldn't believe it – there was this legend, standing in front of us. She was not at all what I had imagined – so beautiful and young. In her remarks to us, Meena told us how important it was for girls to be educated. Back in Afghanistan the strength of the fundamentalist extremists, who believed that only boys should attend school, was already growing.

Afterwards, Meena sat with the students and spoke very kindly to us, asking how we enjoyed our lessons and whether we liked our teachers. She brought us sweets, and she made a special point of welcoming those of us who were new to the school. I was very shy then, and I sat quietly while she spoke with some of my classmates. Suddenly Meena turned to me and told me what beautiful long hair I had. This brought me out of my shell. 'Thank you,' I said, and we exchanged a few more words. I don't remember what we discussed, but I will never forget her thoughtfulness.

In 1987, only a few years after this meeting, Meena became another martyr to the emancipation of Afghan women. She was thirty years old when she was kidnapped right in Quetta and assassinated. She disappeared and it was only six months later that two of her killers were captured and confessed, revealing the location where she had been hastily buried. It is believed that her murder was committed by fundamentalists associated with the party of Gulbuddin Hekmatyar, with the support of the KHAD, the Afghan branch of the Soviet KGB. At least that is what the two men who were arrested in Pakistan confessed before they were hanged. Meena's blood has fertilised the struggle of all Afghan women right up to today. I am very grateful that I had a chance to meet her in person, even if only for a day as a young child. She remains an inspiration to me.

My enemies often claim that I am a member of RAWA. After all, hundreds and probably thousands of Afghan children have been educated in RAWA schools in Pakistan – that doesn't mean they all grew up to be activists with the organisation. I am an independent, but I am not ashamed to say that I share many of the same ideals. If I ever decided that I could be more effective working within the framework of an organisation, RAWA is the first I would consider joining. It is a group that makes Afghan women proud, and I have learned a great deal from their uncompromising struggle for women's rights and democracy.

At boarding school, we were allowed to go home to visit our families a couple of weekends each month. I have very fond memories of one of the drivers who delivered us to our parents' homes. We called him 'Uncle Sayed'. He was a kind and gentle man who volunteered at our school, and I quickly became one of his favourites. When I got to ride with him, I would always try to sit up front. He often gave us chocolate or other sweets, and he would always joke and make us laugh. Sadly, this lovely man would also later be murdered by fundamentalist extremists.

But both of these tragic events were still in the future, and my life at this school was a happy period of growth and discovery. I do, however, have one negative – even traumatic – memory from my time there. One day I was shocked to be told that they would have to cut my beautiful long hair. I tried to run away, but the teachers caught me and sheared off all my precious locks. When I saw my cropped haircut in a mirror, I cried and cried at my loss. These teachers, however, were not being cruel. There was an outbreak of lice and they were forced to cut everyone's hair to curb the spread. I should probably have been grateful that they didn't shave me right down to the roots.

During our family's years in Pakistan, we moved around several times, depending on my father's work situation. We lived first in Quetta, and then near Pakistan's north-eastern border with India in the city of Lahore. Then, finally, we ended up in the huge Afghan refugee camps around Peshawar in north-west Pakistan.

Peshawar is only a short distance from the Afghan border and about 150 miles from Kabul over the famous Khyber Pass, so it was natural for so many refugees to congregate there. The sprawling camps in this region were home to hundreds of thousands of Afghans escaping the war in our homeland, some of the largest being Harakat, Akora Khatak, Shamshato and Jalozai. Just recently, the Pakistani government began to close many of these camps, but for decades they were teeming with Afghan exiles.

We lived in a camp called Pashaee, about a half an hour of bumpy road off the main highway and also a half-hour from the much larger Harakat camp. When we arrived in the mid-1980s, the conditions in these camps were crowded and desperate. Families had to live in a haphazard assortment of shacks and earthen huts. From the camp, we could see clouds of black smoke billowing up from the nearby brick factories where many of the men, and even some of the children, worked long, hard hours. These were hard times for my family, although we were certainly better off than many others. Food and employment were scarce. Many refugees suffered from health problems related to malnutrition, and I have haunting memories of exhausted, emaciated babies in the arms of their anguished mothers.

Most of the camps around Peshawar were controlled by the fundamentalist parties supported by Pakistan's intelligence agency, ISI. Even the international aid was channelled through these groups. The Gulbuddin Party of the notorious Hekmatyar had its own detention centres in Shamshato and Warsak camps, where many democracy activists languished.

The camps run by the three mujahideen groups that were considered more moderate were a bit safer. Fortunately for us, Pashaee was one such camp. It was registered under the Jabhe-Nejat group run by Sibghatullah Mojaddedi. Its council included many open-minded Afghans. Although the camp was named after the Pashaee minority in Afghanistan, many ethnic and tribal groups lived side-by-side in harmony in this camp. Throughout the 1980s, the residents of Pashaee, some of whom were armed for self-defence, resisted attacks and threats from fundamentalist bands, who were not happy with the progressive way the camp was run. Most importantly, in Pashaee there were schools administered by progressive-minded people. At this time, the only education offered at many of the other camps was at boys-only madrassas, where students were indoctrinated in a rigid and militant form of Islam. Most of the madrassas were funded by Saudi Arabia, and they were often the only option for Afghan boys. Orphans were routinely sent to these madrassas, where jihad and extreme fundamentalism were all they knew. This was the so-called 'Taliban factory' that a whole generation of Afghan refugees grew up in. The word 'talib' means student and, indeed, many of the Taliban's fighters received their education in these madrassas in the Peshawar area. In this way, the widespread presence of fundamentalist teaching in Pakistan would come back to haunt Afghanistan.

Amidst these difficult conditions, my parents had found us a place to learn with open-minded instructors. I couldn't wait to walk over to my schoolhouse in the morning with my brothers and sisters. Boys and girls attended separate classes, but followed a similar curriculum. Except for maths, which has never been a strong subject for me, I did pretty well in all my lessons. Again I excelled in composition and reading comprehension in Dari. I remember filling many pages when our teacher assigned us an essay on the meaning of freedom. Since I knew what the rule of fundamentalists meant in the other camps and back home in Afghanistan, I wrote about how freedom meant to have a country with equal rights for all citizens, including women. At home, I would help my younger sisters and brothers with their lessons.

As students, we didn't always realise how lucky we were. I have a vivid memory of how one teacher reacted after some of us complained that we were tired from studying. Her response was firm, 'You should realise that these years, with the chance to focus on your education, will be the best time of your lives.' I know now that she was right. I only wish that all Afghan children could have the chance to get 'tired' by many years of education.

There were also sports programmes for both boys and girls at our school, which I enjoyed because I had a lot of energy. The walled-in yard of the school was the only place for girls' sports –

unlike the boys, we were not allowed to play in the camp itself. I especially liked to play volleyball. Some Afghan parents did not allow their daughters to play sports because it was considered proper only for boys. But mine always allowed the girls to play just as the boys did. Far too many Afghan girls know only work and subservience from a very young age.

My parents followed the progress of the war at home with a small analogue short-wave radio, and from the accounts carried by new refugees as they arrived in the camps. In the mid-1980s, with the whole Afghan population hating them and the resistance growing stronger, the Soviet Union was starting to lose the war. By this time a number of foreign countries – notably the United States, Pakistan, Iran and Saudi Arabia – had become involved in the conflict. The United States wanted to use the Afghan resistance to fight against the Soviets so that it could become the sole superpower. I also believe that it wanted to take revenge on the USSR for its failure in the Vietnam War. And so the Americans made sure the Russians were mired in their own Vietnam.

By 1985 the CIA was funnelling millions and millions of dollars in payments and military equipment to several resistance groups hand-picked by the pro-fundamentalist Pakistani ISI. The leaders of these parties were warlords and religious extremists such as Gulbuddin Hekmatyar, Abdul Rab al-Rasul Sayyaf, Burhanuddin Rabbani, and Ahmad Shah Massoud. Abdul Ali Mazari Karim Khalili, Mohammad Mohaqiq and Sheikh Asif Mohseni were the heads of similar groups supported by Iran. It did not matter to the foreigners that these men used the name of Islam and jihad to make war on their own people and oppress Afghan women.

By the end of the 1980s it looked like that freedom was coming at last. The Russians hoped to improve their chances by replacing Karmal with Muhammad Najibullah, another Russian puppet and former chief of the Afghan secret police, KHAD. But the mujahideen were closing in on Kabul. In 1989, the last of the Russian troops left Afghanistan, but the Soviet Union continued to support Najibullah. He held on to the capital until the Soviet empire itself collapsed and his money ran out.

We learned the true nature of the militias when they finally took over Kabul on 28 April 1992. At first the people celebrated their victory, but soon their hopes turned to ashes when these extremists proved that they could be even worse than the Russians. We did not know it right away, but 28 April would become another black day in the history of our country, as notorious a date as 27 April, the day Russian puppets came to power in 1978.

Although I believe in national unity and I don't like to label people by their ethnic or religious backgrounds, it is necessary to know something about the different groups in Afghanistan to understand the bloody days that were to come. Since the fifteenth century, when it was created as one nation out of many smaller fiefdoms, Afghanistan has been an amalgam of ethnic groups. There are an estimated 32 million Afghans today, consisting of ethnic Pashtuns, Tajiks, Hazaras, Uzbeks, and a number of other smaller groups. The two official languages are Dari, spoken by the Tajiks, and Pashto, spoken by Pashtun people on both sides of the border between Afghanistan and Pakistan. For centuries these groups have coexisted under one flag. But as soon as the militias entered Kabul that unity was destroyed.

It is difficult for outsiders to understand, but our people divide the mujahideen into two types: the real and the criminal mujahideen. In the early days of the Soviet–Afghan War, the majority of those who struggled against the Russian forces called themselves mujahideen – or 'holy warriors'. They were, like my father, Afghan patriots, united to fight against an oppressive invader. The day the Soviet-backed regime of Najibullah finally collapsed on 28 April 1992, the real mujahideen laid down their arms, but it was on this date that the extremists and power-hungry groups began their civil war. It is these criminals that today we call jihadis to distinguish them from the honourable mujahideen.

Even though the mujahideen were battling an atheistic Soviet empire, it is not true that they were fighting just for their religion, which is a personal matter. They were fighting for our right as Afghans to be free from foreign domination.

A couple of years ago, when I was part of a discussion on a talk show, a representative of the Jamiat-e-Islami referred to us having 'fought the Russians for Islam', but I corrected him.

'No, we fought the Russians for *freedom*.'

Most of the main rebel leaders belonged to different ethnic backgrounds. While there were often rivalries between them, as long as they had a common enemy, and the money was flowing in from the CIA, they managed to avoid massive internecine blood-letting. Although it is important to note that even during the years of Soviet occupation, many of the mujahideen factions fought each other for influence, with some even making temporary alliances with the Soviet puppets for the sake of their own power. Once the Russians were gone, these groups started a full-blown civil war, mainly for the sake of power and money – the kind of battle that is called a 'dog fight' by our people.

As soon as Najibullah's troops dispersed, the armies of Hekmatyar, a Pashtun, and Massoud, a Tajik, fought over control of Kabul like dogs over a bone. Gulbuddin Hekmatyar was outside Kabul and rained thousands of rockets on the city. Massoud was joined by the brutal Uzbek warlord Rashid Dostum, who was a powerful military commander in the Russian puppet regime until he realised that they were losing. Then he switched sides and declared himself a mujahideen. The composition of these alliances was changed a number of times, and later Dostum even joined hands with Hekmatyar. The warring factions blasted their way into Kabul, which had survived the war with Russia largely intact. Ours was a capital that was once so beautiful it attracted tourists from around the world and was called 'the bride of the cities'. Other warlords tried to form an interim government, the Islamic Jihad Council, led by Sibghatullah Mojaddedi, to stop the chaos. But the fighting raged on. The militias of Dostum, Sayyaf, Massoud, Mazari and Hekmatyar pillaged the city, robbing families, slaughtering and raping women. Eventually anywhere from 65,000 to 80,000 innocent people were killed in Kabul alone, though there are no agreed 'official' figures for the staggering death toll. According to the UN, over 90 per cent of the city was destroyed. Eventually Massoud and his fellow Tajik, Rabbani, tried to exert authority through a nominal central government. But in fact the country was split into fiefdoms, ruled by the whims of rival thugs and warlords.

During this period, these groups ignited an ethnic clash in the country in which the most innocent and miserable members of all ethnic groups suffered the most. Today these parties are as much hated by their own ethnic groups as they are hated by others.

Unfortunately, after the Soviets left, the world media turned its attention away from Afghanistan, so many of the crimes of these years are poorly documented and almost unknown. One of the worst tragedies, the mass killing of Hazaras and the raping of women in the Afshar neighbourhood of Kabul, was reported by Human Rights Watch. The massacre began on 11 February 1993, led by the forces of Sayyaf, Massoud and others after fighting with Mazari's forces. Within days, the armed forces of Mazari pulled out while hundreds of innocent, poor people died in Afshar, Kabul. The area is still in terrible condition.

In 1992, for a brief period of time, my family returned to live in Farah. I was then fourteen and my memories of those months are frightening. Although most of the devastation occurred in Kabul, even in Farah there was lawlessness and factional fighting amongst the various mujahideen parties. Ismail Khan had installed himself as Emir of Herat, and his forces exerted their influence over neighbouring provinces such as Farah.

Our family moved in with my uncle Babak's family, and the situation got so bad that we could barely ever leave our house. There was anarchy on the streets. Young girls were being abducted, raped and killed by roaming gangs. We were not even safe in our home. At night, armed fighters of criminal mujahideen groups would often walk right into people's homes. When these forces came to town all of the children were locked in a bedroom with the light off and told to remain silent. We were terrified, but we could not cry out as we listened to these men yelling and turning things upside down around the house, taking whatever they pleased.

We could not stay in Farah, and before long we were back in the Pashaee refugee camp in Pakistan. The war with the Russians had forced nearly 5 million of us Afghans into camps, and now the war amongst the mujahideen kept us there. The camps were overrun with even more refugees, especially with people who were escaping the capital, Kabul. And the Pakistani government, which had welcomed the refugees during the Soviet war, was now making it much more difficult for people to flee across the border. Many became internal refugees, forced to set up their camps in Afghanistan.

Most people in the West have been led to believe that intolerance, brutality and the severe oppression of women in Afghanistan began with the Taliban regime. But this is a lie, more dust in the eyes of the world from the warlords who dominate the American-backed, so-called democratic government of Hamid Karzai. In truth some of the worst atrocities in our recent past were committed during the civil war by the men who are now in power.

Women and children were the first and worst victims of the civil war. Under the name of Islam, women were deprived of their very basic rights. Many of the warlords closed the doors of the schools for the girls and even prohibited the sound of women's footsteps.

As early as May 1992, Sheikh Asif Mosheini, the interim governing council spokesman (now a close friend of Karzai and the US in Kabul) and Sayd Ali Javed (now a Member of Parliament) publicly announced a new set of rules governing the conduct of women called the 'Ordinance on the Women's Veil'. As documented by Mr Felix Ermacora, Special Rapporteur of the Commission on Human Rights, it proclaimed that 'A denier of the veil is an infidel and an unveiled woman is lewd' and outlined the conditions of wearing a veil:

1. They must not perfume themselves.
2. They must not wear adorning clothes.
3. They must not wear thin clothes.
4. They must not wear narrow and tight clothes.
5. They must cover their entire bodies.
6. Their clothes must not resemble men's clothes.
7. Muslim women's clothes must not resemble non-Muslim women's clothes.
8. Their foot ornaments must not produce sound.
9. They must not wear sound-producing garments.
10. They must not walk in the middle of streets.
11. They must not go out of their houses without their husband's permission.
12. They must not talk to strange men.
13. If it is necessary to talk, they must talk in a low voice and without laughter.
14. They must not look at strangers.
15. They must not mix with strangers.

In most parts of Afghanistan women now had to wear a burqa because of the fear of being kidnapped, raped and murdered. Young girls were forcibly married to the jihadi commanders. These so-called Muslims married four women in public, which is permitted in Islam, but most of them had more than four wives. They used rape as a weapon to dominate and terrorise people. Their men raped children as young as four, and cut off the breasts of women. There were even reports reaching Pakistan of these criminals raping the dead bodies of women and the old grandmothers – which is beyond imagination.

Nahid Hassan is a well-known martyr of this brutal period of our history. When she was a thirteen-year-old girl, her family's Kabul apartment was attacked by a jihadi commander and his men in early 1993. After they gunned down her twelve-year-old brother and other male relatives, Nahid chose to leap out of the sixth-floor window to her death rather than be raped. Today, there is a shrine to her memory at the spot where she fell.

It was not only the women who were made the victims, but men were also subjected to rape and abduction. Nails were driven into people's skulls and they were left to die. They were put into containers and were burnt. There were public beheadings. Whenever people raised their voices against injustice, they were either insulted and beaten or killed. The insecurity in Kabul was so bad that Amnesty International reported an instance where one family, whose young daughters had been abducted and murdered, had to bring the bodies back to their house and bury them there because it was not safe to take them to the graveyard. The Amnesty 1995 report was simply titled 'Women in Afghanistan: A Human Rights Catastrophe'.

The criminal mujahideen torched public schools and univer-sities. The Kabul National Museum was one of the richest cultural repositories in the world, but during these years it was used as a bunker and 70 per cent of its 100,000 items that dated back several millennia were looted or destroyed. The National Archives were looted. They burned the libraries and even the Holy Quran. They stole the doors and windows of the government offices even as they ransacked private houses. They also stole the precious gems of Badakhshan. Massoud was a famous trader of these gemstones and sold them to Russians. Massoud was later killed just days before the attacks of 9/11. Today this infamous criminal is portrayed as a hero by the Karzai government and the French government, which had close ties with him when alive, and works especially hard to portray him as a legend and even nominated him for the Nobel Peace Prize.

Even though Islamic teaching promotes tolerance of others, the fundamentalist warlords purged all other faiths. The majority of our people are Muslims but a small minority are Hindu and Sikh. The fundamentalists not only insulted the Hindus but also banned their religious festivals and forced them to wear a yellow cloth around their arms so that they could be identified as Hindus – the same way Hitler did to Jews. They even circumcised the Hindu males, even though it is not part of their culture. Today, Hindus in Afghanistan have even been prevented from having a facility to cremate their dead, as is required by their tradition. They have held protests, threatening to leave Afghanistan entirely if they are denied this basic right.

Even though the civil war years were among the most bloody and oppressive of Afghanistan's past three decades, the media and most of the international community had almost no interest in us at the time. Some people even say that the United States wanted a civil war in Afghanistan, as it was afraid of the huge quantity of weapons in the hands of the mujahideen. It wanted them to fight each other and consume the remaining weapons and ammunition. Not until after 9/11 did the world's attention really return to Afghanistan. Until then, the atrocities against our people were considered an internal matter.

I was lucky that my father was wise enough to take us back to Pakistan before we, too, became victims of the civil war. It would have been impossible to continue my education in Farah. We returned to Pashaee camp and my siblings and I returned to the same school.

When I was in my ninth year at school, I heard that an NGO, which had programmes in the camp, was looking for people to teach basic literacy to adults and to assist with the classes for the children. To help make ends meet for my own family, I applied for a position and soon started work as a teacher. I was paid 500 rupees per month (the equivalent of about 17 US dollars).

Most days I would go to school for my own lessons, and then stay on afterwards to teach adult women to read and write in the evening. Only fourteen or fifteen years old myself when I started, it was quite a challenge to teach my elders. I wondered if I could be a good teacher. At first I was very nervous and shy when speaking to the class. It took time and effort to overcome my fear.

I had to win the respect and confidence of my students, otherwise they might stop attending my classes. One day I was sick and I asked a friend to fill in for me, but apparently this replacement was unable to engage properly with these older students. The next day, one of the women in my class scolded me. 'Don't you ever miss class again!'

Many of my students were very poor women and this was their first real chance to get a basic education. I knew that, for many of them, attending class was something of a luxury and that they could only take time for themselves if all their housework was done and all of their children were fed and cared for. They often missed classes and some stopped attending altogether when times were particularly tough for their families.

Because of these circumstances, I suggested to the school's administration that they purchase some basic household supplies that we could then offer to those who attended and completed their lessons. I thought this would be a great incentive for the women to keep up their attendance. From then on, at the end of each week's classes women were sent home with bars of soap or rice or other basics – and the size of my classes quickly grew!

One of my students was a housewife from the neighbouring refugee camp, where there were no literacy classes for women. She was very interested in learning, but her husband was against it. He told her she had to take care of the children while he worked all day in the local brick factories. But while her husband was working, she let her oldest children take care of the younger ones while she secretly took my course. In six months she learned to read and write, without her husband knowing.

Later she started her own class to teach women in her camp, and was getting some money from her students. When her husband found out about it, instead of being angry, he was happy that his wife was helping him to bring in some money to make ends meet. Since then, this husband has been encouraging other women to get an education.

My teaching also had an impact on my own family. My

mother never had the chance to go to school as a child, but now she decided to join my class. It was a special feeling to be able to help my own mother learn to read and write. I treated her just like the other students, a number of whom were even older than her.

I really enjoyed teaching, but I was still young and eager to learn more myself. I especially wanted to learn English but, unfortunately, the only class available was at the same time as the one I taught right across the hall. Before heading home at the end of the evening, I would cross the hall into the empty classroom where the English lesson had been held in the hope that there would still be some words left on the blackboard. If there were, I would copy them down and try to make sense of them.

My experience in the refugee camps taught me a lot about the Afghan people. I saw suffering and injustice with my own eyes, and I learned about the power of education. These experiences affected how I thought about the world. I was reading a lot on my own, as well.

My father loved reading and always encouraged me to read as many books as I could. He used to recite the proverb 'Tell me what you read and I shall tell you who you are.' Once he bought me a gift at a second-hand bookstore: it was a book he had read and liked when he was in jail. Written by Mir Ghulam Muhammad Ghobar, it was called *Afghanistan in the Course of History* and it is still regarded as one of the most credible history books on Afghanistan. My father guided me to read important books that helped to shape my life and my ideas. My father had a good collection of books in Persian, and I would stay awake and read late into the night by the light of our propane lamp.

Ashraf Dehghani's *The Epic of Resistance* had a particularly strong impact on me. She wrote this book to document and expose the horrors of the Iranian jails where she and many others had been detained as political prisoners. Dehghani's steadfastness in the face of abuse and injustice has always inspired me. Maxim Gorky's books *Mother* and *My University Days* and many of the novels of

Jack London were also very memorable, especially *White Fang*.

I loved poetry, too, and I soaked up the delicious language of Iranian and Afghan poets. I also discovered a great African-American poet, Langston Hughes, whose eloquent writing illuminates the injustices endured by black America. Bertolt Brecht wrote inspiring words for social activists around the globe, and I memorised many of them, passages such as:

> *There are men who struggle for a day and they are good.*
> *There are men who struggle for a year and they are better.*
> *There are men who struggle many years, and they are better still.*
> *But there are those who struggle all their lives:*
> *These are the indispensable ones.*

I even posted a copy of Brecht's poem 'Praise of Learning' for women who feared it was too late for them to begin their education.

> *Learn the elementary things!*
> *For those whose time has come*
> *It is never too late!*
> *Learn the ABC. It won't be enough,*
> *But learn it! Don't be dismayed by it!*
> *Begin! You must know everything.*
> *You must take over the leadership.*

Biographies fascinated me as well. I read about Mohammad Mossadegh, the democratically elected leader of Iran, whom the United States and Britain helped to overthrow in 1953. I learned about the life of Mahatma Gandhi, Che Guevara, Patrice Lumumba, Bhagat Singh, Saeed Sultanpur, Víctor Jara and others. The story of Nelson Mandela's life in particular struck a chord. He spent twenty-seven years in prison, but he never let his captors break him or change his ideas. Prison walls could not contain Mandela's determination, and his biography was a revelation.

There were not many films available in the camps, but I remember watching the movie *Spartacus*, the story of a slave uprising during Roman times, on a VCR. It's the story of one of the oldest and most important rebellions in history, and it shows the importance of fighting to the end even when the odds are stacked against you. It made a lasting impression on me.

Another movie that I really enjoyed and that actually changed my life was *The Gadfly*, a story of romance and revolutionary heroism based in Italy. I was about sixteen or seventeen the first time I watched it, and I must have seen it at least three times. I also enjoyed the book it is based on, which is written by Ethel Lilian Voynich. I was moved by the character Arthur (the titular Gadfly), who was motivated by love of his country and a commitment to struggle for justice even at the cost of his relationship with his own father.

At the time I was also listening to music on a tape player. I was especially a fan of Daruish, the Iranian freedom-loving singer, and I had all of his tapes.

All of this – the conditions in the camps, my teaching, the reading I was doing – was changing my perception of the world, and I had taken Brecht's words to heart. I wanted to do something. Above all, I wanted to participate in efforts to improve the situation of the Afghan people.

During the civil war, the Taliban were training in the mosques of Pakistan and sending recruits to fight against the former mujahideen warlords. They planned to establish their own type of Islamic state in Afghanistan, with the help of the Pakistan government. In September 1996, they drove some of the warlords into exile and others into Northern Afghanistan, and took power; by 1998, they controlled almost 95 per cent of the country. The Taliban promised our people security. They were so exhausted by the years of war and anarchy that once again our people welcomed the new regime with hope that they might bring a positive change. But unfortunately their hopes quickly turned into ashes. The Taliban repeated the same crimes committed by their jihadi brothers. And their security was like that of a graveyard.

While we lived in the camp, we followed the news of the outside world on radio. I was always so sad to hear about the latest atrocities in Afghanistan. There were also regular reports about the intifada in Palestine and how their children were bravely fighting against the aggression of Israeli troops.

I asked my father, 'Why are we not from Palestine, where even the children are so brave?'

'If that's the way you feel,' he replied, 'why don't you think about becoming like a Palestinian in your own country?'

This had a deep impact on me. I thought about what he said for days. I wanted to work to end what was going on in Afghanistan, and perhaps my father was showing me the way.

———

Around 1998 I first met the founders of the Organisation for Promoting Afghan Women's Capabilities (OPAWC). They were just getting started – not yet registered as an official NGO – but were eager to do more work inside Afghanistan. They had heard about my teaching in the refugee camps by word of mouth, and they introduced me to their plans. They wanted to improve the health and education of women and girls – the first and worst victims of poverty. Initially their main focus would be to improve educational opportunities for women, and they were looking for volunteers.

These OPAWC leaders convinced me to join their cause. After grade 12, I had been eager to go to university and continue my formal education, but financially this was impossible in Pakistan. I believed in OPAWC's goals, and working with them sounded like another way for me to continue my education. I was not yet truly political in my thinking, but I identified with the idea of activism to serve the needs of the people.

So I joined OPAWC to work as a full-time social activist. They were looking for someone to send into Herat Province to start classes there for girls in defiance of the Taliban and its edicts.

I decided that I wanted to take on this project and to accept the risk involved. This is when I adopted the surname Joya to protect my family's identity.

With the exception of a few months, I had spent almost sixteen years living in exile. It was time to go home to Afghanistan.

CHAPTER 3

THE SHADOW OF
THE TALIBAN

*T*HE ANCIENT CITY OF HERAT in north-western Afghanistan is famous for its towering fortresses, wide tree-lined avenues and beautiful tiled mosques. It is the country's third most populous city and one of its important centres of culture and history. Herat's people are known for their open-mindedness and the value they place on education.

Unfortunately, like the rest of the country, Herat has long suffered from war and abusive, corrupt governance. The first battle of the Soviet–Afghan War took place here in 1979 after the people of Herat rose against Soviet advisers in the city. The air force responded by bombing Herat without mercy, killing 24,000 people in one week. During the civil war of the 1990s, Ismail Khan became governor of Herat Province and ran it as his fiefdom. A strict fundamentalist and close ally of the mullahs who run Iran, Khan is one of those former mujahideen leaders who fought the Russians but later turned on the Afghan people. For instance, he was sending gunmen to support the Jamiat-e-Islami forces who were ransacking Kabul. Because of warlords like Khan, the civil war years were unspeakably dark.

When the Taliban took over the city in 1995, he fled to Iran and began to plot his return.

Like the fundamentalist warlords they replaced, the Taliban leaders misused Islam and imposed strict rules and repressive, medieval measures in the name of religion. All men were compelled to grow beards, and women were forcibly shrouded in burqas. And as most people are no doubt aware, the Taliban strictly forbade any formal education for women and girls. But the educated and proud people of Herat simply would not tolerate it. They wanted all their children to learn. So it was natural that OPAWC requested that I go to this particular city to work as an underground teacher.

It was very sad to leave behind the camps of Peshawar where I had grown up, and the students and friends and neighbours I had worked beside for so many years. But I was an adult now and Afghanistan was where I wanted to be – back in the home country I'd had to leave when I was only four years old – even though I knew it would be very dangerous.

The Taliban dealt fierce punishment to anyone who broke their rules. Lashings, beheadings and hangings were carried out in public, with the victim's body often left out on display for days. In Kabul the Ghazi stadium became infamous as the site of grisly executions. Even the dead were not safe. Some Afghan refugees in Pakistan preferred to take the bodies of their relatives home to bury them in their own country. Once, when a family tried to take the body of a young teenage boy to Afghanistan through the Turkham border crossing, the Taliban stopped them and demanded to check the coffin. When they opened it, the Taliban saw the dead body of a young boy who had no beard. They told the relatives that the boy who died was an infidel because he had no beard, so according to their rule he must be lashed. They actually took the corpse out of the coffin and whipped it in front of the family. Then they allowed them to cross the border.

Everyone in the refugee camps had heard this story and others like it.

Despite what they knew about the Taliban regime, my family decided that they would support my decision and move with me to Herat. Our family piled into a truck for the long trip back home.

This was an emotional journey for our whole family. For my youngest siblings, it was the first time they would see Afghanistan. The moment we crossed the border, we could see signs of the destruction wrought by so many years of war and repressive governments. The roads were in total disrepair, and burned-out tanks and other army vehicles littered the landscape. When we stopped for breaks, children were warned not to stray too far from the road, lest they join the ranks of the thousands of victims of land-mines that remained from previous wars. The Taliban stopped us and searched our luggage at checkpoints along the route. This was a frightful experience, as I remember these gruff men interrogating my father, and even asking questions to make sure we were Muslims. By the end of the journey, the heat and tension had left all of us exhausted, and even my skin colour had changed from all the dust along the roads. What began as anticipation at seeing my dear Afghanistan again turned into sadness when I saw the sombre expressions of men and the silent, burqa-shrouded women drifting along the streets of Herat like ghosts.

It took our family a while to be accepted into the community. Of course it was natural, given the conditions, for people to be suspicious of their neighbours at this time; everyone had to be on guard against Taliban loyalists and informers. This is why, when my family and I arrived in Herat, it was a long, difficult process before I could begin teaching. It was not an easy thing to set up an underground school, especially in a heavily populated city, and many precautions had to be taken.

First of all, the men in our family had to let their facial hair grow, something they hadn't done before. Soon my eldest brother and my father had thick beards as long as 'a clenched fist', according to the rules for male grooming. In fact, they had to start growing their beards even before returning to Afghanistan, because they could have been denied entry if clean-shaven. In those days we joked that a beard was like an entry visa for

Afghanistan. One of our neighbours in Herat later confided that they suspected my family was Taliban because of those beards. But my father and brother were just trying to blend in.

It was during these years that I had to learn to wear the burqa, and I didn't like it. Not one bit. It's not only oppressive but it's more difficult than you might think, and it took me a while to get the hang of it. My father always said he could spot me in any crowd of women wearing burqas because of the way I walked. He said I looked like a penguin. You have no peripheral vision because of the netting in front of your eyes. And it's hot and suffocating under there. The only useful thing about those long blue robes was that they could be used to hide school books and other forbidden objects.

In addition to the harsh restrictions on clothing, many other things were banned under the Taliban. Television, movies and recorded music were illegal, as well. If the Taliban searched your house and found any of this type of material, they would destroy it. Even having books other than the Quran in your own house became dangerous, especially if they carried photos of human beings. The taking and publishing of human photos was considered un-Islamic; the Taliban's daily newspaper had no photos in it.

The Taliban sent bands of men out to enforce their rules, and if we saw them around or thought that they might be coming to do a search of our home, we would hide our books and our writings. On one occasion, I even burned two notebooks full of my personal memories because I was afraid they would be found when our house was searched. I cried as I watched them burn, but I could not risk them falling into the hands of the Taliban. It would have put my whole family at risk.

The Taliban continued to prevent small religious minorities in Afghanistan, such as the tens of thousands of Hindu believers in Kabul and in other provinces, from practising their faiths publicly. But their intolerance was so extreme that even our country's unique cultural heritage fell victim. They considered it a crime against Islam to depict any human image. The Taliban's most infamous act was blowing up the 2,000-year-old Buddhist statues in Bamyan Province, which were the largest in the world. The video of the falling Buddhas was shown over and over on international television. But there were many other smaller desecrations that took place every day. Faces were scraped off paintings and photographs. Heads were lopped off store mannequins as well as priceless museum pieces.

Daily prayer was strictly monitored. It was compulsory for all men to attend the mosque for prayers five times each day. If the Taliban suspected that someone had missed one of the times, they would be taken back to the mosque. Sometimes men and boys ended up praying seven or eight times in one day, because the Taliban wrongly accused them of missing one of the prayers. Other times they could be beaten, or worse.

Even though their religious observations and ordinary behaviour were so closely monitored, the people's spirit was not broken. Trusted friends and family quietly ridiculed the Taliban. They had been hoping for better conditions following the civil war but instead, as the Afghan saying goes, when the earth tore apart, the donkeys came out. I know some people, even old men, who when they had been beaten by Taliban for not obeying their rules, shaved as a show of protest – even though they had never shaved before in their lives.

Young people rebelled in different ways against the Taliban. Some neighbourhood girls became good friends of mine. Sometimes we would invite them over and all of us would dance to amuse ourselves. And dancing was strictly forbidden. Some of us secretly dressed up in modern clothes, which tailors would make if you paid them for a special job. Sometimes girls would even wear Western-style clothes and put on make-up underneath the burqa. I liked to see this, because I felt it was a way for young people to show their resistance to the Taliban.

After teaching in the refugee camps and seeing first-hand how learning brings confidence and pride to women, I was eager to begin my classes in Herat. With the help of other OPAWC activists, we first got to know our own neighbourhood and to identify potential supporters. Many of my OPAWC colleagues were young, educated women who turned to activism because they were forbidden from continuing at university. The hardest part of all was simply finding a secure site for a school. Often, the classes ended up being held in the basements of educated people's homes. And, once established, it is difficult to hide a school, however modest its location. So as not to arouse suspicions, I would tell the students not to come to school in groups larger than two or three, but sometimes they would be afraid and all walk together. It was natural – the girls were nervous about the Taliban so they travelled in groups. But on a number of occasions this behaviour raised the Taliban's suspicions and they discovered the location of a girls' school. Those caught harbouring a girls' school were jailed, or worse. It was very upsetting when this happened, and it would often take a month or more to locate another house where classes could be established. I know of one man in Herat who was sent to Kandahar and imprisoned and tortured for years for the crime of possessing a RAWA magazine with anti-Taliban articles. He was only released from jail after the fall of the Taliban.

Initially, though, crowds weren't a problem. Finding students took time. In Herat, my first classes were made up of my younger sisters and just a few other children of families that OPAWC was in contact with. But word began to spread, and we slowly found more and more girls who wanted to learn. Of course, the daily security situation in the area affected attendance. One day I taught a class with only three students.

Unlike in the refugee camps, here my students were all children. I taught girls from elementary school age until grade 12 – all different ages and subjects, with the exception of maths. Mathematics was the one subject I had always had difficulty with, so other teachers would come to teach it.

Even though these schools were unofficial and very ad hoc –

with very young and inexperienced teachers – I'm proud of the quality of education we were able to provide for the girls. I know in fact that the girls who attended OPAWC's schools received a better education than the Taliban provided in the madrassas for boys. I say this because one of my younger sisters, whom I taught, is very close in age to one of my younger brothers who went to school during the Taliban years. He fell behind his sister in almost all subjects. His lessons were almost exclusively in Arabic on religious subjects, and the teachers at the madrassas could be harsh. He would sometimes come home in tears because he had been beaten for forgetting to wear his turban or for having committed some other punishable offence.

I have a terrifying memory of an occasion when Taliban patrols nearly discovered one of our schools. I was teaching a class in a room in a family's basement, when one of the women of the house yelled down that the Taliban were coming. I instructed my students to lie down on the floor and remain silent, and I switched off the lamp. We listened in the dark to the footsteps above us. Fortunately, they never came down to the basement. After a close call like that, we had no choice but to find a new location.

My family rented a string of houses, moving when we felt our security was at risk. Sometimes we discovered that neighbours were Taliban supporters, and in those cases we had to move. It was difficult to find a good place to live. For one thing, the safer the area was, the higher the rent. You could find a very cheap house, but often only in very dangerous neighbourhoods.

In fact, soon after we arrived in Herat we decided it was necessary to split up the family for a while. I needed to be close to the location OPAWC had identified for a school, but the house we were to live in wasn't suitable for our whole family. So my oldest brother, who was in his mid-twenties, and a number of my older sisters lived with me in the one house, while Mother and Father lived in another house with the younger children. But, of course, my parents still helped us out. My father would come over and bring food. They always took care of us.

At this house we became friendly with the family next door. They noticed how often I was leaving the house, so they asked me somewhat suspiciously, 'All that coming and going … What are you doing?' During these years, most women stayed in their houses all the time.

Because I trusted these neighbours, I told them that it was because I was a teacher. But before I let them in on this secret, some of them thought that maybe I was not a good girl.

Once they knew the truth about what I was really up to, they were interested and wanted to know more about how the schools worked. Their children respected us and sometimes the little boys even helped us carry our schoolbooks. When we came around the corner to our street, they would see us walking home and struggling because of all the big black notebooks of student homework under our burqas, and they would run out enthusiastically to meet us and offer, 'Can I help you, my sister?'

And I would respond politely, 'Yes, thank you!'

This is a poignant memory for me – a show of solidarity from young boys, children who did not share the attitude of the people who ran our country.

The neighbours' daughters became our friends, too, but one of them couldn't believe that I really was a teacher, so one day I told her, 'Come with me and see!'

Perhaps this was a bit mischievous of me, but I also thought it might be a way to get more students into my classes.

And it worked. She came and observed me teaching and then, on the way home, she asked if she could enrol her younger sister and her niece. This is the way we recruited new students. A slow process, but one that was immensely rewarding every time a new girl joined us.

Mostly I taught in the city but sometimes I also travelled to nearby villages. This was not a regular occurrence, maybe twice a month. Often when we had to go outside town, my father would give my sisters, their classmates and me a ride on his motorbike. It was amazing: with only one leg he could give as many as five of us girls a ride on his bike. Three of us, burqas and all, would sit on the back, two small sisters in the front.

My father worked at many odd jobs during these years to feed our large family. He did whatever work he could find. Because of his education, he would also sometimes help the neighbours out with medical advice and check-ups, and some of them started calling him 'Doctor'. Mother joked that even though he never got to become a physician because of joining the struggle against the Soviets, now people were calling him a 'doctor' anyway.

My father's own health often suffered because of how much he worked. Some days he would come home from work and the stump of his leg would be bloodied and sore. At night he would often be in pain. The only cure for this was rest, but this was not possible as only he and my eldest brother were able to work to provide for the family. The neighbours noticed how hard Father worked, and they joked that he worked harder than an able-bodied man with two good legs. For our part, women were forbidden from getting jobs, so my sisters and I helped out at home. These were difficult years, as drought had led to a sharp increase in prices of basic necessities.

At the various houses we lived in during these years, my father liked to plant flowers and some vegetables, whenever it was possible. He always wanted to have a garden. This caused Mother to joke with him again. She said that maybe instead of a doctor he should have been a farmer, because he was always planting and watering.

There was still ice cream under the Taliban, but the shops that sold it were not the same as before. There were usually a few benches or seats for men to sit down with their ice cream, but women had to stay in a separate area, usually standing up. We also had to keep our burqas on while we ate. It was a challenge to learn to eat ice cream under the burqa. You had to use a hand to hold up the material enough to eat. It certainly made ice cream less enjoyable.

Of course, despite (and because of) all the restrictions, there was still a black market, and it was during these years that the Hollywood film *Titanic* became a huge underground sensation in Afghanistan. People smuggled copies of the film, and other contraband, across the Iranian border. Young people were especially big fans. Children and young adults would organise secret '*Titanic* parties' to watch this movie.

I think I was twenty-one when I first saw it in about 1999. My sisters and I were invited over to watch it with the neighbours' children, the ones with whom we had become friendly. This family had a secret room where they had a TV and a VCR. Father thought that only one of us girls should go over and watch the movie, and that if we all went we would cause problems for the neighbours. But we convinced him and I think five of us girls went over to watch it. We were nervous about being found out by the Taliban, and every time there was a knock at the door we turned off the movie. We did not want the Taliban to destroy the TV!

I enjoyed the movie, not so much for the love story but because it was a story about sacrifice and it showed how the rich were arrogant and mistreated the poor. I said at the time that this movie showed that everyone must have a goal, a dream, and strive to achieve it, and in Afghanistan we could have a goal to be free of the Taliban. The other girls joked that I would try to find some political message in everything, even in a Hollywood love story. I remember that we were all so shocked when Jack (Leonardo DiCaprio's character) died at the end of the movie – it was unbelievable! We wished that Jack had survived and he and Rose had got married.

The movie *Titanic*, for its part, was so popular that even in the open markets many things started to be called 'Titanic'. There were Titanic clothes and even shampoo! Some merchants even went so far as to name their vegetables after the movie. So you could go to the market and buy Titanic onions, Titanic tomatoes, eggplant, potatoes, and so on. I found the idea of vegetables named after a Hollywood movie especially funny. It was a nationwide craze. The Kabul River crosses the middle of a rowdy bazaar in the centre of the capital. In the summer, when there is no water in the river, people move their small shops onto the dry riverbed. One summer, people started calling the new market the 'Titanic Bazaar' and the name stuck for years. There were even reports that a mullah had given a religious sermon in which he argued that those who disobeyed God would be destroyed like the *Titanic*. From this, we understood that even those who banned the film were watching it.

After the Taliban regime fell in 2001, one of the first things people did was buy cassettes and DVDs – they became bestsellers at the markets that were suddenly full of them. On every street, people would blast their music during those first weeks after the Taliban fled. In Kabul, aside from Afghan music, Indian songs could be heard everywhere, and in Farah it was Iranian music that was especially popular.

In my opinion the most important rebellion against the Taliban was the underground schooling for girls. OPAWC was not the only group trying to organise in this way. Many others throughout Afghanistan were taking similar risks, sometimes with minimal financial help from groups abroad, but most often on their own.

OPAWC did other support work for people who were poor or in difficult conditions, and I participated in some of these activities. Once we brought supplies to refugees who were living in tents at a camp called Maslakh outside Herat. They were internal refugees from the region of Chikhchiran, where there was a very bad drought. These people were starving. It was very painful to see such suffering. One dying baby in particular, I will never forget, was just skin and bones. Memories of such deprivation still motivate me today to be politically active and to tell the truth. When I joined OPAWC, I was still very young and not interested in politics in the way I am today, but I wanted to be a social activist and I liked the fact that this organisation focused on women, health and education.

All this activism made for a very tough schedule. If I was lucky, I would arrive home in the evening just in time for supper, and then I would usually be the last person in my house to go to sleep. Often, when we weren't living in separate houses, it was my father and I who would stay up late, preparing for the next day's classes by lamplight. For the high school subjects I had to prepare well, or else I could not teach properly. Father would often help me prepare my lessons.

When I had time, I would stay up late reading for my own interest as well. For me, reading has always been very important. In addition to my experiences, it has made me who I am and helped me understand the importance of the values we are struggling for. Even so, my life now does not leave me much time for reading.

I was not the only one in my family who took risks during these years. My brother was also an activist in his own way. He had a camera with which he liked to go out and secretly take pictures. He had a special pocket where he kept his camera hidden, and he would quickly take it out when he wanted to take a shot and he felt he wasn't being observed. This was my eldest brother, the one with a long thick beard. He also spoke excellent Pashto, the language most Taliban were speaking. These things helped him get out of many potentially dangerous situations.

Once, however, my brother got himself into a terrible predicament. He had been out for a walk and came across an execution victim whose corpse had been hung upside down from a lamppost. This was done to send a message of fear to others in the city. My brother took out his camera and took a quick picture. Taliban soldiers must have seen him do this because they grabbed him and beat him and then took him to the police station. After questioning him, they went with him to a photo shop to get his negatives developed.

While the photographs were being developed, my brother was detained with two other men who had also been caught taking pictures. After a long wait, the Taliban men brought out some pictures and took my brother aside to question him first.

'Are these your photos?' they demanded.

They weren't. They were pictures from someone's wedding. But my brother said yes, they were his photos.

The Taliban hit him a few more times for good measure but then let him go. Once he got safely away though, my brother started to worry about his photograph and what might happen to the other men if they were accused of taking it. So he stayed outside to see what would happen. Fortunately, the other men were let go as well.

We later learned that the photo shop owner had tricked the Taliban by giving them the wrong pictures. He knew that if the Taliban had seen the photo of the hangings, they would do the same thing to my brother. It was another example of the quiet resistance of people who were risking their lives to rescue their fellow countrymen.

Meanwhile it was late at night and we were all worried. My mother, who suffers from bouts of depression, was extremely upset. She was shouting and crying and thinking that my brother had been killed. When he finally arrived home safely, she slowly calmed down. My father told him to stop taking photographs, but he continued because he wanted to document the crimes the Taliban were committing.

During the Taliban years, it was risky for a woman to move around the city, since she could be stopped and challenged at any time. If she was seen in the market without Mahram – a close male relative, either a son, husband, father or brother – Taliban enforcers would flag her down on the spot and she could be badly punished. But I have seen for myself and heard from others of many cases when a woman was caught without Mahram, a man who was passing nearby would rescue that woman by coming forward and saying, 'Here, I am her Mahram.' This was dangerous for a man if the Taliban found him not to be a real Mahram. But contrary to the perception that all Afghan men are against women, many men are very sympathetic and risked their lives to help them.

It was especially dangerous for a young woman like me carrying clandestine schoolbooks to travel on the street. Sometimes I would walk with my father so that I was less likely to be bothered. I remember once we were stopped and searched, but my burqa saved me. They ordered me to stretch out my arms but, because they did not pat me down, they never found the schoolbooks hidden beneath. This was when it first occurred to me that wearing the burqa had *some* advantages. This was the first time but it wouldn't be the last.

On days when classes were late or I was otherwise delayed, my solitary journey home from teaching could be a dangerous one. In Herat, as in all cities and towns across Afghanistan, the Taliban imposed and policed a 6 p.m. curfew after which no woman was to be outside by herself. If you were picked up for breaking the curfew, you could be jailed, beaten, even killed.

One night when I was running late, the school's hosts offered to let me stay the night. But there was no way for me to call home – my hosts didn't own a telephone and neither did we – and I didn't want my parents to worry about why I had not come home. So I decided to walk, even though I was alone and it was past the curfew hour for women.

I covered myself and the small stack of books I was carrying with my burqa, and stepped out into the evening. Rather than walking straight home, which normally took about thirty minutes, I took a longer route, using the side streets in the hope that I would escape detection. I kept right to the side of the road and tried to walk as quickly as possible without drawing attention to myself. I wished I had some peripheral vision so that I could watch for Taliban patrols, but with the burqa it was an effort to turn my head at all. Then I thought, *Forget the peripheral vision. I wish I could be invisible.* All the better to reach home safely.

The dusty streets of Herat were quiet and, even though the sun had just gone down, the heat was oppressive. From behind the mud walls of houses, I could smell the garlic from *bolani* being cooked and I could hear the din of men's voices in conversation.

All alone on one of these narrow, poorly lit streets, I suddenly picked up the engine noise of a vehicle approaching behind me. Without looking, I could tell it was one of the Toyota pickup trucks full of young Taliban men on patrol. I knew that these men were well armed and that they weren't likely to ignore a woman out on her own at this hour. If they stopped me and found my schoolbooks, there was no telling what they might do to me.

I quickened my pace, but the truck was gaining ground. Its headlights shining on me, I imagined my mother's pain and anguish if I did not make it home. I had had a few close calls with Taliban patrols before, but on those occasions my older brother – with his impressive beard and polished Pashto – had been there to get me out of trouble. This time I was alone, and my heart raced as I tried to think of what to do next.

As casually as I could, I turned into the yard of the next house I came to, opening the old wooden gate and walking up to the front door. It was a very modest home, the yard surrounded only by a wire fence. I knocked on the door and held my breath, aware that the truck had slowed right down and that the Taliban were watching me from the street. I tried my best to remain calm.

An older woman opened the door of this strangers' home. As quietly and politely as I could, I asked, 'Forgive me, Mother, may I come in to have a glass of water.'

Without saying a word, she motioned for me to come in, and immediately I could tell that she understood my situation.

Inside, she brought me the water. Then she waited with me for several minutes until the Taliban had left the street. 'My child, it is dangerous to be out at this hour,' she chided me.

'I know, Mother, but I must get home to my parents.'

She did not ask me any questions even though she could see that I was carrying books. Who knows what would have happened to me if no one had come to the door, or if it had been the man of the house who had answered when I knocked.

As I headed back out to finish my walk home, she simply said, 'God keep you safe, my daughter.' She understood that she had helped me out of a dangerous situation.

Really though, there was nothing too unusual about this interaction. Every day in Afghanistan, even now, hundreds if not thousands of ordinary women act out these small gestures of solidarity with each other. By necessity, after decades of brutality, we are our sisters' keepers.

Back on the street that night, I walked even faster the rest of the way home, almost tripping over the burqa's material at my feet. My ears listened nervously for the sound of that engine, but thankfully I did not hear it again that night. A few side streets and alleyways later, and I was finally home.

I burst into the house, found my father and hugged him. My mother was lying in bed, but she wasn't asleep. I was upset with myself for having made her worry and I apologised to her for being so late. I didn't tell either of my parents about my close call with the Taliban.

Most of my brothers and sisters were already asleep, so Father and I stayed up by the light of our propane lamp with some of my schoolbooks open. Like so many nights, he helped me to prepare my lessons for the next day, answering all the questions I had about my subjects.

Teaching at an underground girls' school was a dangerous job, but I never even considered giving it up. I felt I was doing something good and positive for my people, and I was filled with energy and enthusiasm. I felt it was a great injustice that Afghan girls were being denied an education. The Taliban wanted to keep them in the dark, because any time a group is denied education it is harder for them to know their rights and to fight for them. When I was a young girl I was able to go to school even though we lived in refugee camps. Why couldn't that basic level of schooling be available to the next generation?

Over their five years in power, the people of the world slowly became more aware of the crimes of the Taliban regime. Some very dedicated women's activists in other countries worked hard to support the struggle of Afghan women. Eve Ensler, for instance, a famous American playwright and artist, visited Afghanistan at this time and tried to raise awareness about our plight. In general though, the world did not pay too much attention to Afghanistan. All that would soon change.

In the summer of 2001, I was named the director of OPAWC in western Afghanistan, which was a big responsibility. At the time, OPAWC was still an underground, unregistered NGO. After a few years of working for them, I had gained their trust. My new job put me in charge of OPAWC's operations in the provinces of Herat, Farah and Nimroz. I was happy about my new position, but also anxious to meet the challenge of these new responsibilities.

Of the three provinces under my direction, Farah was the most remote and needy of these regions and faced the most serious challenges so, after some personal reflection, I decided that I should move there. This move was also a return home, and I didn't go alone. My family was as supportive as ever of my work, and also keen to return to Farah where the economic opportunities were better for them. So they decided to go back with me to the province where I had spent the first four years of my life.

It was not easy for me to leave Herat, but it was necessary. I was very close to my students in the schools that had so painstakingly been established, and I have great memories of those children, and of the brave people who let us use their homes as classrooms. The people of Herat taught me a lot. I was a young woman starting my work as a social activist under dangerous conditions, and countless people in Herat had given me a helping hand.

The decision taken, once again our family was on the move. We packed up our belongings and made the trip to Farah City. We moved back in with Uncle Babak before finding a place of our own. We were just getting re-established when, on the night of September 11th, the radio broadcast some horrifying news. Planes hijacked by terrorists had been flown into the World Trade Center in New York City and the Pentagon in Washington, DC. There were thousands of American dead and injured. Within days everyone knew that there would be a war.

CHAPTER 4

A CLINIC,
AN ORPHANAGE
AND ANOTHER
OCCUPATION

MOST OF THE TALIBAN were long gone before the first bombs fell on Farah. Some of them shaved off their beards to make themselves less conspicuous as they ran away – and exposed themselves as hypocrites who broke their own 'sacred' laws to save their hides. Most of our local officials had also fled by the time the United States and its allies began its invasion. And so, in Farah as with the rest of my country, many lives were needlessly lost.

Every radio in Farah was tuned to the news day and night, and we knew there would soon be an attack. Some people had panicked and left their houses, only to return after the Taliban had fled. For days people were moving in and out of town, not knowing where to hide, often camping with relatives. Those who lived close to Taliban military installations were particularly worried, and with good reason.

The first target was Farah's radar tower, blasted to pieces by a cruise missile fired from a US submarine in the Arabian Gulf. It may have been the first air strike in the entire war. The devastating explosion shook the fragile mud-brick houses in the city, damaging some near the installation and injuring a few civilians. Luckily nobody was killed, most of the houses had already been evacuated.

The next day, US bombers roared over the city and hit the radio and TV station, along with the house of a Gulbuddin Party commander. The noise was terrifying, and children covered their ears and screamed and cried. Smoke and dust rose and lingered in the air with every bomb dropped. Luckily no civilians were killed in these first attacks on Farah, but there were many injuries. And the news reaching us from other parts of Afghanistan was terrible.

Just as many innocents died on September 11th, the initial invasion of Afghanistan also took many blameless lives. And in the years since, thousands of civilians have died from gunfire, mortars, aerial bombings, suicide bombings and the ubiquitous IEDs (improvised explosive devices). They call this death and destruction 'collateral damage' – a very clinical name for the carnage I later saw with my own eyes. One day, while I was walking through the centre of Farah City, I came across the aftermath of a bombing. Several low buildings had been damaged and, to my horror, there were still dead bodies of Taliban fighters lying in the street in pools of dark blood.

In Farah we did not see any ground troops for months to come after the invasion, because the United States and NATO mainly depended on air attacks. Once they arrived they established a fortified base outside town and they had no interaction with people. We only saw them as frightening, heavily armed soldiers riding in vehicles that were too dangerous to approach or overtake on the road. In the first years after Afghanistan was invaded, as they removed the oppressive regime of the Taliban and many promises were made, many people seemed sympathetic to the American and allied forces. But in the later years, as they did nothing for the people, installed a corrupt government, and killed many civilians, they lost support. And people discovered that behind the nice name of 'International Security Assistance Force' is in fact just another foreign occupation of Afghanistan.

While most people in Farah were pleased to see the flight of the Taliban, they were not at all happy with what emerged to fill the power vacuum. The warlords, many of whom had been run out of the country, came back to plunder the ruins. And, like the Taliban itself, the warlords were partly the creations of the US government.

Since they came to power, the Taliban had – like the funda-mentalist warlords before them – been offering sanctuary and support to the Saudi Osama bin Laden, the Egyptian Ayman al-Zawahiri and their foreign al-Qaeda followers. For years the United States had courted the Taliban, ignoring their cruelties while trying to make deals with them on behalf of the oil company UNOCAL, for an energy pipeline project through Afghanistan. The United States also encouraged the regime to crack down on opium production. (As recently as May 2001 the Taliban were given 43 million dollars as a reward for controlling the poppy crop.) At the same time, the United States turned a blind eye to what was happening in the terrorist training camps along the Pakistan border.

But in 1998, after al-Qaeda followers bombed two American embassies in Africa, the CIA turned its attention back to the monsters it had helped to create. After a cruise-missile attack failed to kill bin Laden, American agents began pouring money into the pockets of Ahmed Shah Massoud to hunt and kill bin Laden. This supposedly pious Muslim, Massoud, had been holed up in the Panjshir Valley north of Kabul while he took money from heroin traffickers and illegally exported precious stones recovered from mines in Panjshir.

Massoud was the military commander of a loose coalition of warlords and militia leaders who had been ousted by the Taliban and were now calling themselves 'The United Islamic Front for the Salvation of Afghanistan' – better known as the Northern

Alliance. Many of them had escaped to neighbouring countries and were supported by Iran, Russia, France, India and some other countries. They claimed to be mounting an armed resistance, but in fact, they barely controlled 5 per cent of the country when the 9/11 attacks suddenly changed their fortunes.

While the United States bombed from the sky, the CIA and Special Forces had already arrived in the northern provinces of Afghanistan to hand out millions of dollars in cash and weapons to Northern Alliance commanders. They were the same warlords whose militias had pillaged Afghanistan during the civil war. Abdul Rashid Dostum, Abdul Rab al-Rasul Sayyaf, Karim Khalili, Burhanuddin Rabbani, Qasim Fahim, General Arif, Dr Abdullah, Haji Qadir, Atta Mohammad, Daoud, and Hazrat Ali among others. The only one missing was Massoud, who was killed days before 9/11. His place as military leader of the Northern Alliance was taken by Massoud's closest crony, Mohammad Qasim Fahim, another ruthless man with a dark past. The Western media tried at the time to portray these warlords as 'anti-Taliban resistance forces and liberators of Afghanistan', but Afghan people believed that they were no different from the Taliban.

The Northern Alliance forces quickly took control of cities and provinces in much of the country and advanced on Kabul, ready and eager to collect the spoils of war. As soon as they returned, they started a new wave of crime and brutality. In the early days of the US occupation, thousands of Taliban fighters were surrounded at Kunduz in northern Afghanistan. Under the eyes of the media and US forces, the prisoners were handed over to the Uzbek warlord Rashid Dostum to be transferred to a prison in Sheberghan. But Dostum's men crammed them into sealed metal containers on the backs of trucks. When the trucks arrived, around 2,000 people had already died of suffocation. Dostum's men just bulldozed them into mass graves at Dasht-e-Leili near Mazar-e-Sharif. This war crime was kept secret until journalists uncovered it. Years later, there has still been no official investigation of the massacre.

On 19 November 2001, the *New York Times* reported, 'The galaxy of warlords who tore Afghanistan apart in the early 1990s and who were vanquished by the Taliban because of their corruption and perfidy are back on their thrones, poised to exercise power in the ways they always have.' As the warlords marched back into power, they returned to their old habits of using rape to punish their enemies and reward their fighters. Human Rights Watch and other organisations have documented terrible cases of rape against Pashtun women, simply because they were the same ethnic group as most Taliban. In one case, a fourteen-year-old girl named Fatima was raped by two soldiers in Northern Afghanistan. Then three other soldiers raped her mother. According to a report in the *Washington Post*, when the mother asked them why they were raping innocent women, they said it was because 'you are Talibs and you are Pashtun'.

Once the Northern Alliance had taken control of Afghanistan, the American administration had a problem: how to set up a lasting pro-US government? They knew they needed to include the Pashtuns, the most populous ethnic group in Afghanistan. But they had no reliable Pashtun warlords to put in power. The CIA couldn't turn to one of its favourite former clients, the virulent extremist Gulbuddin Hekmatyar, because he had joined the Taliban and Arab terrorists in attacking Western forces.

They looked instead to a minor Pashtun tribal leader from southern Afghanistan named Hamid Karzai. Karzai had been deputy foreign minister during the bloody civil war years. He was also believed to be a top contact for the CIA since the 1980s and was rumoured to be an adviser to UNOCAL, although he has denied it. Before bringing him to power, the US media had already started a campaign to portray him as a main anti-Taliban resistance leader. The 5th US Army Special Forces had already been sent to protect him in Uruzgan Province, where apparently he was fighting the Taliban.

In late 2001, the Western allies flew leading Afghan exiles, including many of the most notorious warlords, for a meeting in

Bonn, Germany, to set up a framework for installing a 'transitional' government and new institutions. Most Afghans believe that it was the start of a new era of disaster.

Although the meeting was supervised by the United Nations, the most powerful man in the background was the US State Department official and neoconservative icon Zalmay Khalilzad. The Afghan-born Khalilzad had been an American citizen since 1984, and he was a leading foreign policy adviser in the Reagan and both Bush administrations. Khalilzad had been promoting the warlords since he urged the American government to support them as mujahideen. He was also a consultant to UNOCAL during the 1990s, pushing for the gas-pipeline deal with the Taliban. In Bonn, Khalilzad was involved in the closed-door dealing that resulted in some brutal warlords being installed in the main posts of the new government. Today many people in Afghanistan see Khalilzad and the Americans as the creators of the current system that is in place in Kabul and thus sharing responsibility for the plight of Afghan people.

By the time it was over, the Bonn Conference had endorsed a new occupation army in Afghanistan – the International Security Assistance Force or ISAF – and had replaced the fundamentalist regime of the Taliban with another fundamentalist regime of warlords, along with some pro-US technocrats and monarchists. Hamid Karzai was named interim chairman. And an emergency Loya Jirga was scheduled for the following spring to legitimise the transition.

Throughout our history, whenever Afghanistan faced important reforms or changes in government, tribal elders and other leaders have assembled in a traditional gathering called a Loya Jirga. Some Loya Jirgas have been very colourful, others quite unruly. According to one account, a Loya Jirga took place in the southern city of Kandahar in 1747 to elect a king. After talking in circles for nine days, the Loya Jirga finally chose Ahmad Shah Durrani – because he was the only member who had said nothing during the long debate. Durrani went on to unite the various tribes and fiefdoms into one Afghanistan.

Another Loya Jirga was called in 1928 by King Amanullah to win support for a package of reforms – including more freedom for women. The king asked Queen Soraya to remove her veil at the Loya Jirga to prove his point – but the move backfired and the assembly dissolved in an uproar.

The first post-Taliban Loya Jirga convened in Kabul in June 2002. Fifteen hundred delegates attended the chaotic meeting, which was dominated by members of the Northern Alliance. This Loya Jirga was in fact a complete mockery – and like the Bonn Conference, it was run from behind the scenes by the US through their representative Zalmay Khalilzad. And although he was not often seen in public, the Americans were directing everything in Kabul.

Predictably, the attendees at the Jirga elected Karzai president of the Transitional Islamic State of Afghanistan (TISA). Most people knew he was the man that the Americans wanted for the job and, from the very beginning, his hold on power was dependent on their support. Even his security detail consisted of heavily armed American soldiers.

The Jirga was called to give legitimacy to the US presence in Afghanistan and to the government of Hamid Karzai. They also wanted to keep the Northern Alliance warlords happy. So, against the wishes of our people, and with the direction of America, this Jirga declared the slain warlord Ahmad Shah Massoud as a 'national hero'. And to placate the Pashtun royalists, the former king, Zahir Shah, by then more than ninety years old, was flown in from his exile in Italy to be declared 'Father of the Nation'.

Once again, the warlords set about re-establishing their fiefdoms, often despite the hatred of the local people. Ismail Khan returned to Herat with his armed militia and became governor. And as the head of the north-western zone of Afghanistan, Khan installed some of his men in key posts, men who were also in contact with the Iranian regime, which wanted to play a role in Afghanistan's new US-backed government. Several fundamentalist groups competed for power in Farah Province after the Taliban left. The first governor installed there, Abdul Hai Nemati, was an ally of Khan and fellow member of Burhanuddin Rabbani's Jamiat-e-Islami Party.

Although people were happy with the fall of the oppressive and medieval rule of the Taliban, these new developments were very disappointing for them. The central government had little or no control over the province. Corrupt warlords were looting Farah, and the reign of the Taliban was replaced by a reign of fear and anarchy.

From the beginning, the local officials in Farah were not happy about the projects that OPAWC and I were trying to implement. Basic human needs in Farah had been neglected for many years, and there was a severe shortage of health care. When we announced we would be opening a free medical clinic in the city, they were furious. They objected to the fact that I, the director, was a woman and against the warlords. They thought the clinic might also be used as a centre for anti-warlord propaganda.

In 2002, I met the governor's representative about this plan to open a clinic and register it with the Health Ministry. I explained that what we were doing was not a crime and we only wanted to help and serve the local people. I began to give a detailed description of why the facility was necessary, explaining the lack of health services, but the man cut me off abruptly.

'Don't take any more of my time!' he said. 'Don't talk any more. Open your clinic, but we will not guarantee your security.'

After he cut me off, I didn't even say goodbye. I just left the office, frustrated and disillusioned. Clearly this was an indirect warning – a threat and, as long as these types of small-minded men are allowed to remain in power, all of Afghanistan will remain disenfranchised and insecure.

The day we opened Hamoon Health Centre, in 2003, we had a great celebration. Elders from nearby villages took part in the ceremony, and people made speeches and brought messages of support from different parts of Farah Province. Ordinary people stopped by to express their support, to suggest future projects, and to condemn the governor's negative attitude. When I told a small group of people of the threat I had received about 'not guaranteeing' my security, their reply was encouraging.

'The people will guarantee your security,' they said.

It was an optimistic time.

There was a huge crowd of people inside and outside the building during those first days, but people had not just shown up to celebrate. This was, after all, a clinic offering free care and medicine in a very poor and deprived region. In fact, we had a difficult situation on our hands. Patients had travelled from far away on donkeys and on foot. There were so many people who desperately needed medical treatment that they camped out overnight in the courtyard to wait their turn to see a doctor. We had only three doctors and a half-a-dozen nurses, although we saw every kind of illness and injury. If the cases were very serious and urgent we would have to send them to Herat or Kabul to find a better-equipped hospital. It was heartbreaking to see so many people and to know that we simply could not help them all – a frustrating reality that tempered my excitement about the opening of the clinic.

In these early days, people were routinely surprised and even shocked by how young I was. I myself was concerned about this factor. After all, I wanted to gain the respect of my clients and staff. I was only twenty-five, but looked even younger – more like a child. And so I worried about whether the doctors would accept me as head of the clinic. I remember on a few occasions an official would come to the clinic and ask me, 'Where is the person in charge?'

'I'm in charge,' I would respond, and they would always look at me in utter disbelief.

Usually the director of a medical clinic is both a doctor and a man, not a tiny young woman with only high school as a formal education. Some visitors who came to the clinic would ask, 'Can we meet Dr Joya, the director?'

I would be very serious in front of these guests, keeping a straight face, but afterwards my colleagues kidded me about it. 'Hey, Malalai,' they would say, 'you're a doctor without even going to medical school?'

Serving as the director of the clinic soon made me a fairly well-known figure in Farah. Our services were much in demand, so much so that we decided to buy an ambulance. We managed to purchase a van and found someone to work as its driver. This poor man – our driver – was very dedicated, and always overworked and exhausted. The area was so lacking in infrastructure that in addition to transporting the sick and injured, he was called upon to move dead bodies for funerals, and also to help people who couldn't otherwise manage the long distances home from the clinic. In Farah Province, this ambulance is famous. It doesn't look like much, but it does an important job.

The fuel expenses for this vehicle were too much for our small budget. The government didn't support us, and we only had a handful of major donors. What we *did* have, though, was the support of the local people. They helped out however they could, and somehow we managed to keep that ambulance running. Mechanics even volunteered to take care of its maintenance for free. They said they were happy to help. 'This is the car of the people,' they said.

Later that year, a terrible earthquake destroyed the historic city of Bam in south-eastern Iran. More than 20,000 people are believed to have died in this tragedy, and many Afghan refugees were among them. Many more were left injured and without electricity and running water. Some refugees from Bam made their way to Farah and came to the Hamoon Health Centre for help. One day some survivors arrived with a tragic story. A man and a woman brought a child with them – they told us that their seven other children had been killed in the earthquake.

Because of the attention Afghanistan was getting around the world at that time, OPAWC was able to raise more funds. Now, besides the clinic, we also established an orphanage. Afghanistan is sadly a country full of orphans as a result of so many years of war and poverty. Hard as it may be to understand, some parents chose to leave their children with us. They had no other option really. Because they were so poor they found it impossible to care for their children, so they came to us for help knowing that their children would be adequately fed until their financial situation improved. This was a mixed facility, with an age range from about seven to fifteen years old, and we were able to accommodate and care for about thirty to fifty of these needy boys and girls at any one time.

During these years, I lived right behind the orphanage. I had a simple one-room hut where I had decided to live instead of with my family so that I could be close to my work. I just had a mattress and no electricity. For reading at night I used an oil lamp.

The children at that orphanage were a great joy. Whenever I appeared, they would surround me and jump on me, full of excitement. At first I worried about how to control them – they had so much energy – but, day by day, this part of my job got sweeter and sweeter.

Most of these children came from extremely deprived backgrounds. It is common in Afghanistan to eat with the hands but we wanted to teach them to use utensils. Of course, many had been traumatised by the horrific incidents that had taken their parents from them. Their tragic stories saddened me, but also inspired me to do something for them to heal their wounds. Death is no stranger to the children of Afghanistan, but we tried our best to provide them with a chance in life.

And we tried to have fun. I remembered the importance of letting children have their childhood, and we tried to create a space where they were not constantly thinking about their own suffering and the problems afflicting the country. We encouraged them to play and have fun. They especially enjoyed birthday parties, so we would always be sure to organise something for these special occasions. Sometimes we gathered them together and told jokes, but we also had more serious discussions where they could share their problems and feelings. They even had the chance to criticise each other and learn to resolve conflict. Of course, there was a classroom for them to have lessons. We had a teacher working with them, but sometimes I would join in and, on special occasions, give chocolates to students who answered questions correctly.

Occasionally I would read the stories of Samad Behrangi aloud to them and describe the lessons I had learned from them. This is the Iranian writer I loved when I was a child, and I think he has written some of the best stories for children. They are all very educational and encourage children to be productive and think about how they can make a better world. But they are also fun. Our students loved these stories and were always filled with questions when I read them.

These children changed my life and touched my heart. It was my first experience working with so many young children, and they were like beautiful flowers. If I found myself feeling tired or depressed, these kids always lifted my spirits. When you see children who are happy and full of life, it makes you happy as well.

There were heartbreaks as well with the children of the orphanage. It was always sad when one of them had to leave. Sometimes their family members or relatives would come to collect them and take them back, often once the child was a little bit older, around thirteen or fourteen. On many of these occasions we worried that the relatives may have been planning to sell or marry off the girls, but of course there was nothing we could do legally if they wanted the child back.

One girl who had spent time in our orphanage later challenged her parents when they tried to bargain for a higher dowry from men who wanted to marry her. She told them that she was a human being and not an animal to be sold for the highest price. This was the lesson she had gained from being in our orphanage, and it had an impact on her family, too.

My most painful memory of the orphanage was the case of a girl named Rahella. Her father had died just before she was born. Her mother, who was very poor, became sick after childbirth and died. So Rahella was left alone. An uncle was responsible for her and one day this uncle decided it was time for Rahella to get married – to his son, who was a drug addict. This is when Rahella ran away to our orphanage in Farah. She was sixteen and was very upset, as she did not want to be forced to marry her cousin. She wept as she explained her predicament. Of course, we took her in and did our best to educate her and look after her.

Then one day, Rahella's uncle came to the orphanage. He seemed very kind and polite in speaking with us, and asked if Rahella could just come home to visit her family for a few days. Rahella did not want to leave the orphanage even for one day, but we told her that it would be OK. It would only be for a short time. We consented to this visit, not knowing what this man really had in mind for his niece. As soon as they got Rahella home, they had a mullah come in and perform a quick marriage ceremony, forcing this union of cousins. Then the young couple were spirited off to live in Iran.

We learned some time later that Rahella, despondent, had committed suicide by burning herself to death. Self-immolation is a new phenomenon in Afghanistan. It is a tragic and increasingly common method for women and girls to escape their misery. There is a very high suicide rate amongst women in our country, because of all the abuse and mistreatment that they suffer. I still feel like we killed Rahella. We sent her to a fate that she could not bear to live with. I still deeply regret that we didn't have enough experience to see through the lies of her uncle and handed her back to her family.

There were other difficult times during my early years of social activism. Once we had gone to distribute supplies – food, flour, cooking oil – in a desert region of Herat where it was hot like an oven. We were caught in a terrible windstorm, and my lungs felt like they were filled with sand. For two days I was sick.

When I ate, I tasted sand. But I was very happy that we had made this trip to bring supplies to these people. It's my wish that everyone realises what a positive difference even small actions of assistance can make to people in need. In these early years, unfortunately we did not document our work, and there is no photographic or video record of the people who were in need, and how they were helped. But we would soon learn to document everything.

———

In 2003, a year after the first Loya Jirga, the United Nations was called in to oversee elections to a second Loya Jirga that would approve a new constitution and determine the future of our country. Nine delegates – seven men and two women – would be chosen from my district to travel to Kabul to determine the future of our country.

I knew that the US-led, so-called war of 'liberation' had caused the deaths of many innocent civilians and, like most Afghans, I was distrustful of foreign occupiers. Like other democratically minded people, I sensed that the United States was repeating the same mistakes of the past by relying on the Islamic fundamentalists. Afghanistan and its people had once again fallen victim in a strategic game played by the United States and its allies. Everyone knew that a truly democratic election could not take place under the shadows of guns, and we knew the majority of the delegates would be warlords or pro-American puppets. Someone had to get inside this corrupt assembly and condemn it to the world.

I was only twenty-five years old at the time but I had already worked among the people of Farah since my teens. They knew me, and I had come to know first-hand their extreme suffering – especially that of the women. I felt that our people needed their voices to be heard. This was what motivated me to get involved in the new political process in Afghanistan. I was determined to help put an end to the rule of the warlords and fundamentalists, and I knew the great majority of Afghan men and women shared this aim. My mission would be to expose the true nature of the Jirga from within it. Since I was so young, I was not at all confident that I would be elected, but I thought, *Let us see what will happen if I put myself forward.*

I did not understand at the time how this decision would change my life for ever.

CHAPTER 5

'ANOTHER MALALAI, ANOTHER MAIWAND'

*I*N FRONT OF ME more than a hundred women were gathered in a dimly lit hall, at the main United Nations compound in Farah, covered in the black veil, or chador, that is so common in western Afghanistan. These women, all of them my elders, had travelled to represent the women of small villages and towns in every corner of the province. Many of them knew me as the young director of the free clinic. And I knew them, as well. I had heard their stories of loss and violence, and – in spite of my age – I had become a friend and counsellor. The women of Farah, like all the women of Afghanistan, had borne the brunt of oppression before, during, and after the savage era of the Taliban, and I desperately wanted them to put their hopes and trust in me as a representative at the Loya Jirga.

Men and women were separated for the delegate selection meetings, which took place in Herat and Farah City. This gender segregation was done partly to prevent men from intimidating or otherwise influencing their wives' decisions. Many men in Afghanistan, sadly, still do not agree at all with the concept of women participating in politics. The women would choose the two female representatives and the men their six male counterparts. One extra delegate was to be appointed by Hamid Karzai, head of the interim government. We would later learn that he would use this power to load the Loya Jirga with warlords whose involvement he asserted was key to making the new system work.

There were six other female candidates, and we were each given three minutes to speak to the convention. I already had a lot of experience of talking to small groups about the trials and tribulations of the people of Farah. It came quite naturally to me. I had always liked to travel around, to learn about people and to listen to their concerns. I picked up this trait from my grandfather, who ran a medicine shop and loved to roam around the countryside on his donkey, and who was known in every part of Farah Province. But this was different; this was my first real speech.

I was in the middle of the line-up. The first speakers talked in general terms about how they needed the votes of women, and what they would do to help women if elected. But they didn't touch on the real tragedy of women in Afghanistan and our need for equal rights.

I stood up at the table in the front of the room, wondering if my thoughts would be as dry as my mouth. But then I remembered the oppression we face as women in my country, and my nervousness evaporated, replaced by anger.

I had a lot to say, and I wanted to cram those few minutes with everything I had ever done in my life, with everything I believed possible for the future, with everything I wanted for the women of Afghanistan. I stressed that I would never compromise with those criminals who had bloodied the history of our country, and that I would always stand up for democracy and human rights.

As I spoke, I knew my message must be getting through, because when the other women were speaking, members of the audience were chatting and making noise and not paying much attention. But as soon as I began to speak everyone quietened down and listened. They even clapped a number of times during my speech so I felt sure I would win their votes.

I can hardly recall what I said in that speech, but remember most clearly the hush of the women in that hall when I was finished. And in the silence, I heard hope and understanding. These women were not highly educated. In fact, many were illiterate. Yet they could relate to my message because I was speaking about their reality and the hardships they had faced. I felt the privilege of their attention but, more importantly, I felt a connection with them, and a deep responsibility to take on their hopes and dreams.

After all the female candidates had spoken, the votes were cast and counted and the UN officials who were co-ordinating the vote returned to the hall to make the results public. When they announced that I was the winner, the crowd broke into applause. Out of the approximately hundred delegate votes cast, I received forty-five, and my friend Nafas finished in second place with twenty-five votes. The fundamentalist women who were running against us finished well behind. I was not surprised, because when I was voting I could see that my box was over-flowing, while many were nearly empty.

When I heard the results, I knew that a great responsibility had been placed on Nafas and me, and I thought to myself, *Now I must do something to live up to the trust of these women.* I took this election very seriously, and it weighed heavily on my mind for days to come. I thought: *What must I do to repay their confidence?*

Afterwards, the organisers of this local election came up to give me their congratulations. The head of the United Nations' mission in Farah, a middle-aged man from Africa, kissed my head and told me that my words were the truth and that others had been scared to speak out in such a way. He and the rest of the organisers were excited that such a young person had been chosen. These people were very emotional. One Afghan woman worker gathered a bunch of flowers from the bushes in the yard of the UN compound and presented them to me. Another woman went out of the compound and bought a packet of toffees and, as a custom in Afghanistan, threw them over me. Some of them had tears in their eyes and some were praying for me: 'May God give you every success, I wish you will be successful ...'

But a few members of the UN election committee took me aside and told me, 'You are young and, for your own good, you should not speak this way at the Loya Jirga in Kabul.' Most of them seemed sincerely worried. I'm not sure, but it is possible that some of them wanted to scare me into silence.

My mother wept when she heard what had happened after the vote. She was already worried about my decision to get involved in this level of politics, and the warnings from the UN observers only heightened her anxiety. My mother was brought up in a conservative home, and she was always nervous about my outspoken nature. Like any daughter, I didn't want to upset my mother, so I cradled her face in my hands and wiped away her tears. I told her that I would be careful and assured her that I would be safe. What I really wanted was for her to be happy for me, and to think about the fact that so many people believed in her daughter's words.

My family's life began to change the moment I was chosen to attend the Loya Jirga. It was decided that my mother, who had rarely travelled outside the home, would accompany me to Herat. A few days later, my father, along with the rest of my friends and family, were seeing us off on our journey. The delegates had to find their own ways to Herat, and from there they would be flown to Kabul. My mother and I travelled with Nafas and her husband on a public bus. It was a bumpy six-hour drive to Herat, and the road was very unsafe for women. The warlord and governor of Herat, Ismail Khan, had remade his own version of the Taliban's 'Vice and Virtue' squads to enforce his primitive fundamentalism. Like the Taliban, Khan's men roamed the province harassing men for dressing in Western clothes, smashing and burning video and music cassettes at the markets and terrorising women. They even dragged women off the streets – if they were found with a male companion who was not a close relative – to conduct humiliating medical examinations to make sure they were 'virtuous'.

So we had to cover ourselves with burqas while travelling to Herat. Since there is a mesh of cloth in front of your eyes, it's very hard to see what's around you. But when I turned my head to the window, sometimes I could see the wreckage of war machines along the roadside.

When we arrived at Herat airport, more election officials greeted us warmly but almost immediately they were asking, 'Which one of you is Malalai Joya?'

'I am,' I replied. 'Why are you interested?'

'We have heard a lot about you from Farah,' said a UN election worker from Herat. 'You made a good speech there, and bravo for your courage.'

Then he lowered his voice, 'But please be careful in Kabul.'

With my mother standing beside me, another UN worker responsible for organising things for the delegates came up to me and told me bluntly that I should not repeat my words in Kabul, as no one would stand up for me there.

'You are very young,' she said. 'This is dangerous for you.'

But before I could answer her, my mother stepped up and told her, 'Why won't anyone support her? I will be there to support her, and I am sure many more will be on her side.'

I was so proud of my mother for speaking up for me. We had all come a long way.

I kissed her goodbye and boarded the plane with Nafas.

———

All the media, including CNN and the BBC, descended on Kabul to watch as hundreds of elected delegates from every province debated the future of Afghanistan. There were 502 delegates in total, and 114 of them were women. A whole section of the capital city had been taken over for the festivities and a big part of the main university campus was turned into 'Loya Jirga City', where housing normally reserved for students was occupied by delegates. Nafas and I shared a dormitory room together. Normally, four delegates had to sleep in one room, but I was told that everyone but Nafas was afraid to share with me!

Germany had provided a giant tent – like the ones used as

bars during Oktoberfest – for the main plenary hall. The grand hall at the polytechnic university was now the venue for the debates that would decide on a new constitution for our country.

There was a massive security presence, provided by the Afghan police but also by the foreign armed security forces who were part of the United Nations' ISAF mission that had followed hard on the heels of the invasion of 2001. Traffic in Kabul was routinely stopped or diverted for ceremonies and festivities related to the Loya Jirga. All the stops were being pulled out for this big show of democracy and the 'new Afghanistan'.

Immediately, however, it was clear that much of the *old* Afghanistan had not gone away.

Most of the nine delegates from my province of Farah were not warlord supporters, although the same could not be said for the representatives of many of the other provinces – especially the northern provinces of Afghanistan, where warlords had full control. Some of them, in fact, were among the worst abusers of human rights that our country had ever known.

I was shocked and appalled to see warlords and other well-known war criminals seated in the first row at this important assembly. All my life I had heard of the horrible things they had done, and some I had seen with my own eyes. In the refugee camps where I grew up, stories of their savagery were commonplace and, in my home province of Farah, the orphanage I ran was full of children who had lost their parents to these men and their allies.

Hamid Karzai had the right to select fifty-two delegates. Many of the warlords were picked by him. Some were here because they had manipulated delegate elections and intimidated other candidates from running against them.

And, just as shocking to me, no one was talking about this in the speeches heard in the assembly over the course of the first few days. For the most part, delegates were just congratulating each other. Nobody wanted to talk about the elephant in the room: that the assembly was full of the men who had – for the past decades – destroyed Afghanistan, waged civil war, and killed tens of thousands of innocents in their quest for power. In front of the cameras of the West, the warlords now wore the mask of democracy. But we Afghans knew them for the criminals they were. I had feared that this assembly would be merely a showcase of 'democracy' for the benefit of the Western powers, but what I was witnessing was even worse than I had expected. It was painful to see these enemies of our people making decisions about our new constitution.

There was Abdul Rab al-Rasul Sayyaf, with his long white beard and his fascist mind. Sayyaf is a fundamentalist with a bloody past. He was, in fact, the person who first invited the international terrorist Osama bin Laden to Afghanistan during the 1980s. He also trained and mentored Khalid Sheikh Mohammed, the man whom the United States claim was the mastermind of the 9/11 attacks on the World Trade Center. And in Afghanistan, ordinary citizens know Sayyaf all too well because his forces rampaged and massacred thousands in Kabul during the early 1990s. Yet here he was – a man who should be investigated for war crimes – at this supposedly democratic assembly. Human Rights Watch reported that Sayyaf's men used threats and bribes of up to 500 dollars per vote to get him elected to the Jirga.

Also right up front was Burhanuddin Rabbani, who had followed Mojaddedi as president of the fractious mujahideen regime that engaged in civil war in the early 1990s. It was Rabbani, a mullah and leader of the Jamiat-e-Islami fundamentalists, who had issued the rules for women that were as bad as the Taliban's. And as political leader he was allied to Massoud and his militia, who deliberately massacred thousands of civilians in Kabul.

Abdul Rashid Dostum was there as well, also appointed by Karzai. The notorious Uzbek warlord from the north of Afghanistan stood out in the sea of turbans and beards with his short-cropped hair and his bushy moustache. Known as 'the wrestler' because of his thick physique and aggressive manner, he was legendary for his ruthlessness on the battlefield and for the joy he took in terrifying his opponents.

Many of these warlords were key figures in the Northern Alliance that had partnered itself with the United States in its drive to oust the Taliban. Senior among them was Mohammed Qasim Fahim, who inherited the overall leadership of the Northern Alliance when Ahmad Shah Massoud was assassinated. It was Fahim who commanded the forces that first entered Kabul after the flight of the Taliban. Other top Northern Alliance leaders in attendance included Younis Qanooni, who would later become Speaker of the Parliament; and Abdullah Abdullah, who became President Karzai's first Foreign Minister. There was Karim Khalili, future vice-president, and Mohammad Mohaqiq – as leaders of the pro-Iran Wahdat Party both should be held to account on human rights issues. Near him was General Mohammed Daoud, a warlord who would later be appointed by the Interior Ministry to head the 'anti-drug effort'. Controversially – an allegation he laughs off – he has been linked to the drugs trade himself.

Siddique Chakari, another former warlord, was also in attendance. Chakari had been the Information Minister during the civil war, who famously justified the destruction of Kabul on the grounds that the city had become 'un-Islamic' during the Soviet puppet years, and so needed to be levelled and rebuilt as an Islamic city. Years later, I would debate with Chakari on a television programme, and when I stated that he should be prosecuted for war crimes he invoked a former American president who had supported the mujahideen. 'Instead of awarding us medals of honour like Ronald Reagan, you want to prosecute us!'

As I scanned the crowd I could also see the silver beard and black eyes of Ismail Khan, someone who I passionately believe should have been answering questions about his role in the civil war. Instead he was being given a voice in deciding our new constitution.

Among the delegates, there were also technocrats and monarchists, even some former Soviet puppets – many of whom were exiles returning to the country for the first time in decades. Nevertheless, they acted like experts on Afghanistan, while maintaining a cowardly silence about the warlords. Their indifference was almost as agonising as the presence of the war criminals themselves.

Some delegates dressed like Western businessmen; others wore more traditional clothing. But just as you cannot judge a book by its cover, you could not tell who was a fundamentalist and who was a democrat by what they wore. Dostum had chosen to don a suit and tie for these proceedings, while Sayyaf wore a turban and robes. Many extremists and criminals had shaved off their beards to try to hide their true faces, perhaps in the hope that people would forget their crimes from the past. In Afghanistan, there is a saying: 'It's the same donkey, but with a new saddle.'

The voices of the countless widows who had told me of their suffering rang in my ears as I looked around the room. It was terrible enough to hear about these men and their crimes, but seeing them in person running this Loya Jirga and listening to their speeches was like torture for me. I had to speak out.

For days I desperately tried everything I could think of to get the opportunity to address the gathering, but I was the youngest delegate in attendance, and being a woman made it even harder to get the attention of the old men convening the meetings. The sympathies of the chairman of the assembly, Sibghatullah Mojaddedi, were obvious, as a string of fundamentalists and warlords took their turns at the microphone. He was only calling on his friends and allies.

Frustrated after four days of waiting to hear someone talk about real democratic change, I came up with a plan to have my voice heard. Although the literal translation of Loya Jirga is 'gathering of the elders' I thought I could turn the disadvantage of my age around to my benefit.

On 17 December 2003, I approached Chairman Mojaddedi

at the dais in front of the assembly. He wore a turban, a white beard and a stern expression. Mojaddedi had been the first president of the Islamic Republic of Afghanistan established after the Soviet withdrawal, but now he was old and primarily a figurehead. I knew that he and others had already heard about the outspoken ways of the young delegate from Farah Province. But his eyesight and hearing were not very good, so I tried to trick him. Keeping my face at an angle and using my hijab to camouflage my identity, I told him that I was from Bamyan Province – and that, as a representative of the younger generation, I should have a chance to speak. There were many other delegates crowding around him, trying to get his attention. But he finally agreed, somewhat reluctantly, to give me a turn, announcing to the whole assembly that, 'The kids insist that they have not had enough chance to speak.'

This was my opportunity. The main tent was packed full of hundreds of delegates, as well as international observers, and foreign and local media. Although it could not be said that the *whole* world was watching these events, it was close. And every moment of the proceedings was being broadcast live on Afghan television and Radio Kabul.

Unfortunately, there was a line-up of delegates who were equally intent on taking advantage of this rare opportunity to speak. A young Uzbek from the north was ahead of me. Desperate to have my chance, I said to this serious-looking young man, 'Please, my brother, could you let me speak first?' I was extremely polite.

He introduced himself as Nuriddin (not his real name), and asked me my name and what it was that I so badly wanted to say.

I responded, 'I am Joya. What I have to say is a secret, but you will like it.'

Nuriddin seemed intrigued. He wanted to know what I thought of the Loya Jirga and, like me, said he was disgusted by the presence of so many warlords. He even suggested that we organise a protest demonstration.

'No, my brother,' I argued with him. 'First we must try our best to use this tribunal to expose them. If they won't let us do that, then I will help you organise that demonstration.'

Nuriddin let me go in front of him in the line and the chairman told me that, again, I would have three minutes to speak. This was very different from my first speech in Farah. Here in Kabul, there was a huge, mixed audience in the grand hall, and the atmosphere was charged and tense. My heart was racing. As I struggled to compose myself and to remember the key points I wanted to make, my black hijab started to slide back off my head, and I had to adjust it. Because I am only five feet tall, an official lowered the microphone so I could reach it. I spoke as rapidly as I could, and directly from my heart.

'My name is Malalai Joya from Farah Province. By the permission of the esteemed attendees, and by the name of God and the martyrs of the path of freedom, I would like to speak for a few minutes.

'My criticism of all my compatriots is why you are allowing the legitimacy and legality of this Loya Jirga to come into question due to the presence of those criminals who have brought our country to this state. Why would you allow criminals to be present here? They are responsible for our situation now!'

Nuriddin was smiling, and I knew that he liked what I was saying. In the video recorded that day, you can see the other young delegates behind me also grinning nervously as they began to grasp the impact of what I was saying. Many in the crowded tent erupted into applause but most of the warlords seated right before me remained silent and glowered at me with faces hard as stone.

'The chairman of every committee is already selected. Why do you not take all these criminals to one committee so that we see what they want for this nation! It is they who turned our country into the centre of national and international wars! They are the most anti-women elements in our society who brought our country to this state and they intend to do the same again. I believe that it is a mistake to test those who have already been tested.'

Now Nuriddin had dropped his notes. He was laughing and clapping his hands and others joined in the applause. But there were angry voices, too. By now a number of the warlords were on their feet, yelling and shaking their fists in my direction.

'They should be prosecuted in the national and international courts!' I said, raising my voice to be heard. 'Even if these criminals were to be somehow forgiven by our people – the barefoot Afghan people, our history will never forgive them. Their names are all recorded in the history of our country ...'

Suddenly, I could no longer hear my voice echoing over the PA system. I had been speaking for barely ninety seconds when the chairman cut off my microphone.

'That is enough. Thank you,' said Mojaddedi. 'You had asked for three minutes which is now over. Sister, I have been saying since the beginning that all speeches should be courteous and expressed in a good manner. No one should be insulted, and if you have any complaints you could submit your written complaints to the secretaries of the Jirga and we will then follow them up.'

At first I continued speaking, but soon realised that my words had provoked a very serious situation. There was an enormous commotion. Angry men were lurching in my direction. Chakari was the first to raise his voice against me, shouting 'Down with communism!' to provoke others. Even one of the female delegates threatened me, pointing and shouting, 'Take the pants off this prostitute and tie them on her head!'

At first chairman Mojaddedi seemed not to fully understand what had happened. The microphones were still on and recording the proceedings, and they picked up the chairman saying, 'I just did not understand her words, and what she said.'

Someone sitting next to him muttered, 'She hit a hard blow to the reputation of jihadi people, saying they are treacherous ...' Mojaddedi's face grew angry.

'Sister, look what have you done!' he yelled. 'You have upset everybody here! Do you think one should say such words to affront and disappoint everyone? You made a mistake!'

But Mojaddedi was wrong. I had not upset *all* the delegates, and many of them flocked to my side. In the midst of the pandemonium a widow named Ayeesha grabbed me and shielded me with her body. She placed herself between my attackers and me, yelling, 'This is my daughter, do not put your hands on her!' As one man reached out to strike me, she screamed, 'It is against Islam to put your hands on a woman!'

Ayeesha knew full well the kind of depravities of which these angry men were capable. They could have torn me to pieces. I later learned that her brother had been killed by the warlords. She was trying desperately to save me from the same fate.

Meanwhile, Sayyaf, the senior warlord and one of the most notorious men from the civil war years, pushed his way to the front of the room and launched into a vitriolic harangue against me, claiming that, 'When you are calling those heroes who liberated this country *criminals*, that in itself is a crime!'

He went on and on like this for minutes, inciting the crowd to turn on me.

Mojaddedi waited for Sayyaf to finish, then threw me out of the assembly.

'This sister has crossed the line of what is considered common courtesy,' he said. 'I tell the gathering to expel her from the meeting, and she can't attend the discussions.' He waved his hand in the air, as you would brush away a fly. 'Go out! Security officer, security, take her outside!'

Some women in the assembly rushed forward to beg him to forgive me.

'Sit down in your seats, please,' he said. 'No! She should not be forgiven ...'

While Ayeesha and other supportive delegates encircled me, one warlord in the gallery shouted that I should apologise. Mojaddedi agreed, and demanded that I apologise to the assembly. I was too exhilarated to feel afraid. I offered to return to the microphone, but I planned to continue my speech rather than apologise. Sensing what I was determined to do, my friends held me back and made me sit down. Ayeesha begged me not to get up, as she understood that my life was in very real danger.

When he saw that I would not take back my words, Mojaddedi grew angrier.

'Oh, you still do not apologise?' he said. 'Oh, my God, she does not even apologise!' Then, when he called me 'communist' and an 'infidel' I knew it was time to leave.

My supporters and a group of UN facilitators huddled around me, arms locked, to protect me as they escorted me out of the tent. We made slow progress through the mob that was still screaming insults and threats. We finally made it outside and into a UN vehicle that quickly drove me away.

From that moment on, I would never again be safe. At the time, I was not thinking about this, but rather I was pleased that I had been able to expose the true nature of the proceedings. I also began to realise just how much words are powerful weapons and that I had to continue speaking the truth for the sake of the Afghan people who have been silenced for so long. One of the reasons that my speech had sparked such a rabid reaction is the fact I am a woman, and a young one at that. For fundamentalists, a woman is half a human, meant only to fulfil a man's every wish and every lust and to produce children and toil in the home. They could not believe that a young girl was tearing off their masks in front of the eyes of the Afghan people.

After escaping from this chaotic scene, I was taken by UN officials to a safe house in a secure and expensive neighbourhood of Kabul. I was sad to be apart from my colleagues, but it was now too dangerous for me to stay in the dorm room that I shared with Nafas, my friend and fellow delegate from Farah.

Sure enough, that night a group of people angered by my speech went looking for me in the university residence where I had been staying. They carried sticks in their hands to beat me.

Screaming insults, they stormed in on my friend Nafas.

'Where is that prostitute girl?' the men demanded. 'When we find her, we will rape her and kill her!'

'Joya is not here,' Nafas replied defiantly. 'Whatever you would do to her, go ahead and do to me.'

They didn't believe her, and tore the room apart, searching for me behind the beds and in the bathroom. Finally the mob retreated. It was clear by now that not even the Loya Jirga itself was immune from the violence of Afghanistan. My life was in danger – from my fellow delegates and their allies – and Nafas had risked her own life to defend my honour and dignity. She is like a sister to me.

After this incident, the United Nations team brought Nafas to live with me in the safe house, or houses, since we stayed in several locations. They tried to post American soldiers outside our room, but I rejected the idea. I told them that the guards should be Afghans. The Afghan soldiers they brought in were very kind to me and praised my speech. One of the soldiers, named Sayed Akbar, brought me a jacket, as it was winter in Kabul and very cold. He also gave me a small copy of the Quran, telling me that if you hold this, it will keep you safe. This soldier became one of my good supporters and has kept in touch.

The next day I could not go back to the Loya Jirga. But while my location was kept secret, my words and my name became known all around the world through the international media coverage of my speech. I was given a mere ninety seconds to air my message, but now it was reaching millions of people. I was able to monitor all of the coverage in the Afghan media, the BBC, and in other outlets on the TV and radio at the safe house. One of the UN woman guards came and took me to a room with a television set, then turned on the TV and said, 'Watch what you've done! It's breaking news everywhere.' She flipped through the news channels, one after another, and my speech was the lead story on every one.

Chairman Mojaddedi always held a news conference after the

end of each day of the Jirga. On the day of my speech, the whole session was about me, and journalists asked him some tough questions. I was amused when he had to lie that he did not call Malalai Joya a 'communist' and an 'infidel'. The journalists told him that they had a recording of his comments!

Radio Azadi, the Afghan service of Radio Free Europe, the Persian and Pashto services of BBC radio and the Voice of America all carried live programmes about my speech and people could phone in their comments. I was particularly inspired by the responses of ordinary Afghan people who expressed their support of my speech. Many were saying that Joya is a hero.

In my speech I did not name anyone as a criminal, nor did I use the word 'jihadi' or even 'mujahideen' – but the Afghan people knew exactly who I was talking about. As the proverb says, 'The thief has a feather in his hat.' The warlords could not hide their crimes.

On 20 December 2003, around 300 women and girls held a protest rally in Farah in support of my speech and to denounce Chairman Mojaddedi's threat to expel me from the Loya Jirga and to demand that he apologise to the people of Farah for abusing their representative. This was the first women's protest of any kind that people in Farah could remember.

In the days following my speech, all the newspapers and weeklies in Afghanistan ran front-page stories about me. One weekly newspaper even published a special issue dedicated to me full of positive articles and interviews. Their cover story was titled 'Another Malalai, Another Maiwand' (referring to my namesake, the heroine Malalai of Maiwand). One woman's magazine with my face on the cover (but, unfortunately, no story inside!) sold out all of its copies. Of course, the jihadi publications ran articles denouncing me, but I'm told they were not so popular.

The *New York Times* ran an article entitled 'A Young Afghan Dares to Mention the Unmentionable' and the Institute for War and Peace Reporting published another titled 'Joya Speech Breaks

Wall of Silence'. The BBC even called me 'the bravest woman in Afghanistan' and all of the Western media soon started repeating this line. Overnight, I had become known around the world.

For me, telling the truth was not a choice. I did not want fame or special recognition, but I had to speak out. It was my duty and my responsibility to the people who voted for me, who gave me their trust. I had promised them that I would never compromise with the enemies of human rights and, so, I had no other option. It was for this reason that I put myself forward as a delegate in the first place.

One of my favourite quotes is by the German writer Bertolt Brecht, from his play *The Life of Galileo*: 'He who does not know the truth is only a fool. He who knows the truth and calls it a lie is a criminal.'

I could not allow myself, through silence, to sink to the level of the war criminals I despised. And so I did a number of telephone interviews inside Afghanistan that reached every corner of my country. One of the Afghan journalists who interviewed me in the days following my speech was Zakia Zaki, a women's rights activist and the manager of a station called Peace Radio. When she asked me how women could best protect their rights, I answered that once women understand that the key to their freedom is in their own hands, they will dare to be brave, remove the obstacles in their path and be prepared to make sacrifices.

Rights are not easy to obtain and, once we understand this, we must work attentively and persistently – and never become careless or lazy. In our country we have a long tradition of women who have fought courageously for our rights, some of whom have been martyred. Tragically, on 6 June 2007, Zakia herself joined the ranks of these martyrs when gunmen connected to warlords murdered her in her home in Parwan Province. Zakia had received many warnings from the warlords that she should stop spreading her message, so they finally killed her. Her only crime had been to use the media to spread the message of women's rights and justice.

The day after my speech, it was reported in the media that the Afghan Intelligence Agency, which has been in the hands of jihadis, announced that Malalai Joya is a member of the Revolutionary Association of the Women of Afghanistan (RAWA) and they intend to investigate her and her family. Even though RAWA is not an illegal organisation in Afghanistan, it is still underground because it is the most outspoken and staunch critic of the Northern Alliance and the Afghan government. Although I am not a member, whenever anyone talks publicly and without fear against the warlords, they are stamped – positively or negatively – as part of RAWA. Although the Intelligence Agency never carried out its threat to investigate, it was still very stressful to put my family in the spotlight.

When I managed to reach my mother and father back in Farah by telephone, my mother cried and she told me that I must be careful and protect myself. My father told me that he was proud and that he would support me whatever I decided to do.

I felt many different emotions during those days after my speech. Many people, including some UN officials, told me I should never go back to the assembly. I understood the risks but I also knew that my life was no longer just my own. I had a responsibility to my people, not only in Farah but throughout Afghanistan. I did not want to let my enemies win by silencing me, so I insisted that I be allowed to return to the Loya Jirga. I argued that it would be a victory for the enemies of democracy – a victory for the warlords – if I stayed away.

Human rights' organisations took up my cause and issued statements in support of my continued participation. Amnesty International made a particularly strong declaration:

> The Constitutional Loya Jirga presents the people of Afghanistan with the opportunity to turn away from the abuses of the past and create a new system in which the rights of all are ensured. If delegates are threatened or otherwise prevented from expressing their views,

this process of building a new future for Afghanistan will be severely threatened.

Eventually, after arguing with me for some time, UN officials agreed that I could go back. I am sure that the only reason I was allowed to return was because of the great support by Afghan people from every corner of the country. One example of this mobilisation by ordinary people took place in Kapisa Province. After hearing about an interview with BBC radio that I gave after my speech, villagers raised money to send one woman 75 kilometres by bus to Kabul to relay their support. This woman from Kapisa travelled to the capital city and searched for a few hours to find the BBC office. Once there, she told the broadcasters she had come to say that the people of Kapisa supported my message. They put an interview with this woman on the BBC Radio Persian Service. My solitary voice was spreading day by day, as it was raised and amplified by many more Afghans.

In the end, I believe it was easier for the interim government to allow me to return to the Jirga rather than let the resentment against them grow stronger.

From now on I would have to be surrounded by bodyguards, but I would return again to face those who had ruined my country, and I was determined that I would stand straight and never bow to their threats.

CHAPTER 6

A Homecoming
to Remember

A FEW DAYS AFTER MY SPEECH I returned to the Loya Jirga, this time transported in an unmarked United Nations vehicle and surrounded by big muscular bodyguards I did not know. These security people followed me everywhere I went. The other delegates were surprised to see me again. Some were delighted that I had come back. Nuriddin, the Uzbek delegate, saw me and excitedly came over to talk. 'Letting you speak was the greatest thing I have done in my life,' he said, very sincerely. 'Even though I am a man, I did not have the courage to speak the way you did. You have made history.'

Many other delegates, however, were not happy at all. A few murmured threats as I walked by, and at lunch in the cafeteria that first day, some angry female delegates shook their knives and forks as they harangued me about my speech. My bodyguards seemed worried that this would happen again during lunch a few days later, when I was approached by the woman who had called me a prostitute after my speech. But this time she had a look of shame and apprehension on her face.

'Please forgive me,' she pleaded. 'I had to threaten you with death and attack you. I was forced to. But I agree with what you said. I too lost many members of my family because of these criminals. But they campaigned for me to come here as a delegate, so I had to do as they wished. They could kill more of my family.'

I could see that this woman was now showing her true feelings, and it was hard to believe that she was the same person who had insulted me so viciously just a few days earlier. She handed me a government newspaper that contained an article written by one of her close relatives to prove that she was actually on my side. It was a long, powerful article supporting me and quoting the text of my speech. She said, 'Call this man and he will tell you how I have suffered. My relative may have to resign from his government job because of this article, but he supports you very much. And so do I.'

I listened carefully as she told me how these warlords had brutally killed two of her sons. 'If you do not forgive me, God will not forgive me,' she said, reaching out for me. 'I will feel guilty for the rest of my life. Please let me kiss your feet.'

My bodyguards moved to step between us. Because of security concerns, they would not let anyone get close to me, let alone hug me. But on this occasion all those around me, including my bodyguards, had been touched at hearing this woman's story. I said, 'She is a victim of these warlords and I believe she is telling the truth.'

My security people stood back, and I embraced the woman who only days earlier had screamed at me and called me the most awful names. We both cried.

I urged her never again to behave the way she had, and told her that she must stop compromising with the warlords and find the courage to say no to them. I told her that God and history would not forgive her if she continued to let these warlords control her – and that those beloved family members she had lost wouldn't either. This conversation was very important to me. It helped me understand how the warlords maintained their control, to see up close how they used fear to manipulate tormented women like her.

A couple of days later, an old former mujahid – a veteran of the resistance against the Soviets – from Mazar-e-Sharif, came to see me. He explained that he had been so angry at the moment of my speech that he had picked up a chair and wanted to beat me with it. 'I would have hit you with that chair but I could not get close enough to you,' he admitted. But later when he heard one of my long radio interviews, he realised that I had only spoken the truth.

He also asked me to forgive him. 'Tell me what I can do to support you. I have a large family and I will tell my girls to attend a demonstration to support you. What else can I do to help support you?'

'Thanks for your support,' I said to him. 'It's not too late that you understand what I am saying. Please do not trust and work with these warlords.' I shook his hand, something that is extremely uncommon for a woman to do in Afghanistan.

I heard from many people – friends, family and strangers – about how they felt when they heard my speech. One family friend, whose father Ahmadi is a great man who had taught me in the refugee camps and before that had taught my father at university, told us that after my speech was the first time in her whole life she had seen her father cry.

There was huge support for me among poor people everywhere. A widow who had lost one of her hands and who had found menial work at the Loya Jirga, gave me her scarf as a gift to show her appreciation. I remember she cried and prayed for me when she gave me this special present. One of the representatives from Farah told me that a day after my speech, he took a taxi to attend the Loya Jirga sessions in Kabul. On the way he and the driver were talking about Joya and her speech. When the taxi driver found out that this delegate was also from Farah, he told him, 'As you are from the province of Joya, I will not take the taxi fare from you.' He dropped him for free.

Another time a woman delegate named Suraya Parlika, who was formerly an active member of the Russian puppet regime, warned me that no one would support me for my stand, and they might kill me. I told her, 'Please don't worry. I've told the truth and I am sure the majority of my suffering people will be behind me.' I added lightly, 'Even if no one else supported me, if they kill me there will be six more people like me, because I have six more sisters!'

She nodded with amusement, and said, 'Oh, I see! All of your sisters are like you?'

And I explained, on a serious note, 'Remember, those who have given their lives as martyrs in the past have always found new hands to carry the flag they raised during their lives along the path of truth.'

———

Although I was able to return to the assembly, they were not going to let me speak again before all the delegates. Once, when I approached one of the chairman's deputies to request an opportunity to speak, he replied scornfully, 'No, you conspired to make a bad situation here, so go and sit down.' I was for all intents and purposes banned from speaking.

Despite the waves that my speech created, the Loya Jirga carried on as before. No expense was spared. Every day there was a plentiful variety of food available for delegates, and Hamid Karzai hosted big receptions with food and drinks for all representatives. On these occasions Karzai would arrive after everybody else, make a speech and then promptly leave. He did not stick around to field questions. Every minister and all the different factions were also throwing receptions with good food where they would negotiate and make deals.

A number of other democratically minded representatives joined me in speaking out against all the money wasted on hospitality at the Loya Jirga. I asked why they were doing this, why all this expense for the delegates when in every corner of Afghanistan there were hungry and poor people? I explained to anyone who would listen that those of us who had come to Kabul from poor, faraway provinces, did not come here to this Loya Jirga only so that we could be fed. We came to work on the new constitution of

Afghanistan. And they could better spend all this money on orphanages and schools. We often tried to raise these points, but it seemed that nobody was listening. I would have liked to ask Karzai about this at one of these fancy receptions, but of course he was always on his way to another appointment so there was never any time to ask him.

A number of us would have liked to have asked Karzai about the fact that the Loya Jirga seemed to be intending to rubber stamp a constitution that had already been drafted behind the scenes. As delegates, many of us felt we were being used to legitimise a document that we were not able to influence. To propose an amendment, for instance, it required at least fifty delegates to sign a petition. Fifty-two of us signed a letter to challenge the new constitution's provision that officially named our country the Islamic Republic of Afghanistan. We wanted to have a discussion about how Islam had been misused in our history, but our petition was dismissed out of hand. In fact, we were told that to question using the word 'Islamic' meant that we weren't really Muslims.

Even after I returned to the main assembly, the UN officials didn't want me to attend committee meetings because of the risk. But I persuaded them to allow it, because it was important for me to be present there.

Loya Jirga delegates were divided into ten different committees, with many of them headed up by fundamentalist extremists like Burhanuddin Rabbani and Abdul Rab al-Rasul Sayyaf. Before my speech, I had been assigned to be in Rabbani's committee. Some of the representatives who knew my views about these warlords made jokes and laughed out loud as they congratulated me on my position. But I was serious when I said that I did not want to be part of a committee headed by someone like him. I urged the UN organisers at the Loya Jirga to find me a committee without warlords. Finally they found one whose members welcomed me, but it turned out that even this committee was headed by Haji Farid, someone from Hekmatyar's party.

Some of the only productive work on the constitution was done outside of this formal committee structure. There was a hall for female delegates, where at the end of each day we would gather to drink tea, debate and discuss. It was in this setting that we worked on the part of the constitution that dealt with women's rights. I contributed to the debate, talking about violence against women and how women's rights were not clear in law. In the end, we even managed to have the following sentence included in the constitution: 'The citizens of Afghanistan – whether man or woman – have equal rights and duties before the law.' This would have been a great triumph, except there was no provision to enforce it. Furthermore, the new constitution also stated that, 'In Afghanistan, no law can be contrary to the beliefs and provisions of the sacred provisions of Islam.' This provision left the door wide open for fundamentalists to invoke religion to justify the denial of equal rights for women. The Taliban and the warlords had for years been twisting and misinterpreting Islam to oppress women and to justify their many crimes. Now a new opportunity to embrace a secular constitution that respected the rights of all religious groups had been squandered.

This missed opportunity meant that the most marginal sections of the population were left open to discrimination. For example, the small Hindu and Sikh minorities have continued to face systemic abuse in recent years. At the Loya Jirga, the sole Hindu woman representative, Anarkali Honaryar, defended my speech in her committee against warlords who were condemning it. For speaking up, some fundamentalist female delegates attacked her, hitting her and pulling her hair. They did this to Honaryar not only because she sided with me, but also because Hindus are viewed by many as second-class citizens in Afghanistan. I later had a chance to meet her, and I told her she was like a sister to me.

Chairman Mojaddedi made his own interpretation of the constitution clear when he told the women delegates at the Loya Jirga, 'Even God has not given you equal rights because under his decision two women are counted as equal to one man.'

One day, Mojaddedi was doing the rounds, checking on delegates in each committee. When he walked into our committee room with his team, everyone stood up as a show of respect – except me. On behalf of my people, I wanted to show him my hatred of the fundamentalism that he defended.

Shortly after my speech at the Loya Jirga, the US envoy Khalilzad – the man I believed to be the real power behind the throne of our showcase democracy – invited all the women delegates for a meeting. During this meeting some women condemned what happened to me in the Jirga, while others spoke against me. Khalilzad responded that everyone who wants to talk in the Jirga must talk in the framework of politeness and respect, and they should not insult each other. At that time I wanted to respond to him, but the representatives didn't let me speak, as they were worried that the fundamentalist women who were present would rise against me. They told me that I could give an interview later and say all I wanted. But I wanted to answer directly and I wrote a letter to Khalilzad, which was delivered to him by a friend at the UN. It said:

Mr Kalilzad Salam,

If these criminals raped your mother or daughter or even your grandmother, or killed seven of your sons, let alone destroyed all the moral and material treasure of the country, what words would you use against such criminals and puppets that will be inside the framework of politeness and respect?

Signed, Malalai Joya

———

By the time the Loya Jirga ended in January 2004, Afghanistan had adopted a new constitution and plans were in place for a presidential election. Although I knew I had done my best to represent the people of Farah, and I had never backed down from my beliefs, I felt that the assembly had been a failure. The warlords had shown their power to the world, and most of the important decisions about the constitution were made in backroom deals. Human Rights Watch reported that US officials met privately with certain factional leaders, including General Rashid Dostum and Abdul Rab al-Rasul Sayyaf, to negotiate support for the Karzai government's draft of the constitution. As John Sifton, a Human Rights Watch researcher who had observed the Jirga said at the time, 'The atmosphere of fear and corruption at the convention, and efforts by US officials and the Karzai government to secure bloc votes from factional leaders, affected how robustly some provisions were debated. The entire process casts doubt on the elections that are to be held here later this year.'

As I prepared to head home to Farah, I braced myself for a life that would be very different. I had made powerful enemies now, and I would always have to be careful. But I had gathered many supporters, some of whom had created the Malalai Joya Defence Committee to promote my message and to raise funds for my protection.

At the conclusion of the Loya Jirga, there was a closing ceremony broadcast on television, in which a male and a female delegate from each province went up and received an award presented by Karzai. I was to be the female recipient from Farah. I would not have gone up to accept this award, except for the fact that many of the warlords in attendance were angry that I was receiving it. They remained completely silent when I received the award; only the progressive-minded delegates applauded. I later gave this award away to an orphan whose parents had been murdered by fundamentalists. I wish that an orphan or a widow could have, in fact, spoken in my place at the Loya Jirga, and felt the love and support that I did. Too many of the women and children of Afghanistan have had very little love in their lives. Many have lost everything, and so I dedicate everything I do to them.

In the days following my speech and after the Loya Jirga, I received dozens of phone calls from all over Afghanistan, and even from Afghans abroad, thanking me for speaking up. I was especially touched by the support from the poorest of my countrymen and women. Their response hardened my conviction that in any land ruled by the gun and by powerful interests, where democracy is only a mirage, it is nonetheless crucially important to use whatever rotten institutions exist to spread awareness and to tell the truth to the public.

The last night Nafas and I spent in Kabul was nerve-racking. I started to worry that perhaps someone had discovered the location of the safe house. Also, the Afghan soldier who was assigned to guard duty that night was behaving very strangely. He kept looking in on Nafas and me in a suspicious way. We did not get any sleep that night, but luckily nothing happened.

The next morning we were due to fly from Kabul to Herat, as there are no direct flights to our province, then travel by road to Farah. But before we boarded the flight, I received a call from a supporter in Farah who had reliable information that 'one of the warlords' had a plan to kill me on the way to Farah. The report came from people who secretly supported me but were close to this man, so I had to take it seriously. There is a village called Shewan in an area called Daristan, between Herat and Farah, which is usually under the control of the Taliban. People are often abducted and killed in that region. The idea, we were informed, was for me to be killed there so the Taliban could be blamed for it.

When I told representatives of the UN Assistance Mission in Afghanistan (UNAMA) about the threat, they took it very seriously. They quickly organised a special UN flight to fly me directly to Farah. The return trip to Farah was very different from the journey I had made less than two months earlier. The UN arranged for a small plane with just my friend Nafas, a handful of the other delegates from Farah, and the flight crew on board. I had flown in an aeroplane only a few times in my life, but I wasn't nervous about flying, nor was I particularly worried about the assassination threats. I was just excited about returning home from a successful mission, seeing the people I loved again and resuming my position at the orphanage and clinic.

Minutes after taking off, the sprawling city of Kabul suddenly looked miniature as we soared above the beautiful mountains that surround the capital. Looking down at the vast, arid landscape of my country, I thought about how the democracy we were supposed to be talking about at the Loya Jirga was still a distant dream for the people of Afghanistan. Almost none of my fellow Afghan women would ever get to drive a car, let alone fly in an aeroplane. Life expectancy is still barely forty-five years, and many women die much younger during childbirth. Almost 20 per cent of infants never reach the age of five. And then there are the hundreds of women who kill themselves each year to escape their violent husbands or the shame of being raped or abused.

I knew that these people of Afghanistan had heard something of themselves in my words and that they knew things had to change. During the flight, I thought about all this, and especially about the people in my own province of Farah. They had suffered so much, and this put a great burden and sense of responsibility on my shoulders.

As we approached the airport in Farah, all of a sudden the pilot – a relaxed, middle-aged man – started yelling with excitement. 'Look! Look at that crowd!' he called back to us from the cockpit. As the plane came in lower to the ground, Nafas and I saw what he was talking about: a huge mass of people had gathered near the airport to await our arrival. At first, I couldn't believe that all these people had come out to welcome us back. It was an incredible thing to see, and I was overcome with emotion. The pilot even flew an extra circuit for the crowd's benefit. After we landed and were preparing to leave the plane, I noticed that even the pilot was emotional and he was smiling widely, almost in disbelief, as he looked out at the throng.

There were so many people outside the plane that it was difficult for me to move through them. Young girls had brought flowers for me, and many people shouted kind greetings. As I walked slowly through the throng, women called out, 'Thank you for telling the truth!' From every direction, I heard warm cries of gratitude and words of friendship and solidarity. People were holding placards with my picture on them. Old women and young girls, in particular, clamoured to hug and kiss me – these are among my warmest memories of this homecoming.

When one of the organisers of this reception found me and explained that they had organised a rally for me, I had to explain that, before attending their rally, I first I had to make a visit to the governor's office, where I had been invited to a reception. Somehow I made my way through the crowd to a waiting vehicle, and we were on our way.

Governor Abdul Hai Nemati certainly did not support the theme of my speech nor my political views, but the governor wanted to give the appearance that he supported democracy, and so I was invited along with the other local delegates to the Jirga to attend his event. This governor was part of the Jamiat-e-Islami Party of Burhanuddin Rabbani, one of the warlords I had denounced in Kabul. Naturally his people were reluctant to let me give a speech, but I insisted. After I had spoken a few words, the faces of Nemati and his allies changed and became less friendly as we sat down to have tea.

Accompanying me on this visit to the governor's was a male supporter and his teenage daughter. When the tea was brought in and placed in front of us, this young woman did something very brave. Before either of us had a chance to take a sip, this girl quickly moved in and switched my cup of tea with the governor's. This was clearly done to protect me from a possible poisoning. The governor did not say anything. But to me, this act showed great courage and audacity for a young female in Afghanistan.

All day long, I saw other examples of this kind of heartfelt support for me in Farah. After we left the governor's palace, we went back to attend the welcoming rally that had been organised just outside the offices where I had been working for years as a social activist. I could hardly make out the orphanage and surrounding buildings that had been my home in recent years. A big tent and stage had been set up in the courtyard, and a huge crowd had gathered in our honour. My dear Uncle Azad – who in the coming months would take charge of my security – greeted me warmly and helped me up to the front of the crowd.

Waiting for my turn to speak, I watched and listened to a number of speakers and performers on stage. There were tribal elders and young students making speeches, musicians dedicating songs to me. People performed local traditional dances. The whole scene was almost unbelievable. I knew many of these people, but for every face I recognised there were many more strangers. These were the ordinary people of Farah – the poor and forgotten who had inspired me to get active politically – and they had obviously been moved by my message. Many had travelled great distances to attend the ceremony.

I scanned the crowd in front of me looking for my mother and father but I couldn't see them anywhere. My mother never liked crowds, so I thought she might have stayed home, but I was sure my father had to be out there watching and listening.

When it was my turn to speak I was, for the first time in my short political career, almost at a loss for words. This audience was much larger than the group of women who had heard my first real political speech just a couple months earlier, but it was emotion, not nervousness, that almost overcame me. I remember gathering my thoughts and trying to convey my gratitude to the crowd while also emphasising some key points.

'Unfortunately, with the backing of their foreign masters, many warlords and criminals have been given positions of great power at the Loya Jirga, and so our struggle for real democracy in Afghanistan will be a difficult one ...' I said. 'We must continue to work to demand that these warlords be removed from top positions, and be held accountable for their crimes against our people ...

'I want to warmly thank everyone for their incredible support, and I promise you all that I will never compromise with those who have destroyed our country.'

As I spoke, I was making an effort not to cry, but it became very difficult when I could see that people in the crowd were crying. This moving response from the people of Farah showed me just how deep their hatred of the warlords runs, and how much they hope for a future when Afghanistan will finally be rid of this terrible burden.

After the rally, I made my way over to the main building of the Hamoon Health Centre. As I made the short walk with a few bodyguards, the crowd marched along behind in a cloud of rising dust, even chanting slogans of support. This was one of those moments where I could see the depth of support I had, and it confirmed for me that the power of people is like the power of God. In front of the clinic, waiting for me, was my father. I had never seen him so emotional. He was beaming and he gave me a big hug. I asked him if he had been at the rally.

'Of course,' he responded. 'I was behind the stage, but I heard everything.'

Inside the clinic, I found my mother and some of my sisters and I hugged them. After a day of being welcomed by crowds of well-wishers, it was a relief to just be greeted as a sister and as a daughter. There was no time to really talk, however, because there was a constant stream of other families and village elders coming through to speak to me.

At some point later that day, some villagers arrived pushing an extremely old woman in a rickety wheelbarrow. A couple of men in robes and turbans lifted this elderly lady up and sat her down on a chair next to me. They told me her name was Bibi Zulaikha. She was a bereaved women, who had lost two sons, Mohammad Yousif and Mohammad Islam – one killed by fundamentalists and one martyred in the resistance to Soviet occupation. Beneath her black head covering, I saw a tired, wrinkled face – but her eyes were animated.

'My daughter Malalai,' Bibi Zulaikha addressed me in a most respectful tone. 'I am almost one hundred years old, and I am dying. When I heard about you and what you said, I knew you were a special person and that I had to meet you. God must protect you, my dear. Now that I have met you I can die in peace.'

After she said these words, she took out a gold ring and said she was giving it – her only valuable possession in the world – to me, and that I must use it to get funds for my work and my programmes.

When I responded that I could not accept such a generous gift, she was emphatic. 'You must take it! I have suffered so much in my life,' she continued, her voice quivering with emotion, 'and my last wish is that you accept this gift from me.'

I cried and hugged her, and said that I was greatly honoured by her generosity. I handed the ring to my uncle for safekeeping. This ring and others like it, that I received later on, are still kept in a lockbox of valuables to be used for the benefit of the movement. I later heard that Bibi Zulaikha died just months later. Her confidence in me was yet another reminder of my new responsibilities.

Late into the evening, a steady stream of visitors kept arriving to see and talk to me. Villagers who had walked all day long from remote parts of Farah Province to welcome me were now camped out for the night on the cement floor of the clinic's reception hall. At some point in the early hours, when the last conversation was finished, I managed to find a blanket and a spot to lie down among them. Exhausted, I fell into a deep sleep.

A few days later, I was invited back to the governor's for a dinner in honour of all the Loya Jirga delegates. Abdul Hai Nemati was trying to look magnanimous and democratic by inviting even his opponents, and I decided to put in an appearance because there were many visitors in attendance. I made a strong impression on them by casually addressing the governor by his first name, when everybody else was calling him 'Sir'. During the dinner I was able to expose Nemati in front of his guests. When I engaged him in a discussion he simply had no way to answer my accusations. I know this was a blow to him.

After dinner, I had a chance to meet with Nemati's wife and his daughter; the latter expressed her support for my cause. She hugged me and we sat close together and talked, but when the governor came in she moved away from me, attempting to conceal her sympathies from her father. Later, she visited me at my office and even agreed to take part in the International Women's Day activities we were planning – we even worked together on a speech she was going to deliver. Unfortunately, her father got wind of her plans and when the day came, I was told, he locked her in their house and forbade her from participating.

Following my time at the Loya Jirga, I resumed my duties in Farah, although my life and work changed significantly with my new notoriety. There were more threats and attacks, but it also meant that a lot more people were coming to see me, to offer support or to seek help.

I was now a kind of counsellor or social worker as well as the director of the facilities. Women, especially, came to ask for advice and shared very personal issues. They told me their stories of rape, abuse and other violence. The more stories I heard, the more I realised that I had done the right thing by speaking out. Young girls confided that they were suicidal, with death seeming like the only escape from an abusive father or an unwanted marriage. I always sought to encourage them to have hope and to fight for what was right, and to work with other women for equality. More than once I had hard discussions with men who thought that they could treat women and girls like property. Sometimes they justified this by using the excuse of religion, or what they claimed was Afghan culture.

Some men and women came to see me for advice about very, very personal matters. In some cases I was young enough to be their daughter, so it was inspiring that they trusted me to confide in and that they wanted to know my ideas. But some men refused entirely to discuss an issue regarding a woman. They would say that they would not discuss it with the president of Afghanistan himself. 'She's my wife, she is mine,' they said, as if she was a piece of property. In some cases men would even say, 'I bought her.' Unfortunately some Afghan men still do not view women as equal human beings, and this has many ramifications.

It is very difficult for a woman to get a divorce and even if the problems in a relationship are entirely the man's fault, people will have the view that the woman is to blame. The paperwork required even to bring the process of divorce involves a lot of bureaucracy. First a woman must file a letter with the Ministry of Women's Affairs, then they must appear before a court with a male relative. Families almost never give their consent to a divorce if the woman is requesting it, because of the children. This is one of the results of three decades of male chauvinism justified by cherry-picking quotes from the Holy Quran and twisting Islam.

I hope that we can educate new generations to change this bias against women. I take hope from my own experience, which has taught me that despite the widespread influence of funda-mentalism, and despite the common monolithic portrayal of our society in the Western media, many Afghan men are willing to accept the leadership of a woman, if you speak from the heart about the core issues and the miseries that afflict them. Scores of men visited me to tell me they were ready to work for my cause. They wanted to take direction from me, regardless of my age and gender. This gives me confidence that if more women in Afghanistan take up the struggle for our rights and for justice, we will have the majority of poor Afghan men as our comrades-in-arms.

I often counselled rape victims. In Afghanistan the victim is brutalised twice, first when she is assaulted, then again when she is shunned by her community. To say that a girl or woman has been raped is to bring shame upon her whole family. Many consider that a victim of rape is permanently damaged, and she will be unable to marry. Sometimes family members will even kill the woman who has been raped, and often the victim herself commits suicide. Personally, I encouraged women victims of rape to turn their pain and tragedy into something positive by advocating for other women. I urged them not to stay silent, and explained that they had a responsibility to speak out. I would tell them, 'Let us join hands. Women's rights are not something given to you. They have to be taken and this is something that only we can do together.'

Another memorable visit I had was from two young girls who came to me with an important request. At first they had telephoned and I asked them how I could help. They did not want to tell me what their issue was over the phone, so I told them to come and see me. It turns out they wanted me to meet their father in order to convince him to allow them to attend school. I agreed to meet the father, who turned out to be a big supporter of mine. We had a long discussion about the benefits of education for young girls, and the importance of women having their own identity and opportunities in life.

I told him that when you support me and say that my voice is your voice, you should think: If I was not educated then how could I become your voice? When you say that I tell the message that is in your heart, it is because I went to school and read books. And so you should allow your daughters to be enlightened to become like me.

These discussions had an impact on him and he agreed to send his daughters to school. The daughters were very happy. I still remember the big smiles on the girls' faces when they found out they would get to go to school. They thanked me many times.

Other visitors came to see me to ask me a different type of question: 'What can we do to help?'

People were always bringing gifts, and these offerings varied depending on the wealth of the donor. Some brought goats, milk or yogurt; some brought fruit and vegetables from their gardens; some came with religious items to keep me safe. Others brought clothing. One tailor donated clothes for all my bodyguards. Another time, when I was invited to give a speech at a local market, a supporter announced that all of the women who had accompanied me were to be given the most expensive clothes at the bazaar as gifts. Poems were written for me, and they were published in the local papers or sent to me personally. A number of people donated thirty-two different parcels of land – a most precious possession in Afghanistan – so that I could use it to build schools or hospitals. Unfortunately, due to lack of funds, no facilities have yet been built on these lands.

Sometimes people would travel great distances to meet me. I remember one night in particular when two poor women came to visit us. They arrived in the evening after a long journey, so I invited them in and found some food to prepare for them. We ate and talked together, me calling them 'Mother' and them calling me 'my child', as politeness dictates. Then, after dinner, one of them asked me, 'When will we be able to meet Malalai Joya?'

'You will meet her soon,' I said.

Some of my supporters had made posters and CDs to spread the word about my speech at the Loya Jirga, and these visitors asked for some posters of Malalai Joya.

I smiled and said I could certainly get them some of these posters.

When I came back into the room, they looked at the picture on the poster. And then they looked at me, more closely this time. They couldn't believe it.

'Why didn't you say it was you? ... And don't you have any help here?'

They hugged and kissed me as I explained that all my colleagues were away for the evening.

A man that I met days after my return from the Loya Jirga told me that usually only men had radios in Farah. Women had no interest in listening to the radio – until my speech.

'After your speech our women are also interested in listening to the radio to follow your news,' he said. He complained that now he had a problem with his wife, because she wants to hear the radio, while in the past it was only his property!

Residents of Farah from all walks of life made it known that they were behind my opposition to the warlords. Once, a group of elders paid me a visit.

'We wanted to meet you, the one they call "infidel" in Kabul,' one of them announced after I had greeted them.

I waited somewhat nervously for them to continue.

'We are very religious men … but if these criminals in Kabul call you "infidel" and "communist", then we are "infidels" and "communists" too.'

My enemies even tried to use the fact that I was receiving so many visitors against me. For example, there was a rumour that said the reason I was receiving so many guests was that I had been raped, and all these people were coming to express their condolences to my family. They were trying to exploit the terrible stigma rape carries in Afghan society against the victim. But, in my situation, most Afghans, thankfully, were like the group of elders who came to visit me and were able to see through all the name-calling and lies.

There were, however, some dangerous exceptions.

CHAPTER 7

A DANGEROUS
SEASON

*T*HE MONTHS FOLLOWING MY SPEECH at the Loya Jirga were the most dangerous times of my life – even riskier than the years I spent teaching under the nose of the Taliban. Now that my name and face were known in every corner of Afghanistan, there were some in my country who only wanted to do me harm. My enemies had also started a rumour that Malalai Joya had fled to a foreign country, and she only gave her speech at the Jirga to get asylum. Unfortunately, in the past, some people who had said harsh things against the criminal warlords had taken asylum abroad. I wanted to show that I had not run from my country, that I would never abandon the struggle in Afghanistan. And I wanted the warlords to know that I was not afraid of them.

And so when the Ministry of Women's Affairs invited me to attend the events marking International Women's Day (IWD) in Kabul in March of 2004, I accepted. I knew there would be a lot of media in Kabul, and that high officials, including Hamid Karzai, would be at the ceremonies. Since this would be my first public appearance after the Loya Jirga, I thought I would get time to speak, and it would be a good opportunity to put forward the message that I had not been allowed to deliver before. I travelled to Kabul by bus, under the cover of my burqa, accompanied by my Uncle Azad and another bodyguard.

When I arrived in Kabul, the Ministry of Women's Affairs assigned me a security detail – two men and two women – because they knew the threats I was facing. However, my own bodyguards were not allowed into the event themselves. The main Women's Day event was held in a huge hall in the city, with many speakers scheduled to make remarks. Unfortunately, the main official presiding was a woman linked to my enemy Ismail Khan, the Herat governor. When I told her that I wanted a turn to speak, she flatly refused. Then I approached Habiba Sarabi, the Minister of Women's Affairs but she told me that she had no authority there to give me a chance to speak.

So I thought that I had lost my opportunity. But when President Karzai started his speech, I wrote a note saying that I had untold stories to tell, and would he please ask the organisers to give me a turn. I gave the note to one of the organisers who passed it to Karzai while he was delivering his speech. I watched as Karzai looked at the note and put it on the table. When he finished, he gave the note to the announcer and left the event. So I was still not sure whether I would be given a chance.

While I was eagerly waiting in my seat, a woman who seemed to be some sort of guard came up to me and asked brusquely, 'Are you Malalai Joya?' She spoke Dari with an accent common in the Panjshir Valley, a stronghold of the Northern Alliance. Everything about her, including her impolite manner, made me suspect she was working for the warlords.

When I said 'Yes, I am Joya' she told me that I had a visitor waiting for me outside.

'It's someone who says he was your bodyguard at the Loya Jirga, and he needs to talk to you. So please go and meet him.'

I thought it might be one of the kind soldiers who guarded me at the UN safe house. But I could not leave and miss a chance to speak.

'Thank you for telling me,' I said, 'but right now I am waiting for my turn.'

'OK, I just passed the message to you,' she said rudely. 'It's up to you what to do.'

Seconds later, I was called to the podium. My note to Karzai had worked. While I went up to deliver my remarks, my bodyguards went off on their own initiative to check out this man who wanted to see me.

I used this opportunity to, in a sense, complete the speech that had been cut off at the Loya Jirga, reminding the women present that our rights would never arrive as a gift from others, but only through our own prolonged efforts. I also took the chance to rebut some of the slander that my enemies had been spreading in their attempts to discredit me, such as the assertion that my criticisms were only designed to win me fame and asylum in the West. A comfortable exile would never be acceptable for me, and I made clear that I would rather die than abandon my country.

The audience clearly appreciated what I was saying, and every sentence of my speech was followed by clapping.

I finished to loud applause and walked back to my seat where I saw that my bodyguards were all waiting for me, looking very nervous. Women from the audience were trying to reach me to congratulate me and speak to me, but my bodyguards kept them away. I wanted to greet these women, but it was not allowed. Obviously something was wrong. Before sitting down, I told my bodyguards that I wanted to meet the visitor who was waiting for me. They told me no, we should leave now, and hurried me to a room next to the hall. Then one of the female bodyguards finally told me what was going on. When they went outside to check on this man, they became suspicious and decided to search him. They found a concealed pistol and they arrested him. She told me that he was probably sent to kill me.

I had to stay in the room until the event was over and everyone had left. Then my bodyguards checked the area. They asked me to put on a burqa, and while they surrounded me, walked me to a luxury car with dark windows. As soon as I was in the car they raced out of the area to a safe place.

Despite my efforts, I could never find out what happened to the man who was arrested, or even his name. So I suspected two possible scenarios: either the assassin was sent by powerful warlords or anyone else who could easily have him released, or the whole scene was a drama to frighten me to stop speaking out against them.

This incident was unsettling, but I refused to cut short my visit to Kabul. And I continued to make frequent trips to the capital in the months to come. I still had a great deal to do.

My beloved Uncle Azad now devoted himself full time to my protection, and he recruited trusted friends, relatives and others to screen my visitors and to accompany me when I travelled. At first it was very strange to be constantly surrounded by young bodyguards in camouflage uniforms carrying AK-47 assault rifles, but it became the routine of my life. With new dangers facing me wherever I went, it became riskier and riskier for me to move around, but I tried not to let this affect me too much.

It was important to travel to different parts of Afghanistan to see conditions first-hand and to spread my message. And so I accepted an invitation to speak in a mosque in my native village of Ziken.

As we drove along the winding, rutted road to Ziken, a friend told me he thought this might be the first time in Afghan history that a woman had been invited to give a political speech in a mosque. No doubt it was an unusual event. Many supporters with cars and motorcycles joined our convoy and told us that they would take care of my security in case there was trouble. This large crowd followed my every step that day.

When we arrived, the mosque was packed with hundreds of men and there were loudspeakers mounted on the exterior walls so that more people could listen from outside. The crowd included tribal elders, some of my long-time supporters, the simply curious, and a few people who came to listen even though they disagreed with me.

I was warmly greeted by some elders and, along with my security people, I took a seat and waited for my turn to speak. As I looked around at the crowd, I carefully considered my remarks. This was a great honour for me, especially being such a young woman, just three days past my twenty-sixth birthday. It showed that I had broad support in my province, and that my enemies who called me an infidel had not succeeded in discrediting me. Following a welcome from the imam, I was introduced by a village elder. I walked up to the microphone and began by giving greetings to the audience and thanking those who had invited me, but I had barely managed to say a word beyond these courtesies when two middle-aged men, wearing white caps and shalwar kameezs, jumped up from the crowd and shouted, 'She has insulted the mujahideen! Do not let her speak!'

These two, and a handful of other opponents in the crowd, kept shouting and trying to disrupt the event until other members of the audience managed to hustle them out of the mosque. Luckily, I was soon able to continue.

I addressed many topics, including my commitment to basic human rights, women's rights and democracy. I even spoke about the need for secularism in Afghanistan. I explained that I believe religion is a private issue, unrelated to political issues and government. As a social activist and politician, I don't talk a lot about Islam. Too often extremists invoke Islam to justify crimes against the people. And politicians invoke Islam rather than focusing on what policies they will implement. The people of Afghanistan have Islam in their hearts and minds. They don't need those who are a shame to Islam to impose their rules on them in the name of Islam. They don't need it in their government, and they do not need anyone – certainly not politicians – to guide them in their faith.

Instead of this dangerous conflation of religion and politics, I explained that what we needed was a secular government, one that would remain distinct from religion, which is a matter of personal faith. Despite what the fundamentalists claim, secularism is not to be feared. It simply means the separation of religion and politics, and this in fact safeguards and guarantees the rights of citizens to freedom of religion and belief.

As I was speaking I glanced at one of the bodyguards who had accompanied me. He was anxiously surveying the crowd, trying to gauge people's reactions. But there was no need to worry. The rest of my talk was very well received.

Before giving this speech, I had worried that perhaps it was a bit too soon to talk publicly about secularism. But one should never underestimate people's political awareness. Despite the best efforts of the fundamentalists, secularism and democracy can still get a hearing and could still inspire people. The men in that mosque understood that Islam should not be subverted for political purposes. Many of them had, in fact, been victimised by groups who had done just that. In a free and democratic Afghanistan, with a secular government, the image of Islam would be safeguarded instead of distorted.

I completed my speech and took my seat again. Afterwards, as we all rose to leave, the first person to approach me was the imam of the mosque. He was very gracious and he said that he agreed with me. Many of the other religious leaders present also came over and, in their own language, explained that they, too, shared my view. They even asked to have their picture taken with me. All of this was very encouraging.

When I exited the mosque that day, it was a wonderful scene as supporters gathered around to send me off. There were young girls with flowers, and many kind words from the crowd. As I was escorted to my vehicle, I noticed an older man with no legs and I went over to see him. He greeted me and also gave me flowers. He told me that he was a veteran of the mujahideen struggle and that my words had been very meaningful to him. I thanked him for his support and listened to more of his story. He was suffering from extreme poverty because he was unable to work, and he cried as he described his predicament. This man had sacrificed a great deal to fight for our country, and we were later able to help arrange some financial support for him.

After that I visited some boys' and girls' schools to talk to the students and teachers. They all strongly supported my work, and some even read poems they had written for me. I also stopped in at local homes and met people.

At the end of this exhilarating, exhausting day, everyone was waving cheerful farewells as our security vehicle and the convoy of supporters began the drive back to Farah City. But our mood soon changed as we approached the Harot bridge outside town. Just ahead of us a huge bomb exploded with a flash and a shock wave that jolted us in our seats. We watched as a plume of dust lifted in the air and spattered debris from the bridge on the roof of our car like dry rain. My driver quickly checked to see whether anyone had been hurt, then spun the car around and raced back to Ziken. A large number of my supporters surrounded us there, promising they would protect me.

Once we were a safe distance away from the smouldering bridge, I called the authorities in Farah City. When I reached one of the local commanders, he offered no help – not surprising, since he was an opponent of mine, with close ties to the warlords. So, on the urging of some of my local supporters, I contacted Ali Ahmad Jalali, the Minister of Interior in Kabul. Jalali promised to call the Farah police to get them to send some men out to assist us. When they finally arrived, and after much discussion, we decided to take a different route back to Farah. This time our convoy included not only soldiers, but also a pack of young men on motorbikes who surrounded us and shouted words of support and encouragement as we cruised along.

It was not a coincidence that this assassination attempt happened on 28 April 2004 – the date of annual celebrations of the mujahideen takeover of Kabul after the fall of the Russian puppet regime in 1992. I had publicly denounced government officials for holding big celebrations of this so-called 'victory day' in both Farah and Kabul. This was another shameless example of Karzai placating the warlords. The real victory day for Afghanistan was 15 February 1989, the day the last Soviet soldier left our country.

This incident highlighted the gravity of my altered circumstances, and it became harder and harder for me to visit different parts of Farah. Instead, supporters travelled to see me at our headquarters in the city. They often carried disturbing news. In some towns, warlords and their local commanders held total control, with private militias, private jails and private torture cells. We received reports of people being jailed simply on suspicion of supporting me.

This happened to some of those who had come to support me when I spoke at the mosque. Some weeks later, a man came to Farah City to explain what had been done to his elderly father in the days after my visit. His father had been in the presence of a local fundamentalist commander, a man with links to certain warlords, and overheard him saying that I had made the mosque 'dirty with my presence'. This supported my suspicions that allies of these warlords were behind the attempt to kill me.

The son told me that their whole family supported me, and that his father would not stand for these insults and so he had defended me to this man. For this, he was beaten and taken and locked in this fundamentalist's private jail. The son wanted to know what he could do to help his father. He urged me to communicate to Karzai and the government that men like this local commander needed to have their powers withdrawn.

The father was in fact released after several days, and then he came to visit me to explain the rest of the story. The local thug had decided to let him free because he was so elderly, but they warned him to stop supporting me or else he knew what they could do to his son, who was his only son. The old man then explained what he thought of this threat, 'No, to support you I am willing to lose my life, my son's life and my family's life. I will not be silent.'

I responded, 'I am not better than you or anyone else. It is because of you that I put my life at risk. We struggle together and we hope that the blood of none of us will have to be shed.'

One day late in the spring, Interior Minister Jalali called me and told that they had a plan to assign a man called Yousif Baghlani as governor of Farah. He asked what I thought about it. I told him that I had never heard this name. And since my view is only the view of one person, I would need to discuss the appointment with the people of Farah, and I would report back with their opinion. He agreed and soon I gathered some elders of Farah to hold a meeting. Even though it was pouring with rain in every corner of Farah Province, around a hundred people came to the meeting. I asked them for their view of Yousif as governor – and I was shocked to learn from some of them that he was actually a famous war criminal named *Bashir* Baghlani who supported the fugitive warlord Hekmatyar.

Apparently the ministry gave him a new name to try to trick the people, since he was rejected everywhere else they tried to put him. The elders became very angry at the government and refused to accept Baghlani as governor. One of them said, 'What kind of gift is this that Karzai sends us? Are we a laboratory where he sends criminals to be tested?'

I called minister Jalali and told him that people were very angry over his choice and they rejected this criminal, Baghlani. I even sent him a videotape of the meeting. So it was very surprising to the elders and to me when, a few days later, Bashir Baghlani was sent out to be governor of Farah. The appointment sparked a protest among the people, but it did no good. This was just another example of how the government ignores the will of the people by supporting hated criminals.

Earlier in the year I had been honoured to receive the Malalai of Maiwand Award, a prize initially established by a group of Afghans living in Germany called the Cultural Union of Afghans in Europe. It was given to me – for standing up to the warlords at the Loya Jirga. In early July 2004, I travelled to Kabul, once again under the cover of my burqa, where I donated the award to the Afghan Minister of Information and Culture where it would be placed in the government-run National Archives. I did this because I felt this award belonged not to me but to the people of Afghanistan. In retrospect, I realise it was a mistake to hand it over, because it was used to help legitimise a government that has proved to be the most corrupt in our history, and cannot truly be regarded as a 'national' government.

Later that month, while I was still visiting the capital, I received a phone call from an agitated worker at my office in Farah, who explained that a small crowd of fundamentalists, some armed with guns, were attacking the orphanage, which was nearby. This mob did not know I was out of town. There were a few security people at the headquarters who gathered up their weapons and were ready to defend the orphanage, but I gave clear instructions: 'If you have to shoot at them, aim only at their feet. Do not kill anyone.'

News of the attack was reported by the BBC Persian service and on Radio Azadi in Pashto and Dari. In fact Radio Azadi aired it live as breaking news, and many people called the radio station to condemn the attack as it was happening. I was interviewed by Radio Azadi and I used the opportunity to condemn the warlords I knew were behind the attack. Meanwhile I followed the news anxiously while getting updates from my colleagues in Farah. Shopkeepers and neighbours came running to help defend the orphanage with their bare hands, some of them throwing stones at the attackers. Eventually the fundamentalists were driven off.

In the battle, some of the attackers were injured and couldn't run away. Our people put them in the clinic's ambulance to take them to a hospital. They were very ashamed when they realised that, despite being enemies, our team was still willing to care for them.

Later some of them became my supporters, and they visited my office to explain what had led to the attack. They said that Bashir Baghlani, the infamous warlord who Karzai had appointed as the new governor of Farah, had planned the attack. He lied to them, saying they should attack our facilities because I had insulted the mujahideen and Islam. He told them I had hoarded money in my office, and that they could keep this wealth if they carried out the plan. Now they felt misled and misused. The people of Farah had already protested about the appointment of Governor Baghlani. The lies he and his associates spread that incited the attack on our facilities in Farah made him even more hated. There was widespread protest and President Karzai was eventually forced to replace him.

After this assault, more neighbours offered to be my bodyguards. Any time people in the area heard so much as a single gunshot, they would rush out to make sure we were safe.

Former mujahideen travelled to visit me, offering to help protect me with both manpower and weapons. Some even offered to take up arms against those who had targeted me, and those who terrorised our region. They wanted to avenge these local extremist commanders. They expressed their support for me, and my ideas, very strongly.

'Whatever you ask of us, we will do,' they said. 'Malalai, give us guns. We want to kill these enemies.'

I told them that I believed that the gun was not the way for us now. It was not the best way to achieve peace and democracy, and that we were against war and violence. We only carry guns for the purpose of self-defence. But this is just one example of how tired and frustrated people were with the situation, one that still exists today. They are angry that no government and no people in power have listened to them. They are ready to put their lives at risk and take up arms if they are asked.

I believe it is very important, in any struggle for justice, to analyse carefully and logically the contemporary situation in one's country when determining tactics and strategy. For instance, the situation of the 1980s and the armed resistance that my father took part in against the Soviets is not the same as the struggle in which I am engaged. Today, we have tried to use non-violent means to raise people's awareness about the mockery of democracy that has been imposed in Afghanistan.

However, if the situation were to change for the worse and

leave us with no other choice but that of freedom or death, I would be ready to pick up the gun to defend my country, to defend freedom and to defend the values we are working for. This is the choice, after all, that many martyrs of my father's generation made. I have promised to my people that I will always defend the freedom of our country, and this is very important to me. Those who fight for freedom love peace, but at some moments in history there is no other choice but to take up arms, no matter how much we dislike what they represent.

I personally do not like being surrounded by men with guns for my protection, but it is necessary, and I am honoured to have friends and supporters all over Afghanistan who are willing to take risks and sacrifice themselves for my security. I have very friendly relations with my bodyguards, and we often have lively discussions and even joke around sometimes. Even those that aren't relatives are like family to me. I worry about their safety, and if something were to happen to them in fending off an attack against me, I would be heartbroken.

Soon after the attack on our facilities in Farah, and the huge show of support that followed it, I received notice that President Karzai wanted to meet me. I accepted the offer because I thought the meeting could be an opportunity to tell him what the people on the streets of Afghanistan thought about his government. Publicly at least, Karzai was saying that he wanted to put an end to the dominance of the warlords, and at this time most Afghans still held out hope that he would live up to some of his promises. I wanted to remind him that the people hated his alliances with some of the most notorious enemies of Afghanistan. Not only was Karzai close to the strongmen of the Northern Alliance, but he also maintained ties to some former Russian puppets, not to mention a number of thugs from Hekmatyar's party.

At the arranged time, I arrived at the presidential palace, accompanied by a colleague from OPAWC, a woman who was one of its directors. At the gates of the palace, we saw many large American soldiers on guard. Some of them asked my name and what we were there for and then they escorted us inside. Then a group of female security guards searched our bags. These women were kind, and in fact they said they supported what I had said at the Loya Jirga.

It had been our plan, if possible, to make a video recording of the meeting with Karzai, or at least to take pictures, but we were told that there was a strict policy against any recording devices. After passing through all of the security checkpoints and procedures, we were ushered into Hamid Karzai's ornate presidential office. This was Afghanistan's version of the Oval Office. There was a big desk, an Afghan flag and a number of framed pictures on the walls, including ones of former kings and Ahmad Shah Massoud, the criminal Northern Alliance leader who was killed just before 9/11, and who was now called a 'national hero'. This was a reminder to me that, despite the pleasant expression on Karzai's face and his impeccable manners, he represented men with dark and extremist minds.

When I came into the room, President Karzai got up from his chair and greeted me warmly. He shook my hand, put his other hand on my shoulder, and then he asked me kindly to sit down. He was very respectful, but I think that he wanted to charm me in hopes that I would stop my harsh criticism of his government.

There were a couple of other officials present, and a server who brought us tea. Sitting across the table from Karzai, the first thing I said to him was, 'Thank you for giving me this chance to share with you the problems of our people. I have a lot to tell you.' I did not want to waste too much time with formalities or small talk.

Karzai replied, 'Yes, I heard about your speech at the Loya Jirga. Do not think that I did not understand your message.' This was his way of opening with an expression of his support. But translating that support into promises of action would be difficult.

I did most of the talking, because I had a lot to say. The meeting lasted slightly less than an hour, and I believe I spoke for at least two-thirds of this time. I outlined the many outrages and deprivations that the women of Afghanistan faced. Karzai listened attentively and I even saw tears fall from his eyes when I told him some horrific details of the rapes, abductions and murders that went on in our country.

I urged him to weaken the warlords' power by denying them appointments to key government posts. I told him that people were saying he was not an honest person and I said to him, 'Our history will ask, and people are asking, why have you made compromises with the warlords?'

'How have I made compromises?'

'For example, you sent us a fundamentalist to be governor of Farah,' I said. I told him that Bashir Baghlani, the new governor he had sent to replace Abdul Hai Nemati, was even worse. I gave him some documents I had collected about Baghlani's corruption, and told him how the citizens of Farah protested about his appointment. They even wondered if Baghlani had been sent to kill me.

Then I told him of another case. 'You know, last night I was in a supporter's house and there one dear old mother told me about the time she saw the video of you putting a medal around the neck of Ismail Khan and offering him a post as a government minister. When this woman saw this she told me she became despondent about you, and she said, "What is the difference between these fundamentalists and Karzai?"'

He answered that he had been put on the spot by Younis Qanooni, the Minister of Education, who called upon him right then and there to come on the stage and put the medal around the neck of Ismail Khan.

Karzai said that he agreed with most of what I was saying, but he avoided making any firm commitments. In fact I got the impression that, whatever I said, in his heart he agreed with me. I suspect now that he may have allowed me to do so much of the talking partly because he did not really have many answers, or real solutions that he was willing or able to pursue. When our time was up, the president rose and was, again, extremely polite. He pulled my chair out for me and walked with me all the way to the door.

The last thing I said to Karzai was, 'Please pass my regards to your wife and also please give her a message that next year she must attend the International Women's Day events. Why did she not attend this year?'

He responded, 'Why don't you tell her this yourself. She is in fact a strong supporter of yours.'

'Where is your wife now?'

'At the moment she is convalescing. She has been in France for an operation, so you should make an appointment for another day to meet her.'

'I have to return to Farah in the next couple of days, so it would be good to meet before I go.'

So he agreed that I could have an appointment to meet his wife the next day at the same time. And then Karzai kindly saw me off.

We would never again have formal discussions.

As my colleagues and I exited Karzai's office, none other than the warlord Mohammad Fahim was on his way in. Fahim, at this time, was the most powerful of all the Northern Alliance commanders, and he stared at me in a clear attempt to intimidate me. I returned his stare as we crossed paths.

The next day, as arranged, I returned to meet Karzai's wife, this time accompanied by a different supporter. After again going through the security procedures, I was ushered into a large sitting room with framed pictures of Karzai and his family on the walls.

Zenat Karzai, the president's wife, greeted me warmly. She asked me to sit down with her and then she pointed to a magazine on her table with my picture on it.

'See, I am a supporter of yours,' she said.

The magazine had in fact been published by someone with fundamentalist ideas, but they had put me on it because it was an issue that at the time could sell copies.

This meeting lasted just under two hours. I explained in detail to Mrs Karzai a number of the crimes of the warlords and, in particular, the record of some of the fundamentalists in Farah. I brought documents with me, which I gave to her, urging her to pass them on to her husband.

She was interested to know about my educational background, and how I prepared for speaking at the Loya Jirga. For my part, I asked her why she was not working as a medical doctor, since that was her profession. She said it was considered too dangerous for her to work in a hospital, as she might be a target for kidnapping.

I also spoke about the role of women in Afghanistan and about the role of the president's wife. I said that even if she was so ill that she could not walk she could have come to International Women's Day in a wheelchair. She accepted this, and said that in the future she would make every effort to attend these events. She related the fact that the First Lady of France had told her that she had a very important role to play regarding women's rights.

Mrs Karzai even said that she was interested in setting up a special group to work on these issues. I told her that if she was serious, if this was not merely going to be a symbolic group, then I might be willing to join her effort. Before leaving, I said I would be waiting to hear from her about when we would be starting this women's group. She said as soon as her health improved she would get to work on this. To this day, I have never heard back from her about this women's group.

Hamid Karzai, of course, went on to make compromise after compromise with the warlords, and I later wondered, *What good were the president's tears if he would not or could not take the necessary measures to solve Afghanistan's problems?* I came to think of Karzai's tears merely as crocodile tears. And today I must conclude that for him following orders from the White House was more important that looking after the well-being of the Afghan people.

Karzai would win the presidential election held in October

2004. Many people voted for him because, at least, they did not see him as a war criminal – as someone with blood on his hands from the past. And since most of the other candidates were warlords, people preferred him as the lesser evil. Karzai himself, of course, was not really the most powerful person in Afghanistan. He might be the man installed in the presidential palace in Kabul, but he relied on the Americans and his alliances with the powerful warlords throughout the country to keep him there. After all, it was the forces of Fahim and other Northern Alliance commanders – not Karzai – who, with the help of US Special Forces, had first taken over Kabul when the Taliban fled the capital in 2001. Karzai was always negotiating new arrangements with the warlords. Often this took the form of new 'opposition' alliances being declared against Karzai. My father, for one, was always distrustful of news about these developments.

'You can't believe or trust these things,' he would say. 'It's like the fighting between a man and his wife.' In other words, even though there were squabbles among them, Karzai's government was still married to the warlords.

Afghanistan has had puppet rulers before. They were controlled by the British and the Russians. Sadly, President Karzai has become a mere puppet himself. And the man many considered to be pulling the strings at this time – often referred to only half-jokingly as the 'real president' of Afghanistan – had his offices near the presidential palace. I was also invited to meet him.

Zalmay Khalilzad, who had helped orchestrate the disgraceful Loya Jirgas, was now serving as the official US ambassador to Afghanistan. He was even more closely protected than Karzai. The day that I met him there were many layers of security to negotiate before entering into the offices of the heavily fortified US Embassy, which was guarded by Marines.

The ambassador's office was decorated with prominently displayed photos of Khalilzad in the company of George W. Bush and Dick Cheney. In fact, everywhere you turned there was another picture of Bush, another American flag. I thought, *At least*

he does not try to hide what he stands for and for whom he works.
There was no ambiguity about his position, either. Many people
in Afghanistan considered Khalilzad the architect of misguided
US policy in Afghanistan, and as he was a supporter of the
warlords I wanted to hear his reasons for dealing with such
criminals. I told him that America was repeating a mistake of the
past by backing Islamic fundamentalists in Afghanistan, a
historical error which has already resulted in the tragic 'blowback'
of 9/11. I told him that the people of Afghanistan would never
forgive the United States for backing such brutal men. And, I
stressed, people's judgements against him would be especially
harsh, since he was an Afghan by birth.

But after exchanging a few words with the ambassador, it was
obvious to me that he was not really interested in hearing or
acting on my message.

In the aftermath of my speech at the Loya Jirga, Ambassador
Khalilzad had told the international media that the fact that I was
able to voice my criticisms illustrated the admirable democratic
process that was being established in Afghanistan. He did not,
however, address the substance of my speech – which exposed
the charade of the 'showcase democracy' the US wanted to install
– nor the many threats it had brought down on me. Now I began
to wonder whether this meeting had only been arranged so that
the ambassador could announce to the media that he had met
with Malalai Joya. I felt this session was a complete waste of time,
as was my meeting with Karzai.

After leaving his post in Afghanistan in 2005, Khalilzad went
on to serve as the ambassador to Iraq and later as the US
ambassador to the United Nations. There were even rumours cir-
culating that he might put his name forward to replace Karzai as
president when elections are held in 2009.

In the months after I returned from the Loya Jirga, I still
considered myself a social worker. The orphanage, the Hamoon
Health Centre and everything else that OPAWC had worked so
hard to establish remained important to me. While in Kabul, I

visited a number of local and international NGOs, as well as the embassies of Australia, Japan, Germany and others in the hope of securing funding for the orphanage and for other projects I hoped to establish. Most of my requests were rejected, or promises were made that were never fulfilled.

I returned to Farah more frustrated than ever with the government, but even more determined to challenge the dominance of the warlords. I felt I had to use any and every means available to denounce the warlords, even if that meant becoming a politician in a country where democracy remains a farce, and where Parliament is still a den of thieves and killers.

CHAPTER 8

A WEDDING
AND AN ELECTION

AFGHANISTAN'S first parliamentary elections in thirty-three years were set for 18 September 2005. It would be the first time that women were allowed to run for election. Naturally many people wanted me to run for a seat, and I asked my father what he thought about this.

'You should decide,' was his simple answer. He had always taught us that everyone must have their own identity, the freedom to decide their own course, especially women.

I thought about it long and hard. A seat in Parliament would allow me to voice my concerns about violence, poverty and women's rights to a larger audience, not only in Afghanistan but around the world. It would also give me a forum to expose the corruption of the warlords and to call for their prosecution for war crimes. I knew that this Parliament would be full of warlords and their proxies, just like the Loya Jirga. I was concerned about fraud in past elections, and I doubted if this one would be fair and democratic. I also knew that my campaign would be dangerous and full of challenges.

But in the end I was willing to accept the risks. I felt I had a responsibility to the people of Farah, in particular, who had shown me so much support. I knew that, even if elected, I would be in a small minority and couldn't expect to pass any laws to benefit my people. But I hoped by being inside the Parliament I would be able to expose Afghan 'democracy' for the hoax I knew it to be. Also I could at least push for more funds for important projects like our orphanage. So I decided to put my name forward.

There would be much to do to prepare for the campaign, but before I got started there was also an important moment in my personal life – this one a more joyous event: my wedding.

When I was a young girl, I decided I would not get married until I finished my education. And then, for many years, I was busy as a teacher and as a social activist. Even though more than half of Afghani women are married before they reach the age of sixteen, my parents knew that I was not ready, and they did not push me. I had seen so many young women forced into early marriages, and I was grateful that my father was not like other fathers, and that he respected women.

In Afghanistan, marriages involve the whole family, even extended families, as they are called in the West. Traditionally, it is up to a female member of the prospective groom's family to approach the family of the bride to bring up the topic of marriage. Over the years, different families had made proposals on behalf of various young men but my parents always had to decline. I asked my family not to even tell me about these proposals, because sometimes they were from family friends or even the parents of my students, and I did not feel comfortable knowing about this.

There was one memorable time when we had just moved to Herat during the Taliban regime. Unlike in Farah, in Herat it is customary that when women from the boy's family come to propose a match, they ask the girl, for whom they are suggesting the marriage offer, to bring them water. Then the girl's family automatically knows what they want. The girl herself does not meet them, and the parents either accept or reject the offer, or ask for time to think about it. But in my case, once when some women came and asked me to bring water, I went right away to get them some water and sat down next to them in the room. As soon as my mother came in, she nodded at me to leave the house. Later everyone was laughing at me because I didn't understand the custom and the women thought that I had agreed to the marriage!

When I finally decided it was time to marry, it was years later to a young man of my own age whose family had been friends with my parents for many years. I cannot tell you his name, because it would put both him and his family in danger. But I can tell you that he lived much of his life in Iran as a refugee while I was in Pakistan. We first met at a press conference in 2004 when he was still a student at Kabul University. I knew that his mother – his father had died long ago – had spoken to my parents about asking for my hand in marriage. But they understood that I had been reluctant to get married because of my dedication to my social and political work.

Later that year my future husband and I sat down together in Farah to discuss our situation. It is, of course, highly unusual for a man and woman to discuss their own marriage. I knew that he shared my commitment to social justice for women and all Afghans. But I had to be sure he understood that our life together would be difficult, and different from the traditional marriage.

'You understand my life,' I said to him. 'You know I may be killed at any time. And, that if we did get married, my political commitments would have to come first?'

'Yes, Malalai,' he said. 'Of course. I understand your life. And I am no better than you. Whatever happens to you, I am willing to accept the same risk.'

'Mubarak!' I said, using the happiest word in the Persian language, meaning 'congratulations!' We Afghans congratulate each other on our birthdays, at weddings, on holidays such as Eid and New Year, and other joyous occasions. It is a way to exchange best wishes for the future. Usually, a woman's parents accept a proposal from the groom's family by saying 'Congratulations!' But in this case, I had to say it myself.

After this conversation, I told my father that now it was OK for him to talk to my suitor. And, out of respect for my parents, I agreed to follow the rest of the traditional process to finalise the engagement and marriage. Everyone in my family was happy with the match, and we decided to throw a brief, simple engagement party to celebrate. My fiancé travelled to Herat Province to collect his mother and bring her to the party. But while he was away, I was told that an important press conference I had already agreed to attend would be held in Kabul the next day, so I'd better leave immediately. I thought the engagement party could go on without my presence. So I left a note for my fiancé to congratulate him on our engagement and to tell him I was sorry that I could not attend the ceremony. I pulled a blue burqa over my head to disguise my identity, and, with two other supporters, left for Kabul by road. When he returned and read my note to his mother, she cried because I would not be there and she could not see me. She was already beginning to learn that I was not going to be a very traditional daughter-in-law.

First of all, I was twenty-six years old, which is well above the average age for a bride in Afghanistan. And although I hoped the wedding would be a very special day for our families, I did not want anything extravagant. In Afghanistan it is customary for the groom's family to buy expensive gold jewellery for the bride. We did not allow the family of my husband to buy anything. They were unhappy about it, but we insisted that they did not spend any money on luxuries.

Material things do not matter to me. I am always encouraging young girls not to spend too much on clothing or jewellery. I believe it is better to live simply, and I wanted to set a good example. Too often in Afghanistan poor families have to go heavily into debt to pay for a wedding. Unlike the custom in Pakistan and India, the groom's family in Afghanistan pays for the wedding. The cost can be enormous – a farmer earning the equivalent of 300 dollars a year might spend 2,000 dollars on a wedding, including expensive gifts to the bride's family. In Kabul, a middle-class family might pay 15,000 dollars or more. In the opium-growing regions of my country, poor farmers have sometimes been forced to give up their daughters to repay debts to the drug traffickers. These 'opium brides' are as young as ten years old. I wanted to show with my wedding that a daughter was not an object to be sold, that jewellery and expensive clothes do not bring luck. Education is what brings good fortune, and that's where the money should be spent.

We decided to get married in Farah on 10 March 2005. The day before, there was a major rally and celebration of International Women's Day (the usual 8th March celebration was postponed because of rain). The organisers had a big tent, some chairs and a sound system set up right in front of our orphanage. People travelled to Farah from all over to take part and to listen to speeches and watch the performances of patriotic songs, poetry readings and a stage drama exposing violence against women. I was honoured to be invited as the chief guest speaker. My supporters asked the Women's Day organisers if they would keep the tent set up for one more day so we could use it for our wedding party. They were delighted to accept. Near the end of the programme, one of the organisers made a special announcement: Malalai Joya was getting married tomorrow and everyone was welcome to join the celebration. Since we had not printed up invitations, it was a good way to spread the word! By using the Women's Day tent we did not run up extra expenses, and the money we saved could be used for OPAWC projects.

The next day my security detail set up a defensive perimeter around the tent as we prepared for the wedding ceremony. Hundreds of people, including neighbours, family, former students and friends, some from distant villages, came to celebrate our marriage. My bodyguards had to implement stringent security precautions to keep my enemies from using this occasion to launch an attack. In fact my only sad memory from this day is that people could not give me their gifts directly – they had to be first checked for bombs.

Although it is almost impossible to find fresh flowers in Farah, especially at the end of winter, somehow a few of my guests managed to bring beautiful live bouquets for me. Many others brought lovely artificial flowers. But for security reasons, my body-guards had to search each arrangement for explosives. We all remembered that Rajiv Gandhi, India's prime minister, had been killed by a suicide bomber presenting him with a garland. I was so sad to be kept away from my wedding flowers, but there was no other option. By the end of the day we had a huge pile of colourful blossoms, so we announced that everyone who needed flowers for any occasion could come to get them from us. Little children ran around singing 'Free flowers!' For days, women and children were picking up the flowers – some even made a joke that I should open a flower shop and make some money instead of giving them away! But I felt that everyone should share in such beauty.

Some visitors who attended my wedding party brought me more extravagant gifts of jewellery and other luxuries, even against my wishes. We decided to donate these to OPAWC to help fund the Hamoon Health Centre. I also broke with tradition by choosing not to wear a shimmering silk bridal dress, fancy scarves and jewels. Even though my husband's family also wanted to bring me these items, I had to say 'No, thank you'. They were shocked that I did not even buy new clothes for my wedding. I just washed and wore a simple, light-blue Afghani-style outfit. This threw some of the guests. Two different men approached the head table and asked my husband, 'And where is the bride?'

I was sitting right in front of them. Later, everyone had a big laugh over this.

Instead of the usual lavish wedding feast of meat and rice and many different dishes, we only distributed juice and cake to the guests. But even with such a modest celebration, everyone had a joyful time. Two famous groups of wedding singers from Farah (one made up of women and another of men) came to my wedding party and performed free of charge because they wanted to show their support for my work.

I planned to give a speech to explain to everyone why we were having such a simple gathering. But my mother objected, and said that this was not in keeping with Afghan tradition. She said that everything else about the wedding was as I wished, so I should listen to her and follow the custom in this one respect: the bride is not supposed to give a speech at her own wedding!

I agreed to Mother's request, but I did write out some remarks for my assistants from the clinic to read out to the guests. They explained why I wanted to set an example of how to have a lovely wedding without throwing away money and going into debt. For months, the story of our wedding was discussed in homes and offices in Farah, and many regard it as a model of how to break with a harmful tradition.

There was no time for a honeymoon after the wedding. I had dozens of visitors to see every day. But my husband stayed with me in Farah for a while and attended many of the meetings I had with people. I am fortunate to have married such a kind and understanding man. He and his family continue to be very supportive, although it can be difficult. We are not able to see each other all that often. When I am in Kabul I have to keep moving constantly between the houses of different supporters to stay one step ahead of my enemies. My husband is not able to tell his co-workers or even some of his friends that we are married. Sometimes he overhears people criticising me but, for both his safety and mine, he must restrain himself and not respond in a way that might make them suspect that he is the mystery man married to Malalai Joya.

———

Because of my high political profile, OPAWC was facing many problems. It was stamped as Joya's NGO, and most donors refused to fund its projects. Its employees' homes and offices have been raided by Afghan intelligence, which is still run by the Northern Alliance. A number of times their employees have been taken into custody and questioned by agents asking them to provide information about Joya. They want to know the names of Joya's associates, and why she hasn't stopped criticising the warlords and the government. This harassment goes on even today.

Sadly, shortly before the election campaign we had to close down the orphanage in Farah. We relied on a few Afghan supporters and donations from abroad, but it was no longer enough to keep the orphanage running. This was a very upsetting day for me and for all my colleagues. It was difficult to say goodbye to these children. Many of them went back to their families, even though they were desperately poor and could not afford to send their children to school.

One of my hopes in running for Parliament was to push for funding for much-needed projects like this orphanage. Distant provinces like Farah were always left behind with no support. In fact, with the domination of warlords and the ubiquitous corruption in our government, very few projects like our orphanage ever received funding. Most international agencies attach conditions to their grants in order to control their recipients. And they won't fund projects run by critics of warlords, the Afghan government and foreign occupation.

There are dozens of political parties in Afghanistan, but I belong to none of them. I have always chosen to remain politically independent because I feel that the membership cards that we carry are not as important as the ideas we carry in our hearts and minds. As an independent, I believe that I have been able to represent and give voice to all the people of Afghanistan. But without a political party for backing, I had to build my campaign from the ground up. Although many candidates spent huge amounts of money on their campaigns, I spent no money and most of the campaigning was carried out by volunteer supporters.

Because of the death threats against me, and an escalation in violence in the province before the elections, it was not safe for me to attend most campaign events. Basically I could not travel anywhere outside Farah City, and many times I was confined behind the thick brick walls of my headquarters, which was like torture.

Throughout the campaign, people were streaming into my office to ask questions and to offer support. Many elders promised me I had the votes of their entire village. Some supporters showed my speech on VCR players at their marriage parties and get-togethers in villages where I couldn't go due to security reasons. Some of them invited me to speak at their parties or other events. A shopkeeper gathered people together and invited me for a speech at the opening of his shop.

To get my message out, I would record brief remarks on cassette tapes, and many of my volunteers put their lives at risk to take these cassettes to every part of Farah Province. Then, in faraway villages, they would gather people together and play the tape so that my message could be heard. A few of them even recorded messages from me on their cell phones, then campaigned in their districts. Some of these election volunteers were physically beaten when it was found out they were helping my campaign.

A lot of these couriers were under the age of eighteen and they would tell me that they only wished they were old enough to vote for me themselves. Children and teenagers were some of my most enthusiastic supporters. Many fought to convince their parents to support me instead of fundamentalist candidates. One young girl told me that her father was backing a fundamentalist candidate and that he had put up posters for this man outside their home, but she was proud to report that she had taken down her father's posters and put one of mine up in their place.

In Afghanistan we have a saying, 'Ask the truth from a child.'

Whether it's in my own country or when I meet members of the Afghan diaspora, it is the young who are my most enthusiastic supporters. This is perhaps even truer of Afghan communities abroad, and it is a positive sign. If Afghanistan is to stand on its own feet as a democratic and independent country, it will require the participation of many who today live in the West. And it will require the return of the estimated 4 million Afghan refugees who still live in Iran, Pakistan and other nearby countries – the majority of whom are young people. Pakistan has recently closed down some Afghan refugee camps forcibly, but for many there is still no safe place to return home to. Many prefer to move to Kabul because the security is a bit better there. That's one of the reasons why Kabul's population is exploding today – it's becoming crowded with internal refugees.

Because of our reduced life expectancy and all the war dead, Afghanistan's population has the highest percentage of young people in the world. And because of our country's tragic situation, young Afghans are very politicised. This is certainly true of my younger siblings. On one occasion, my little eight-year-old brother was at my bodyguards' home when he noticed that one of them was wearing a hat with the image of Ahmad Shah Massoud, who was one of the criminals who did so much damage to the country during the civil war.

'Why are you wearing that criminal's hat?' my little brother wanted to know. 'If Malalai sees that, she will get very angry!'

My bodyguard had not really paid any attention to what was depicted on the hat. He just liked the way it looked. Once alerted to the fact, the bodyguard found a pair of scissors and cut out the picture of Massoud, but friends still tease him about this. They like to remind him how a 'baby' had to point out to him that his hat was not politically correct.

Many of the children I know follow politics closely. I remember being at a supporter's house when his young son caught the fact that a television report had shortened the clip of me speaking, cutting off a key part of my message. Once people gain some awareness, they can sift the truth from the lies. I hope that my success in getting elected as a young person – and as an outspoken woman – has helped in a small way to inspire the next generation.

On one occasion I was with friends and they asked their young son what he would like to be when he grew up. He answered at once, 'The President of the United States.'

'But why the United States?' his mother asked him.

'Because then I will make Malalai Joya the President of the United States to fix everything there. And once the United States is fixed, Afghanistan will also be fixed.'

Children have such vivid imaginations.

I still see many of the children from the orphanage. When I am able to visit Farah, they are always the first – along with their families – to come and see me. There was one girl, Rahima, who lives with a disability that makes it hard for her to walk. She has suffered a lot of discrimination in her life. She told me that her happiest times were the years at the orphanage with us and the other children, where everyone was treated equally. I always try to visit her and bring her gifts when I am in Farah – we still have a lot of fun together. The children at that orphanage brought me a lot of joy, but sometimes the few difficult and sad memories are the things that stand out in our minds and in our hearts. Those we cry with, we never forget, but those we laugh with, we forget too soon.

When I was a young child, I was inspired by the courage of Palestinian children who resisted the occupation of their land. I told my father I wanted to be like these children who fought, with empty hands, for their homeland against soldiers and tanks. Now I believe that, today in Afghanistan, we have whole generations who will struggle courageously for their country.

Children understand right and wrong, and they cannot stand to see their families suffering. It is natural for children to want to challenge the enemies of Afghanistan, those who prevent us from having real democracy and self-determination. Afghans my age and younger have known only war. There has never really been peace in our lifetimes, and yet we are determined to struggle for a better future.

Some from the older generations, unfortunately, have become tired and given up on the possibility of real change. Or they tell me that they are sympathetic to my message, but, even as they say this, they also try to get me to tone down my criticisms.

Sometimes they address me like a child: 'Daughter, please, we understand what you are saying but it would be better if you were less outspoken.'

Often they say they are just looking out for my safety: 'For your own sake, you must moderate your message.'

But of course I did not want to do this. I am echoing the feelings of my supporters who hate the warlords. Many of them have said to me that even if these people are set ablaze their ashes would contaminate the soil of our country.

It was amazing to see the support that many ordinary people in Farah gave to women's participation in politics. Both men and women spread the slogan 'Now is the time for women!' because they felt that men in power had brought nothing good. And many men also expressed their support for equality. One man told me, 'I want to put my hat on your head, and your scarf on mine.' This was his way of saying that it was not right that women were always thought to be lesser than men. The support I received in the election campaign proved that the inequality between men and women was not some kind of permanent part of Afghan culture – things could be changed for the better.

Women, of course, were my most dedicated supporters, because I spoke directly of their struggles and hardships. In some cases, even the daughters and wives of fundamentalists backed me, although rarely openly, of course.

I should note that most of the religious leaders in Farah supported me as well. A number of imams visited me during the campaign to say that they were encouraging people at their mosques to vote for me. Of course there were also some mosques where the mullahs spread propaganda about me.

My enemies spared no effort to block my election, distributing flyers that called me a 'prostitute', 'anti-Islamic', and a 'communist'. Among the worst was a leaflet that showed a photograph of me without my headscarf, falsely saying that the picture was taken at the Loya Jirga. Underneath was the awful slogan: 'She took off her scarf at the Loya Jirga, she'll take off her pants in Parliament.'

Once in a while my security team was able to arrange a campaign event in a nearby village. To travel to these places I always had to shroud myself in the blue burqa and ride between heavily armed guards. In one memorable case I was followed by a Danish film crew who were making a documentary about my bid for election. The women at this village were nervous at first, but were very receptive to my message and nodded as I told them why I was running for parliament: 'I have chosen to run in order to expose the enemies of Afghanistan, the enemies of democracy, the enemies of our happiness who don't want peace ...'

When the documentary came out, the film-maker Eva Mulvad called it *Enemies of Happiness*. It was a great honour to be the subject of a film that I think provides some excellent insight into the suffering of the Afghan people. I was used to having my picture taken, but it was strange being followed everywhere and even filmed in my house, washing my own clothes by hand in the courtyard and reading by lantern-light at night. But eventually I got used to it, and sometimes even forgot that they were there.

During my campaign, visitors continued to come to ask for advice, often on very important personal issues. The film crew was there to capture the story of a young girl named Rahella – another Rahella! – who was inconsolable because a powerful old man in her neighbourhood wanted to take her as one of his wives. When Rahella and her friends or siblings walked by this man, he would say very bad things, taunting her about how she would be his wife. Rahella was an educated girl, who didn't want to marry an illiterate who was also an opium smuggler.

I met this man and tried to convince him that he should leave this young girl alone. After all, he already had wives and he must remember that in fact Islam grants rights to women as well. But he was adamant: he had to marry her or he would be ridiculed, he would lose face. Besides, he argued, it was 'Afghan culture' that it was his right to take this girl even if she did not want to marry him. I could not convince him. He said he didn't care if she was willing to commit suicide by self-immolation if he forced the marriage. He said he would pay 'compensation'.

Rahella's only uncle later tried to intervene with this man in the girl's favour. This uncle was murdered for his efforts. Rahella and her remaining family were then forced to flee to Iran to escape the killer who wanted to take her for a wife. In Afghanistan, there are far too many Rahellas who face the torture of a loveless, forced marriage.

Sometimes the film crew took pictures that are painful for me to see. As the election grew closer, the stress of the campaign was starting to show in my face. Once when a close friend came to visit me at my headquarters to offer her support, I was overcome with emotion and had to turn my head away to hide my tears. Although it is not good to show my enemies any weakness, I am still only a human being. It is hard to be strong all the time. Like everyone, I feel tired and sometimes afraid. There is no shame in that. The important thing is to keep on going despite the hardships.

There were also wonderful, inspirational moments during the campaign. One very old woman, a former mujahideen who had planted mines to blow up Russian convoys, walked for two days to see me. She had heard about me and wanted to tell me she thought I 'behaved in a proper Islamic manner and treated people decently'. This old woman came back to Farah on election day, and together we walked into the polling place to cast our votes.

Along the way we had to pass American soldiers perched on armoured personnel carriers, their machine guns and rifles at the ready. Men and women entered separate rooms, and were frisked for weapons. The International Security Assistance Force's troops were expecting violence from the Taliban, who had sworn to disrupt the elections.

The voting paper was a large piece of paper with forty-seven candidates listed on it. Three of us were women. Since many people are still unable to read, each candidate was given a symbol to identify them. Mine was a house. We dipped our index fingers in purple ink to show we had voted, then marked our papers and stuffed them into large plastic boxes.

The old woman with me shouted out to the crowd that she was filled with hope. But in her face you could also see years of regret, and a hint of fear.

I was confident that I would do well in the election even though my enemies tried to manipulate, intimidate and generally subvert the election process. There were some reports of irregularities and corruption in Farah on election day. It was alleged, for example, that a blind man who wanted to vote for me was tricked into selecting the wrong candidate.

Three weeks later the votes were counted and we heard the news announced on a short-wave radio at my headquarters: Malalai Joya had won a seat in Parliament, with the second-highest number of votes in Farah Province. I would be the youngest Member of Parliament, one of 249 members of the lower house, the Wolesi Jirga, of which 28 per cent would be women.

My supporters shouted with joy, hugged and kissed me and poured sweets over my head in celebration. On the night the results were announced, there was a big celebration of people from my home village of Ziken and the surrounding Anardara district, complete with traditional dancing and fireworks. I was sad that I couldn't attend because of security concerns. But they did make a very good video recording of the festivities and they sent me a copy. It made me very happy to watch this video. It was a wonderful victory for my people, but my heart was again heavy with the responsibility I now carried.

I believe I found my way into Parliament because the power of the people is like the power of God, and because the truth always carries a strong voice. My province sent five representatives in total to Parliament, including me and Mohammed Naeem Farahi, who supposedly got the highest number of votes, although I wonder if that was the case. A few of the election workers were my supporters and they would call me about the progress of the vote counting. They told me that up until the last days of counting I had more votes than any other candidate, and they were happy for it. But on the last day they didn't know what happened but suddenly Naeem Farahi was announced as getting the highest number of votes. Farahi is a former official with the Interior Ministry and a big landlord. He is now a key member of the National Front, a coalition that includes fundamentalist jihadi leaders and some former Russian puppets.

In the days and weeks following the elections, I learned the obstacles that some women in Farah had to overcome to vote for me. A few days after the election, a middle-aged woman explained that when she told her husband she was going to vote for me, he forbade her from doing so – and ordered her not to vote at all.

'But I sneaked out and voted for you anyway,' she confided to me.

She then rolled up her sleeves to reveal terrible bruising all over her arms. 'When he found out that I had been out to vote, he beat me,' she explained through tears. 'But I am so happy that I was able to support you.'

For me this was a dramatic – and inspiring – example of just how eager Afghan women are to play an active role in society. I always remember what Meena, the martyred founder of RAWA used to say: 'Afghan women are like sleeping lions who when awakened … would play a tremendous role in any Afghan social revolution.'

Some of my male supporters paid an even worse price for supporting me than the woman whose husband beat her. There was a young man, Ibrahim, only eighteen years old, who campaigned for me very actively and effectively throughout Farah. He was a very brave and intelligent young man. Soon after the election, he was abducted and killed. His body was burned, and he was brutally abused before he was murdered. The corpse had no eyes, as it appears that his killers had carved them out as a form of torture. I cried bitter tears when I heard the news of his death and the terrible way in which he was killed.

Even though I had security problems, I insisted that I travel to see his family in their village in order to offer my condolences. The family was devastated; Ibrahim was their only son. The whole village was upset; they had loved this young man a great deal. Some in his family spoke of avenging his death but it could not be done. This boy's suffering mother has still not recovered from her grief.

After I was elected to Parliament, once again I had to pack my bags and leave my home and family. My enemies had already tried to kill me and spread terrible propaganda about me, and now I was heading right back into their midst to denounce them again. I would be going to work and sitting in the same chamber as many of the worst warlords in the country.

I knew that the US-installed Afghan government and its stooges might try to benefit from my presence in Parliament – to show the world that there was a real democracy in Afghanistan because even a critic of the occupation and the warlords could be elected. And there were a few Afghans who criticised me for joining this corrupt, warlord-ridden parliament. I simply told them the Afghan proverb which says: 'How can you catch tiger cubs without entering the tiger's lair?'

I was ready to go to the lair, to hunt them in their own house.

CHAPTER 9

HOUSE OF
WARLORDS

O<small>N 19 DECEMBER</small> 2005, the freshly elected Members of
Parliament were ushered into buses and paraded through the cold
winter streets of Kabul on our way to the opening ceremonies.
Before I could even sit down, one of my fellow MPs made a
sarcastic remark. 'Now, I'm going to make trouble, too,' he said,
laughing. I tried to brush him off and make a joke out of it, but
some of the others joined in, criticising me for being too outspoken
before I had even said a word.

'You instigate rebellion in this country if you tell the truth!'
I said.

I looked out of the window at the rows of men lining the
route, some of them holding the green, red and black flag of
Afghanistan. Some looked angry because they had been forced
to miss work to stand by the road. Others seemed filled with
hope that maybe now we would have a government that would
respond to the needs of the people. But I was not optimistic.

As I walked inside the recently rebuilt halls of Parliament I
saw mostly the same old faces from Afghanistan's sorrowful past.
Many warlords had once again strong-armed the process and
forced their way into Parliament. Even though it was supposedly
illegal for militia leaders or combatants to run for office, a Human

Rights Watch report showed that 60 per cent of the new parliamentarians were either warlords or their allies. These people either stole their places in Parliament at gunpoint or bought their seats with US dollars – which they had in abundance because leaders of the Northern Alliance were paid with cash by the CIA for their support of the US war. We heard reports that some warlords paid for the campaigns of sympathetic candidates, and bought votes for them.

Even Hezb-e-Islami, the party of Gulbuddin Hekmatyar – who is listed by the United States as one of its most wanted terrorists – was allowed to have thirty-four members in Parliament. Although the current party leaders try to say that they are no longer controlled by the black-bearded Hekmatyar, there is in fact no difference between them, and they even fly the same green flag of Hekmatyar's old faction. Their main leaders like Abdulhadi Arghandewal, Attaullah Loudin (head of the judiciary commission of the Parliament), Khalid Farooqi, Mohammad Siddique Aziz (currently an adviser to Karzai) and others are the same people who for years worked alongside Hekmatyar. In the past these fundamentalists, and especially Hekmatyar, were saying that democratic elections were un-Islamic and a gift from the infidels. As far as I am concerned they are theocrats and fascists who have never believed in democracy. But today, under American direction, every one of them acts like a born-again democrat, and some of them even talk about secularism! For years we've known there have been behind-the-scenes negotiations to bring them and perhaps even elements of the Taliban into the Afghan government. In fact there are some Taliban commanders already among the Members of Parliament.

Because the MPs are seated in alphabetical order in the parliamentary chamber, I was assigned a spot up in the second to last row – almost as far away from the centre of the action as possible. But I would manage to make myself heard in the months to come. Unfortunately, I was surrounded by some virulent fundamentalists, and I had to constantly look over the turbaned head of the warlord Abdul Rab al-Rasul Sayyaf, who was seated one row below me.

There were many dignitaries on hand for the opening of Parliament. The US Vice President Dick Cheney – who misled his country into war and authorised the torture of prisoners – was seated in the front row, near some of the fundamentalist warlords who had inspired many of the jihadis America was now fighting. It was not only ironic that Cheney should be among the war criminals, but fitting as well. I believe that all of them should be prosecuted for their crimes.

President Karzai delivered the opening address to Parliament. In the speech, Karzai became very emotional, and even shed tears when speaking about the plight of our country. His voice broke when he proclaimed that 'our dear Afghanistan has been resurrected like a phoenix from the ashes of war'.

A few clips of Karzai's speech were included near the end of the film *Enemies of Happiness*. Although I thought the documentary was excellent, and I was honoured to be in it, I would have preferred that it did not end on this note, because it may have given some viewers the mistaken impression that after the elections, everything in our country has turned out fine.

Unfortunately, today I must conclude that Karzai's tears – much like the ones he shed in our earlier meeting – were only crocodile tears, and his beautiful speech was just empty words to deceive the people. While he was talking about the plight of the Afghan people I was deeply hurt and angry. I wished I could stand up and shout at him that his own hands were stained with the blood of the innocent people of Afghanistan because he had put so many warlords and criminals into positions of power. This has caused many authentic tears in the eyes of the Afghan people.

Even one of Karzai's vice presidents, Karim Khalili, was an infamous warlord from Bamyan Province, and the other was a brother of the warlord Massoud. He installed Karim Khuram of Hekmatyar's party as Minister of Culture, Information, Tourism and Youth Affairs – a man who is an enemy of both the free media and women. He once stopped a woman photographer from taking his photo saying he did not want to be photographed by a woman.

Karzai even invited the brutal Abdul Rashid Dostum, whose men were involved in the suffocation of so many prisoners at Mazar-e-Sharif, to be army chief of staff. Dostum's Jowzjan militia forces, one of the largest private armies in the country, have committed unspeakable crimes against the Afghan people, including raping and killing thousands. And yet he and others like him hold the real power in Afghanistan. Dostum even owns his own television station, Aiena TV. The CIA literally handed out millions of dollars to Dostum and other warlords as part of its 'warlord strategy' in invading our country.

Karzai also manipulated the legislature to serve as a rubber stamp for his own agenda. There are two houses in the Afghan Parliament: the lower house, or Wolesi Jirga, with 249 elected members, and the 102-member Meshrano Jirga, or upper 'House of Elders' filled with tribal leaders and political appointees. Karzai was allowed to appoint thirty-four members of the upper house, most of them cronies or warlords, like Mojaddedi, who chaired the Loya Jirga, the Northern Alliance strongman, Fahim, and even some deputies of the Taliban ally Gulbuddin Hekmatyar. Arsala Rahmani, a minister of the Taliban regime, was also among the people selected by Karzai to the upper house.

The very first time I spoke in Parliament my microphone was cut off, a practice I would become accustomed to. As proceedings of the parliamentary session got underway, the MPs all had turns to introduce themselves and to make some initial comments. Many opened their remarks with lines like, 'My congratulations to the chairperson and the esteemed representatives gathered here ...'

I looked around at my 'esteemed' colleagues and I felt this was just too much to take. Sitting just a row in front of me, in fact, was none other than Sayyaf. The room was full of criminals. So when it was finally my turn to speak, I did not offer my congratulations. I began, 'My condolences to the people of Afghanistan ...' I had barely started to list my various concerns with the process and composition of the Parliament when my sound was cut off. There were shouts from other MPs denouncing me and there was a slight delay while the situation calmed down and order was restored. I was not allowed to resume my opening remarks, and in my two years in this elected body, I never once had the chance to speak without my microphone getting cut off.

There is a famous saying in the West: 'If voting changed anything, they would make it illegal.' In many ways, my two years' experience in Afghanistan's Parliament confirmed this bleak outlook. From the very beginning of my term, the proceedings inside the legislature confirmed my contention that we did not have a half-hearted democracy, let alone a real one. What we had could more accurately be described as a 'showcase' democracy for the benefit of the US government.

Some of my enemies tried to use my election victory against me. They asked maliciously, 'Why does Joya say that we do not have democracy, if she herself got elected?' Of course, as I have explained, I had to overcome many obstacles and cheating by opponents during my campaign. Other democratically minded candidates were not so fortunate. Sometimes what matters isn't so much who votes but, rather, who *counts* the votes.

And what democratic country has ever had to witness a race between warlords for the position of Speaker of Parliament? That's exactly what happened in Afghanistan. Some democratically minded MPs stood for the position, but unfortunately it came down to a contest between Younis Qanooni, who had been one of the key leaders of the Northern Alliance, and Abdul Rab al-Rasul Sayyaf, the infamous warlord who had been the first to jump up and denounce me at the Loya Jirga. Qanooni had been the Minister of Education in the transitional government set up after the war. He was a close ally of Fahim, and in fact ran against Karzai for the presidency in 2004. Qanooni hid his medieval mind behind a neatly trimmed beard and modern clothes while Sayyaf, with his long beard and white turban, always looked the part of the extreme fundamentalist. According to a report on the

Afghan Parliament by the International Crisis Group, 'Sayyaf was a leading theorist of global jihad, running training camps in Pakistan that were a magnet for militant Muslims from every country. That he is now able to seek to lead a new Western-backed democracy is one of the ironies of the war on terror.'

As soon as I got to Parliament I came under pressure to support the ambitions of Qanooni and other ethnic Tajiks. Some fundamentalists even tried to tell me that they supported me because I was a Tajik! I said, 'Who told you that I am Tajik? It is shameful for me to feel happy for this kind of support.' Whenever anyone has asked me about my 'tribe' I always answered that I am just an Afghan. The warlords must have thought I was just as narrow-minded and bigoted against other tribes as they were, and they tried every method to get me on their side. But I never accepted them in any way. Fundamentalists who don't have footing among the people always try to play the ethnic card and provoke the ethnic sentiments of people so they can exploit them for their own political benefit.

Nimatullah Jalil's father called and asked me to vote for Qanooni for Speaker. (Jalil is Qanooni's brother-in-law and was an official of the Interior Ministry at that time.) They argued that Qanooni was a Tajik, like me, and otherwise Sayyaf with his long beard would win.

'There is no difference between Sayyaf and Qanooni for me,' I told them. 'Physically they are different, but mentally they are the same. If they apologise to our people and expose more crimes of their bloody parties, and if people change their minds about them, then I may as well. My opinion is that of the people. Tell Qanooni that between me, you and others are the rivers of the blood of innocent people, especially women and children.'

They tried to tell me that I was wrong, Qanooni had changed. But even their gentle persuasion did not work. In the end, when it came down to a vote between Qanooni and Sayyaf I decided I could not take part. When I was asked how I could boycott such an important election, I responded, 'If the choice is between these two, you cannot choose one over the other.' There's an Afghan proverb that says, 'The yellow dog is the brother of the red dog.'

Qanooni won the vote by a small margin.

As I walked out of the Parliament building in protest, some journalists surrounded me and asked me why I was leaving and not voting. I said that I did not want to vote for warlords whose men have committed many crimes in the past. 'First they must apologise to our people for what their parties did in the past and then face the court instead of running for elections in parliament and enjoying a wonderful life ...' As usual, the journalists censored the most important part of my remarks, but some parts of it were aired that night on local television. They also put on Qanooni's reaction, where he rejected my words and shamelessly insisted that the Members of Parliament had a glorious history.

I am very grateful to the majority of Afghan journalists who are kind to me and strongly support me. But almost every one of them says they are sorry that they can't do more, because those who control the TV, radio and other media have their own political line, and censor their reports about me. Many times journalists have done special interviews with me and assured me that they will be aired, only to later have them completely censored by the TV channel. In one case a brave journalist later released the interview on YouTube so at least those who have access to the Internet could watch it. Another journalist told me that he was only working with the TV station to feed his children; otherwise he was very ashamed to work in a medium that does not serve the needs of the Afghan people.

My days in Parliament were always stressful and lonely because I was constantly being attacked and insulted, and there was no one who wanted to discuss the core issues affecting our country. I felt a tremendous pressure to speak out for my people, but I was never given a chance. Sometimes I would raise the red card on my desk in protest, or even walk out in disgust.

It was always a relief to go home at night to a small rented house a few kilometres away where I lived with some family members and my bodyguards. Whenever I left Parliament, despite being very tired, it would always cheer me up to see my bodyguards and to laugh and joke with them. They would often ask questions about what happened that day. We would discuss how the laws being made always favoured the warlords, and I could vent my frustration at not being able to speak. But some days were so bad that when I returned home I would cry for my people who were at the mercy of laws made by their enemies and killers.

Every night I received calls from people from around Afghanistan who supported me and were also reporting the news from their provinces, especially the crimes of warlords. I could use this information to expose the people who represented them in Parliament. On days when TV and radio interviews I had given outside Parliament were aired, there would be dozens of supportive calls from both men and women. These calls always raised my spirits. It was comforting to know that even though I felt alone in Parliament, outside of its halls the majority of my poor and suffering people were with me.

One of my greatest challenges as a parliamentarian was simply getting to work safely. When I became an official elected representative, the Karzai government had to help cover the cost of my bodyguards. A few MPs were assassinated before they took office, so security was necessary and every MP, regardless of their position, was given two bodyguards. But people like Qanooni, Sayyaf, and Mohaqiq had dozens of their own bodyguards and surfed the streets of Kabul in luxury bulletproof vehicles on their way to and from Parliament. Once in a TV interview in Kabul, Mohaqiq showed off three of his luxury armoured vehicles. People joked that he once had no donkey to ride, but suddenly today he owns such expensive cars. In that particular programme he offered a royal feast to the journalist, who commented that this single meal would cost a teacher one month's salary.

Because of the threats against me, I usually have about six bodyguards in Kabul, and another six in Farah City. None of these men are paid by the government. They rotate and are replaced from time to time. In the capital, it was the responsibility of these men to get me to Parliament and back safely each day. The car my supporters had obtained left something to be desired. It was an older model, and it was not in great shape. In fact, this vehicle would often overheat, especially in the summer months. When this happened, my driver had to pull over, get out of the vehicle and use water or some other fluid to cool off the engine. Stopping like this left us vulnerable and out in the open, and these were always harrowing moments for me and my bodyguards.

Sometimes stressful pit stops had to be made for other reasons. Once, driving through Kabul, I urgently needed to find a washroom. Desperate, I asked my driver to pull over to the side of the street in front of an ordinary house. I went up to the front door and knocked, just hoping that the occupants of the house were not fierce opponents. A man opened the door and after a couple of seconds his face lit up. He was a bit shocked, but happy to see me. 'Malalai Joya! I am a big supporter of yours! What are you doing stopping here at my family's home?'

I explained that, in fact, I really just needed to use the washroom. We ended up spending quite a bit of time there as the man insisted we stay and meet his family.

Inside the buildings of Parliament I felt somewhat safer from attack. But I also felt uneasy about what someone could be planning, so I had always to remain alert. One older woman MP named Gulhar, who was a supporter, followed me almost everywhere I went in the Parliament buildings because she was concerned something would happen to me. She was an ordinary woman elected to represent Kunar Province after her husband, who was a respected democratic activist, was abducted and killed by fundamentalists. In Parliament, Gulhar was like a mother to me.

In fact, most of the staff at Parliament supported me, and they kept their eyes open to help me as well. For instance, each MP had a box in the main office where they received mail. On one occasion when I stopped in at the office, a secretary took me aside and informed me that all of my mail was being opened and read by government officials. I put the word out to friends and supporters not to write to me at my parliamentary address.

There were some Members of Parliament who defended my right to debate freely. One of them was Dr Ramazan Bashardost. In a speech he compared me to Galileo, the scientist who in his time was persecuted for arguing that the earth revolved around the sun, and not vice versa. Today, Bashardost pointed out, everyone recognises that Galileo was correct.

Bashardost is independent of the warlords and their factions, and he also boycotted the election for Speaker of Parliament. He was Karzai's Minister for Planning in the original transitional government, but he resigned in disgust at all the corruption. He had wanted to shut down most of the NGOs working in the country – almost 2,000 of them in total – because he felt they were not really working for the benefit of ordinary people. He has announced his intention to challenge Karzai and to run for the presidency in 2009.

One day at the end of a parliamentary session, I was standing among a few other MPs when Mohammad Mohaqiq, a warlord and member of the Hizb-e-Wahdat Party, walked up to me. After saying hello he told me that at four o'clock we would both take part in a round-table discussion on TV.

'Yes, I know,' I said, 'but remember it will be a live interview.'

'What do you mean?' he said.

'You will have to answer the people's questions, especially about the crimes your party committed during the civil war and is still committing today.'

He cut me short and angrily told me that everyone knew I was a communist and a member of RAWA. I told this warlord, 'Please come for this interview. Then we'll see what people will ask. I will answer their questions and so must you. It is the people who will tell you who we both are.'

He stormed out of Parliament in a great fury. At four o'clock he didn't turn up for the interview, but instead sent his representative.

The journalist who was interviewing us joked with me. 'Joya

Jan,' he said, using a Persian term of endearment, 'it seems you have made Mohaqiq sick, because someone called to say he could not make it here due to an "illness"!'

Another of my few funny memories from Parliament involves an animal. One day, as MPs were getting ready for a session, a mouse ran up to the front of the hall. All of us were watching the mouse as it then scurried under some other desks and finally made its way out of one of the exits. I said to those around me, 'Even the mouse runs away from these criminals!'

Most of what I witnessed in the Wolesi Jirga, the lower house of Parliament, was more tragic than comic, however. Many MPs, for example, are not literate. They are in Parliament because they are commanders or otherwise allied with powerful warlords. I remember one fundamentalist commander sitting in front of me with his newspaper open as if he was reading, but the paper was upside down!

The warlords continued to use Islam to justify themselves. On one occasion, I confronted them about this in Parliament. During a question and answer period, I asked them a question that an old man had sent to me, 'Why in your speeches do you swear again and again on the Holy Quran that you are Muslim and mujahid?' I explained that people were tired of this, because so many politicians in the past had invoked our religion to distract from their crimes.

This question, of course, provoked a furious response from some MPs, who knew that I was referring to them. They demanded that the speaker not give me time for questions in the future, since I was 'using abusive words'. I responded that if they were real mujahid then they should not have taken my words personally.

During my time in Parliament I was frequently insulted and threatened with death by other members of the chamber. Sayyaf, who sat in front of me, once turned around and made a menacing motion in my direction and said something to the effect of, 'Shut up! I will make you silent for ever.'

I looked straight at him and said, 'We are not in Paghman here, so control yourself.' Paghman is a district near Kabul that Sayyaf and his men dominate. Traditionally, it was an area where wealthy Afghans lived and many had villas there. Today in Paghman, this dictatorial man takes over people's land, runs his own private jails and his militias terrorise the local inhabitants at will. The people of Baghman protested against this treatment a number of times and even burnt photographs of Sayyaf. But their protests were stopped by police and two protesters were even killed.

I would not be intimidated by anyone, and as I had promised, I used my position in Parliament to expose the abuse of power and corruption whenever I found it. Some of the people of Paghman met me in Kabul and gave me many documents about Sayyaf's occupation of their land. They asked me to raise the issue in the Parliament. When I was not given a chance to talk inside the house, I decided to hand over the documents to the Complaints Committee of Parliament and ask for an investigation. When I went to the committee, I saw that many of the members were hateful men, and they mocked me when I brought up the issue. One of them was Khyal Mohammad Hussani, a warlord and close ally of Sayyaf. He warned me saying, 'Be careful, you are touching very big issues.' Of course, nothing was done after I registered my complaint.

I also raised a question in Parliament about media reports that when Speaker Qanooni was still serving as the Minister of Education in Karzai's cabinet 25 million dollars had gone missing from the budget of the Education Ministry. Again I demanded an official investigation, but nothing came of it.

In May 2006, I was using my turn to speak in Parliament to condemn the celebration of 28 April as victory day and to describe the important distinction between the real mujahideen and the criminal mujahideen, many of whom now sat in the chamber. Some argue that the mistakes of the past must be forgotten. But I believe that there is a big difference between mistakes and crimes. Was it just a mistake to kill more than 65,000 Kabulis during the civil war? Was it just a mistake to use rape as a weapon of war, to murder and mutilate, such as those whose militias cut women's breasts off to terrorise the population? These were not just mistakes, and that is why I use the term criminal mujahideen. The public knows that these men made a mockery of the values of jihad and that they should be punished for their crimes.

The Speaker, Qanooni, cut off my remarks. Qanooni then proceeded to quietly stir up the MPs by implying that I had in fact been defaming the true mujahideen. Then a former jihadi commander, Alam Khan Azadi, whose people in northern Afghanistan call him 'Alam the Black', jumped up and announced that he would not remain in the hall while the mujahideen were insulted.

Soon the Parliament was in an uproar. One excited opponent, the warlord Daud Kalakani, stood up and yelled, 'Down with RAWA! Take them out of here! Down with communism!' Other MPs got up and threatened to storm out, too, if I did not leave. But I refused to be forced out of Parliament for having spoken the truth. One MP came towards me and told me that I should apologise. My response was simple: 'For what?' Then others ran up the steps to surround me. I had to duck behind my desk as they hurled water bottles at me and a sandal flew over my head.

A few MPs including Gulhar, Bashardost, Fazel Rahman Samkanai, Obaidullah Halali and some others rushed and surrounded me for my safety. All of the warlords, Sayyaf, Rabbani, Khalid Farooqi (the leader of the Hekmatyar party MPs) and others stood up and encouraged other MPs to walk out. Gulhar, with all her strength, pushed back one of the warlords who was trying to get to me, and he fell to the ground. Niaz Mohammad Amiri, a man from Sayyaf's party was shouting 'Take this prostitute out of here!' A cameraman covering the mêlée for a local Afghan TV station, was slapped by Khyal Mohammad Husaini, who demanded to know why he was trying to film the

MPs while they were using abusive words. This behaviour provoked a huge outcry from the Afghan media.

The team of female security personnel who worked in the Parliament circled me and held back the MPs who had turned into an angry mob. For my own safety I had to remain in the hall until all the other MPs had gone.

After a few hours' delay, the parliamentary session was resumed. One after another, warlords and pro-warlord MPs, including Qazi Nazir Ahmad, one of Ismail Khan's men, spoke out against me. Sayyaf, in a lengthy speech, resorted to Quranic verses to characterise my comments as 'anti-Islamic'. He announced on behalf of all warlords that there must be what he called a 'red line', where nothing should be said against Islam or jihad in Parliament. But, of course, I had only criticised the criminals – certainly not Islam, the religion of our people, or the real mujahideen who fought for the independence of our country. What really upset the warlords was that I continued to insist they be tried for their crimes, telling the media: 'Russian puppets, mujahideen or Taliban: those who killed our people should be put on trial.'

I returned to Parliament the next morning, and on the doors into the parliamentary chambers, someone had taped up handmade signs with the famous quote attributed to Voltaire written on them:

'I disagree with what you say, but I defend to the death your right to say it.'

A young woman who worked in the reception offices later approached me to say that she was the one who put up the signs. She asked me to keep this fact confidential, because she could be fired for openly supporting me.

After I entered the Parliament hall, I heard some warlords laughing with each other about what had happened the previous day. Daud Kalakani told the others in loud voice so I could hear, 'We suggested many times to give us water in glass bottles but they did not. It would have been such a joy yesterday if the bottles were made of glass!' They all laughed even louder.

I was a hard nut for my enemies to crack. They tried threats and intimidation but that did not work, so they tried to discredit me. Many times their schemes were discovered and denounced by my supporters.

Shortly before I was attacked in Parliament, a man calling himself Najibullah arrived at my office in Farah and told my colleagues that he wanted to support the work of Hamoon Health Centre. I was in Kabul on parliamentary business at the time. Najibullah claimed to be a representative of a German NGO that wanted to deliver a large sum of money to the clinic – but first he needed to get the signatures of the clinic's staff. He said he also planned to travel to Herat to meet officials of OPAWC to support other projects. Some of the people at the clinic were suspicious of this man, and they wisely videotaped their entire conversation with him. It was on the advice of my Defence Committee that we recorded all visitors to Hamoon Health Centre, especially those who arrived requesting a meeting with me or with a proposal for a project. My supporters reasoned that we should try to videotape all visitors, because then in the event that I were to be killed there would be video documentation of the crime.

A couple of days later, Najibullah was arrested in Herat – my supporters helped to identify him to local authorities – and it was determined that he was indeed part of a political conspiracy to discredit me. The local police handed him over to the Afghan intelligence services, where he confessed that he had received 100,000 Afghanis, worth about 2,000 dollars, 'from Parliament' to collect signatures of my staff to create a false document showing that I 'worked with America and against Islam'. The intelligence services claimed that he had been sent to spy against me by the Taliban, but my supporters believe he was paid by someone connected to the Northern Alliance and the government. I never could find out what happened to this man and the case, as the spy agency kept it a secret and most probably he was released as he had the backing of powerful people in the Parliament.

But months later, a secret supporter of mine who worked with the Afghan intelligence service, brought me a copy of a confession signed by Najibullah and stamped by the intelligence agency that confirmed my suspicions against him.

Several other plots of this sort – attempts to discredit me and the work that I do – have been discovered by my allies because, as we say, 'Walls have mice and mice have ears.' Sometimes, even amongst those who work for fundamentalists or government officials, there are people who quietly support me. These secret supporters are surely one more reason I have been able to survive as long as I have. In one case I was tipped off by one of my would-be assassins.

The house where I was living most of the time in Kabul was a small two-storey building located next to a construction site. My room had a window looking out on the construction works, which we thought was safe. One day a man notified my bodyguards that they should not allow me to use that room. He said he was one of three men who had been assigned to monitor Malalai Joya from the building under construction. He said they had a rifle with a silencer, and they had been ordered to shoot me when I entered the room. This informant said that they waited for a whole day yesterday, but fortunately I had only appeared in my room once in the evening. He said it had not been possible for them to fire as they had been ordered to hit me in the head, and they couldn't get a clear head shot that night. We knew he was telling the truth because he was right, I had only entered my room once in the evening. Unfortunately he did not disclose who had ordered the assassination. But we took his warning to heart, and we soon moved to another house.

Around the same time as these plots were being carried out against me, the government stopped funding my security. Even though I was an elected member who had even been openly threatened by other MPs *in* Parliament, the government would no longer contribute to the cost of my security. And I had to be aware and alert at all times.

You would think that, with all the suffering the women of Afghanistan have endured, the women Members of Parliament would stick together, or at least treat each other as sisters, despite our differences of opinion. But sadly this was not the case. Some fundamentalist women MPs were as dark-minded as their male counterparts. And since 25 per cent of the seats were reserved for women, many had been put up as candidates by the warlords hoping to fill the quota with their supporters. Particularly in the areas where the warlords had full control, no independent woman dared to stand for parliamentary elections.

I received verbal threats from some of the female MPs. Once, after some commotion following my remarks, a fundamentalist woman called Noorzia Atmar, who sat right behind me in Parliament, looked down at me and said, 'I will do to you something that no man would dare to do.'

'I'm sorry for you,' I responded. 'I believe you are a victim of these fundamentalists.' It's true. I believe that women who parrot anti-women and extremist ideas are themselves victims of the system.

One day, a fundamentalist MP from a stronghold of the warlords in Northern Afghanistan came up to me as I was on my way to the toilet. She told me that she wanted to say something secret to me inside the washroom. The toilets of the Parliament were on a far side of the main hall, in a quiet, lonely corner of the building.

I said, 'There is no noise so you can tell it to me here. No one will listen to us.' Again she insisted that we go to the toilet.

She pressed on although I showed her various appropriate corners where we could talk quietly.

'No, I must speak with you somewhere more private.'

'What's wrong with speaking about it over in this corner, nobody's around to listen.'

I noticed she was apprehensive and her eyes were fearful. 'Don't be afraid,' she said nervously. 'Don't you trust me?'

I knew that she was a fundamentalist and of course I didn't

trust her. I strongly sensed that something was not right. Why would she leave the huge empty hall and insist on going *inside* the toilet? So I refused to follow her. I told her that I didn't have time to go, as there was an important discussion about to begin in Parliament. Then I turned around and walked away. I had in fact really needed to use the washroom, but that just had to wait. I cannot be sure, but I think she or someone else was planning to harm me.

After I told my bodyguards the story they also agreed that it might have been a dangerous conspiracy. They told me never to go to the toilet of the Parliament again because of its remote location. Long before they had warned me not to drink from the water bottle on my table in the Parliament; everyone's seats are specific and there was a possibility that someone could poison my water. Once I had accepted a cough lozenge from a fellow MP. After I casually mentioned it to my bodyguards they warned me I shouldn't eat anything like that again. It had never occurred to me that someone could really try to kill me with a cough drop. I couldn't even eat in the first month of the sessions when extraordinarily good food was prepared for the MPs. First of all, I protested over the extravagance of such things when my nation was dying of hunger. But there was also the worry that I could have been poisoned by the food. Ramazan Bashardost was the only other MP who didn't eat from the banquet.

After so many years without a parliament in Afghanistan, there was a great deal of ground to cover and many issues to debate. But to really have a democracy, a basic rule needed to be established and enforced that war criminals could not run for office. Instead, the war criminals continued to pass laws in their own interests.

For instance, human rights groups have argued for the establishment of a legal age of eighteen years, for marriage and criminal law. The fundamentalist parties in Parliament were opposed to this, and they argued amongst themselves over how much to lower the age. Fifteen? Sixteen? Eventually, they settled on passing a law to make the legal age sixteen, despite objections from human rights advocates who felt this was too young.

During a number of sessions the MPs were bargaining to increase government salaries and privileges. After some back-door deals with the government, the salary of parliamentarians was increased from around 1,100 dollars to 2,000 dollars per month – double for Qanooni, the Speaker – and many other perks were added on. They were given diplomatic passports, and the government paid for their rent, their drivers, telephone bills and more. But still many MPs were arguing that it was not enough, even though many of them are so rich and do not need this money anyway. It was around the time that all the teachers in Kabul were on strike because their monthly salaries of up to 60 dollars per month had not been paid for months by the government. In response to the call of civil servants for a pay rise, the Parliament – after much debate – approved an increase of 14 dollars to their monthly salary. In Afghanistan 14 dollars can hardly buy a 25 kilogram bag of flour. This was enough evidence for the Afghan people to understand that Parliament was definitely for the benefit of the poor!

Once while speaking out against me in Parliament, one MP suggested that I should be deprived of the privileges of the Parliament because of my 'abuse' of the institution. My enemies thought this kind of pressure might work to keep me silent. They still did not realise that I was not there to enjoy the privileges – I was ready to shed my blood for my people, and their precious privileges were the last thing I cared about for myself!

The warlords who controlled Parliament were indifferent to any appeals from other groups in society, let alone human rights organisations. Early in 2007, they demonstrated their contempt for justice by passing the so-called Reconciliation Draft Law. This legislation called for immunity for all war crimes committed during the past three decades of fighting. Essentially criminals created a law giving themselves amnesty. Supporters of the law claimed that it would help bring 'national reconciliation' and maintain national unity. But all it did was send a clear signal to the Afghan people that this Parliament was corrupt and self-serving. It also signalled how much they were afraid of facing a court of justice. This bill was presented soon after Saddam Hussein was hanged in Iraq, which shocked Afghan criminals too. They discovered that their alliance with the West was simply not enough to protect them.

I continued to insist that no war criminals should be granted immunity from prosecution. The Afghan people feel very strongly about this. On one occasion a man, who was visiting me in my office in Kabul, put this to me in stark terms. 'Malalai,' he said, 'why do you talk about taking these men before courts? No court can properly judge them. They should be burned, and then even their ashes would make the rivers dirty from their crimes.'

I responded that we Afghans have suffered so much under their rule and deserve to have these men face national and international courts. We do not want to respond with violence to these violent men. But should not the lives of Afghans be valued as much as the lives of the victims of Pinochet, Khomeini, Suharto, Hitler, and other criminals throughout history? The blood of these Afghan criminals is not more red than the blood of these other dictators and killers.

If the top warlords and criminals were finally held responsible for their past actions it would have an impact throughout the whole country. Their commanders and others would not feel so free to continue committing crimes against the people. This accountability for war crimes is a key principle and a goal to accomplish if our country is ever to move forward – we have to draw our own line somewhere. But the warlords were determined never to face justice.

Of course, I spoke out strongly against this amnesty legislation. To those who claimed that this was the only way to keep Afghanistan together, I responded that national unity can never be achieved by forgiving national traitors.

When the legislation finally passed in the early spring of

2007, it said that the jihadis 'must be treated with respect and defended against any kind of offence'. I issued a statement denouncing the bill. I said it was 'unjust and went against the will of the people. Those guilty must be tried. In fact, they have already been tried in the minds and hearts of the people and they should be tried officially.'

The warlords responded with fury, some of them calling me 'a traitor who should be severely punished'. One of the most vocal warlords was Niaz Mohammad Amiri, a close man to Sayyaf, who sat right behind me in Parliament with his grey turban and foul mouth. I had to endure constant threats and insults from him; he never missed an opportunity to call me a whore.

To show their power, many of the warlords and former Russian puppets, headed by Rabbani, formed an alliance called 'National Front' in Kabul. This group even included such former Soviet collaborators as Abdul Haq Ulumi, a general of Dr Najibullah who joined the warlords after the fall of the puppet regime. They organised a large gathering in Kabul and spent a lot of money to bring their men from a faraway province to Kabul in a show of their power and to force Hamid Karzai to sign the amnesty bill passed by the Parliament. Thousands of their men marched in the streets of Kabul, chanting 'Down with Human Rights!' and 'Death to Malalai Joya!' I was happy to be considered 'Public Enemy Number 1' by such anti-women and extremist forces.

Almost all the top warlords, including Burhanuddin Rabbani, Qasim Fahim, Mohammad Mohaqiq, Rashid Dostum, Karim Khalili, Siddique Chakari, Younis Qanooni, Abdul Rab al-Rasul Sayyaf and others attended and addressed the rally, which was considered their main show of power in Kabul. One of the women MPs speaking that day was Shakila Hashimi, who also ended her pro-warlord speech with the slogans 'Down with human rights!' and 'Down with Malalai Joya!' Later in a TV interview she denied denouncing me at the gathering, even though the TV station aired a clip of her shouting her slogans!

The warlords had hoped to mobilise 100,000 people in support of their amnesty. But despite all the money they put into their effort, they could only gather 20,000. In TV interviews, some of the participants said they had been brought to Kabul by jihadi commanders from other provinces. Many didn't even know why they were there.

The warlords were also angry with Human Rights Watch for a 2005 report, appropriately titled 'Blood-Stained Hands: Past Atrocities in Kabul and Afghanistan's Legacy of Impunity'. It had listed Sayyaf, Dostum, Rabbani, Fahim and others as having serious questions to answer for what had happened during the civil war. The document also touched on the role of Ahmad Shah Massoud, which has been a taboo subject in Afghanistan in recent years. It concluded 'Ahmad Shah Massoud is implicated in many of the abuses documented in this report.' Human Rights Watch had called for the Karzai government to implement a programme for peace, reconciliation and justice immediately.

Elsewhere in Afghanistan, and internationally, the National Reconciliation Bill came under major criticism, and Karzai was forced to make minor amendments. In the end, victims still retained the right to file a case against any individual criminal. But this is all but impossible, because when there is no rule of law and the warlords are in high posts in the courts, who will dare to file a case against them? In the absence of such a complaint the government was still forbidden from prosecuting war criminals. The impact of the legislation remained: it was a 'get out of jail free' card to the warlords, Taliban and former-Russian puppets. And in our history it will always be recorded that these warlords have the blood of innocents on their hands.

My enemies were always looking for new ways to silence me, and Parliament itself was becoming an ever more hostile and dangerous environment. Sitting amongst so many criminals putting on a show of being democratic was really like torture. But I had pledged to work in this house to expose the enemies of the Afghan people.

My opponents, it turned out, were no longer satisfied with just cutting off my microphone. While the criminals were busy making plans to pardon themselves, they were also plotting to frame me and have me banished from Parliament altogether.

CHAPTER 10

BANISHED

*P*EOPLE QUICKLY UNDERSTOOD that there was something very wrong with our Parliament in Afghanistan. Early on, a man was interviewed on the street by one of our local television reporters and said that Parliament reminded him of a street bazaar because it was so chaotic. After the report aired, many MPs complained about this comment during a parliamentary session. When it was my turn to speak, however, I said that if we continue to do nothing with this Parliament, and not solve any of the people's real problems, today they may call it a bazaar but tomorrow they will call it a zoo. As usual, the MPs started banging their desks in anger, and the Speaker cut off my microphone.

In April 2007 I was on a tour of the United States where I gave an hour-long interview to the US-based TV channel Ariana Afghanistan, which is also available via satellite in Afghanistan. As always, I used strong words against the warlords, and this time I repeated my prediction that if the Afghan Parliament continued on its current path, people would soon call it a zoo or a stable. Many viewers called in to support during the live interview. Since the programme was aired in Afghanistan, it made the warlords very angry.

When I returned to Afghanistan, the privately owned Kabul station, Tolo TV, asked me for a special interview. During that interview, the journalist asked me why I used the word stable or zoo in my previous interview and I explained it in detail. I said there are two different groups of representatives in Parliament. Some MPs are real representatives and some are criminals and warlords, and that my comments only applied to the second group. I even named some of the warlords I was talking about.

When Tolo TV aired the thirty-minute long interview on 8 May 2007, they deleted the whole question and answer about the zoo issue.

But on 16 May 2007, during another Tolo TV programme called *Zang-e-Khatar*, the presenters discussed the censored parts of my interview and made some nasty, abusive comments about me. They aired a small piece of what had been cut out of the previous programme, in which I said, 'To refer to this second group of representatives in the Parliament, who are criminals, as a stable or zoo is even not adequate – because in a stable we have animals like a cow which is useful in that it provides milk, and a donkey that can carry a load, and a dog that is the most loyal animal. But they are dragons.'

But the first part of the statement was left out. Out of context, it sounded like I was criticising the whole Parliament. This programme ended up defaming me in the eyes of the Afghan people while giving my enemies in Parliament ammunition to use against me. One of the commentators said, 'By comparing the Parliament to a zoo or stable, she in fact has insulted the entire nation, because the Parliament is the "house of the nation", where the eyes of the nation, the tongue of the nation and representatives of the nation are there.'

On 20 May 2007, some MPs in the Wolesi Jirga brought up the 'zoo' issue during an ordinary session. A female MP named Qadria Yazdanparast, a member of the fundamentalists' 'National Front', delivered a long speech denouncing me on the issue. I raised my red card and asked to be given time to speak and defend myself. But although many of my critics were given time, I was never allowed to speak. Then Speaker Qanooni announced that the next day would be reserved to discuss this issue, and closed the session.

From the atmosphere that day and the harsh words of the warlord MPs, I knew that they were all burning to suspend me. I also received some calls from other sympathetic MPs who warned me not to go to Parliament the next day because there was a plan to beat me up. Gulhar also called and told me that she had overheard one MP say that I would be killed by a suicide bomber. So I decided it would be wise not to go. I knew that even if I showed up they would never let me speak. So it was pointless to put everyone in danger. On 21 May, instead of attending Parliament, I arranged a press conference in Kabul that would begin as soon as the Speaker announced my suspension.

That day's session was broadcast on live TV and radio. The Tolo video of my interview was shown several times to the whole house. Speaker Qanooni incited the members against me and encouraged one MP after another to denounce me. The warlord Mohaqiq declared that I had committed treason and should be punished in court. A few members urged moderation, and said that I should be given a warning instead of being suspended. But Qanooni finally announced that I should be suspended for 'insulting the institution of Parliament'. Qanooni called for a vote, and each MP held up a sheet of coloured paper – green for yes and red for no. Although there was never a formal count, the majority of MPs voted to suspend me from Parliament for the rest of my five-year term. I never was given a chance to defend myself. Qanooni also said that he would turn my case over to the 'courts', and suggested that I should be barred from leaving the country.

I was watching the proceedings on television, and some like-minded MPs were phoning me from Parliament with reports and updates. A large number of journalists had gathered in the house, where we lived most of the time with my bodyguards, to hear my reaction, and when my suspension was announced on radio and TV as breaking news, I started the press conference. I told them that my suspension was a political conspiracy against me, and that my comments had been censored by Tolo TV. I set the record straight about who I thought were worse than animals.

And I vowed that my suspension wouldn't stop my struggle; it had only given me a larger pulpit from which to speak. I told them I was ready to defend my words in any just court.

Word of my suspension spread quickly, and I was besieged by requests for media interviews. That day a journalist who ran a radio show invited me for a round-table discussion of my banishment with the leader of a liberal political party and another female MP, Sabrina Saqeb, who was closely aligned with Qanooni. Sabrina Saqeb said during the interview that the Parliament is like a mosque, and if someone calls the mosque a zoo it is an insult to all the Muslims of Afghanistan!

I said, 'If the Parliament is like a mosque, and the imam and the people know that some criminals or murderers are in the mosque – especially those who misuse Islam for their dirty ideas – they would beat them up and kick them out in one second. The people would not let a mosque be made filthy by the presence of criminals. Today, these criminals have made the Parliament dirty by occupying most of the seats.'

When the interview was over the people working in the studio came up to me and told me how much they supported me. They also criticised the other MP and told her she should have supported Joya because I was telling the truth.

The MP answered that if she supported Joya openly it would be like committing suicide, and she would lose her position. 'You won't have this seat for the rest of your life,' I told her. 'Think of using it for the benefit of the helpless people, especially women.' Then the journalists and studio technical workers started arguing with her and defending me. Before I could finish our conversation my bodyguards whisked me out of the building. My enemies were stirred up, and my security team thought it was best for me to stay out of sight for a while. We were worried that my enemies were trying to have me arrested and probably wanted to disarm my bodyguards, as I had lost my parliamentary privileges. We changed houses that night and kept moving for a few weeks. But I was in touch with my many supporters in Afghanistan and overseas who were mounting protests against my expulsion.

Not only was my treatment in Parliament unconstitutional, but it was an attack on democracy itself. From the first day that I was suspended, many Afghan law experts, and even some anti-warlord MPs, said publicly that it was completely illegal to expel an elected Member of Parliament for the whole period of their parliamentary term. And the rule that was used to justify the suspension was 'Article 70' of the internal rules and procedures of Parliament, which forbids MPs from criticising each other. When this rule was being made weeks before my suspension, one MP told me to be careful, as this article had deliberately been included in the rule to be used against me. But at the time of my suspension, this article was still under discussion and had not yet been approved. And, of course, none of the other MPs who had shouted out in open Parliament that I was a communist and a whore or that I should be raped and killed was ever punished under this so-called 'rule'. But the leaders of Parliament would not listen to these arguments. I was out.

Human Rights Watch also made strong statements in my defence. Brad Adams, Asia director at Human Rights Watch, said, 'Malalai Joya is a staunch defender of human rights and a powerful voice for Afghan women, and she shouldn't have been suspended from Parliament … Joya's comments don't warrant the punishment she received and they certainly don't warrant court proceedings.'

After a request was sent out by my Defence Committee, the highest government officials, including Karzai, were flooded with emails from Afghans inside and outside the country; my foreign supporters also protested about my suspension. People in Afghanistan and in many other countries took to the streets to support me. In Farah, hundreds of women marched and rallied for my reinstatement. The head of the provincial council in Farah stated that my suspension was 'an insult' to the thousands of people who had voted for me.

There were also rallies in Kabul and in other towns and cities across the country. In Pul-e-Khomri, in the northern province of Baghlan, men and women marched in support of me. In the provinces of Herat and Kunar, police prevented peaceful protests against the suspension, using the excuse that they were protecting demonstrators from potential violence. Students of Balkh University issued a strong statement in my support, which had a huge coverage in the Afghan media. Many other Afghan writers in Afghanistan and abroad wrote articles to support me.

Those who publicly protested on my behalf took great risks with their personal safety. I believe they did so because in standing up against my suspension they were in fact standing up for their own rights, for real democracy. The fact that women took these actions, protesting with empty hands, is evidence that we are not only victims, and that women have the power to make changes in their lives and in their country.

In Jalalabad, women and men marched together to the United Nations office and presented a letter calling for my reinstatement. They carried banners and chanted slogans, with women – many covered in their burqas – playing a leading role. One female protester named Shabana said, 'Joya is not only the representative of the Farah people, she is representing women all across the country.'

The demonstrations also crossed international boundaries. On 21 June 2007, one month after my suspension, rallies were held in cities including Rome, New York, Barcelona, Milan, Vancouver and Melbourne. Seven female MPs from Spain – representing seven different parties – signed a letter expressing condemnation of my suspension. Eight members of the German Bundestag (Parliament) also wrote a letter to the Afghan government, making four demands:

1. That the Afghan government and in particular the President explain the reasons why Malalai Joya has been ousted.
2. That the security and the physical and psychological

integrity, as well as the free exercise of her political activism be guaranteed.

3. That the voice of Joya and other outspoken women's rights activists be heard and acts of intimidation against women be investigated and judged in an exemplary manner.

4. That the restriction of movement against Joya be lifted and her return to office which is consistent with the democratic elections be initiated.

Soon after my suspension, I officially handed over a protest letter to the Afghan Supreme Court, but they did not address the issue. It was difficult for me to find a lawyer brave enough to represent my case, but I was finally able to retain a young attorney who worked for a small fee. I filed a case against the suspension, but many months passed without receiving any answer from the court. I know that the fundamentalists who wield so much influence in this highest body of Afghanistan's judiciary are trying to prolong this appeal process until the end of this parliamentary term. They no longer want me to be able to use the Parliament as a forum to describe the miseries and oppression of our people.

The Inter-Parliamentary Union, a Geneva-based organisation with the membership of 254 sovereign states has issued three resolutions on my behalf, urging Afghanistan to quickly resolve my appeal for reinstatement and expressing concern for my safety. The IPU Secretary General spoke with the Permanent Representative of Afghanistan to the United Nations in Geneva. He agreed that Malalai Joya's suspension was unlawful, but said that this was a purely parliamentary matter in which the government could not intervene because of the separation of powers. IPU also spoke to the Afghan delegation, led by Deputy Speaker Mirwais Yasini. The delegation left no doubt that my mandate should be restored as quickly as possible, and as soon as they returned would put the issue on the table. But still no action was taken, causing the IPU to refer to the situation as 'very frustrating'.

Gul Padshah Majedi, head of the Immunity and Privileges Commission of the Afghan Parliament, said in an interview with the Pajhwok Afghan News that the decision of the Wolesi Jirga to suspend Malalai Joya was not within the House rules of procedure. He said that, according to the principles of duties of the Wolesi Jirga, if an MP commits a mistake once, he or she is given three chances. If the member repeats the offence, the speaker of the House should expel him, and if he does not comply, he should be removed by the security forces. According to Majedi, the Wolesi Jirga did not go through this process and immediately expelled me. He also pointed out that at the time of the expulsion, I was not given the chance to defend myself.

A number of intellectuals and social justice activists in the NATO countries signed a letter in support of my case for reinstatement, which reads in part:

> ... As activists and writers living in countries whose governments are at war in Afghanistan and back the regime of Hamid Karzai, we wish to express our support for Malalai Joya ... We believe that the governments of the NATO countries bear a great deal of responsibility for Malalai Joya's security, as they created and prop up the government that has allowed her to be expelled from Parliament... . The world is watching the case of Malalai Joya, and she has great support amongst all those working towards genuine democracy and women's rights in Afghanistan.

A petition to reinstate me was initiated by stopwar.ca and signed by Noam Chomsky, the author Naomi Klein, Canadian MP and party leader Jack Layton, and many others.

All of this support from people in other countries is meaningful to me – we know we are not alone in struggling for our rights. But, unfortunately, nothing has been able to change the mind of the Afghan government. Most of the leaders of the

NATO countries have never made any public comment on my case – even though they say their militaries are in Afghanistan to help build democracy.

Recently some Members of the European Parliament came to meet me on their visit to Kabul and told me that they raised the issue of my suspension with the delegation of the Afghan Parliament. They were told that this was an internal matter for the Afghan Parliament and others should not interfere. The Europeans responded that when you need money, soldiers and anything else, you don't regard it as an internal issue, and you invite other countries to help. But when we call your attention to an illegal act, you call it an internal issue.

Many, many people, including even some of my fellow parliamentarians, have approached me to discreetly tell me that they support me, but that they cannot do so publicly. This type of support is essentially meaningless. It is why I have said many times that the silence of the good people is worse that the actions of the bad. I condemn those who sit silently when they know the truth.

Once again, some people have suggested that if I simply apologise, my problems will be solved. 'Joya has offended the parliament,' Noorzia Atmar, a female Member of Parliament who had once threatened me, told a reporter from the Institute for War and Peace Reporting. 'If she really wants to serve the people of Afghanistan and be the envoy of the people, we respect her and her ideas. If she apologises, she can come back to work.'

But I will never apologise for speaking the truth, even when I describe some Members of Parliament as belonging in a zoo or stable. If anyone deserves an apology, it's the animals! As I told the same reporter, 'If animals had tongues with which to speak, they could sue me for comparing them to these parliamentarians.' It is something that many of my supporters have told me, as well. They say that at least a hungry wild animal feels full. Yet, some of the criminals in Parliament appear to have an endless appetite for victimising people, and they never seem to get tired of killing, looting and pillaging.

For the sake of Afghanistan's future, it is no longer good enough for us only to voice our criticisms in polite, moderate tones. The real safety of all democratically minded people in my country can be ensured only if we all raise our voices together. We all need to show the courage of lions. I imagine this could be like the wonderful show of solidarity at the end of the film *Spartacus*, when the leader of the slave army rises to turn himself over to face certain death. Before he can be singled out his comrades rise in chorus, 'I am Spartacus!'

We should all use whatever position we have to speak out. If we do this, and if we unite together with democratic leadership, our actions will mushroom into something even more powerful that will make it much harder for the fundamentalists to continue their fascism. Right now, with corrupt people in so many key posts, it's a hard and risky struggle. Even if in the beginning we only create a small spark of light, at least there will finally be some light. As Brecht says, 'Those who do struggle often fail, but those who do not struggle have already failed.'

I disagree with those who tell me I should mix some sugar and honey in with my statements about the warlords. This may be good advice for someone struggling in a democratic society, but it does not work for Afghanistan at all. I also dream of such a society in Afghanistan where I will not need to be so harsh, and present my criticism as a bunch of flowers to my opponents. But for the time being we are far from being a just society. How can we be diplomatic with criminals who do not understand the meaning of diplomacy? Political dealing and compromise may be a good choice with opponents who believe in democratic values, but those who only know the language of the gun regard any compromise as a weakness. To offer them compromise only makes them more rabid and aggressive. One of the reasons the Afghan fundamentalists are so bold is the fact that people who call themselves 'intellectuals' always seem to compromise with them. In a country like Afghanistan those who compromise with such brutal people need to realise that they should share the responsibilities of the warlords' past crimes.

Unfortunately there are thousands of others, many of whom consider themselves progressives and intellectuals, who choose to compromise with the warlords and those who occupy Afghanistan. But most people don't regard them as their true representatives. Among those I believe to be 'compromised' politicians are: Foreign Minister Rangin Dadfar Spanta, Interior Minister Hanif Atmar, Ashraf Ghani Ahmadzai, a former Minister for Planning and current candidate for the presidency, Azam Dadfer, the Minister of Higher Education, Anwar Ahadi, the former Treasury Minister, and many others who have worked alongside the warlords to make up the current corrupt narco-state of Afghanistan. Some of them are as hated by the Afghan people as warlords such as Sayyaf or Qanooni. They are willing to compromise with the warlords to save their seats. The day that I tone down my message, or join those who compromise with the fundamentalists, will be the day I lose all value to the Afghan people. It would be the day of my political demise.

A famous Italian journalist once asked me why don't I try a more diplomatic approach with my enemies in Afghanistan and reduce the risks to my life.

I answered, 'Would you allow me to answer your question by asking a question of you?'

'Yes, of course,' she said.

'Would you have compromised with fascists like Mussolini in your country?' I asked.

'No.'

'Then why are you asking me to compromise with the Mussolinis of Afghanistan, who are just as dirty?' I told her that the day I compromise with my enemies, I may not be in danger any more, but I will be regarded as a traitor to the Afghan people, who are the real power in the country. Without them, I would be nothing.

The support that my own cause has garnered is evidence that

things must not always remain the same in Afghanistan. I have been backed and welcomed by the suppressed people of Afghanistan in every corner of the country. They see me as their real representative, which is a source of inspiration and honour to me. Many people from faraway provinces come to meet me in Kabul and share their problems and feelings and announce their support for our common cause.

I am very honoured by the support I have received, even in our society where women are seen as second-class citizens and where fundamentalists preach day and night that 'a woman should be in her house or in the grave'. But as a woman I challenge the most powerful people in the country who only speak in the language of guns, and my voice is echoed and welcomed by the vast majority of my people.

As I have written, the Parliament workers are very sympathetic to my cause, and even after my suspension some of them stayed in touch. Sometimes they would phone me to report what was happening there. A while after the suspension, one told me that Qanooni had specially ordered the guards not to allow Joya to enter Parliament. He ordered all the office workers not to do any job related to Joya, such as writing or delivering letters. She told me that one day Qanooni was attending a meeting of MPs in a conference room when someone rushed inside and said with wonder that 'Joya has entered the Parliament house!' Everyone in the meeting became very nervous and got up from their seats to stop me from entering – only to find that it was a false alarm, and I was not there. My friend told me that she enjoyed seeing how flustered they became.

'All of those warlords were even afraid of your name, never mind your presence,' she said.

Freedom of speech is a fundamental tenet of any democracy, but in Afghanistan it does not exist. While I was being kicked out of Parliament, others were being thrown into jail for exercising their right to speak.

In October 2007, a twenty-three-year-old journalism student

Sayed Pervez Kambaksh from Mazar-e-Sharif was arrested and sentenced to death. His crime? He had allegedly downloaded an article and circulated it among his friends at university. He was convicted of 'blasphemy' because the article was critical of women's rights in Islamic societies.

When he was still facing the death penalty, I wrote in the UK newspaper the *Independent*:

> I utterly condemn this undemocratic act of those in power against Sayed Pervez Kambaksh. This situation has exposed the corruption of the government, which is inherently undemocratic, which does not believe in women's rights and which is willing to go to extreme lengths to prevent freedom of speech. If Mr Kambaksh is killed for his 'crime', then tomorrow it will be someone else. The situation that the press is faced with gives you a clear indication of the level of freedom and democracy in the country as a whole.
>
> I would like to appeal to the UK and democratic countries around the world to speak up in defence of Mr Kambaksh, who must be released as soon as possible. He is an innocent man whose life is in real danger.

After a major international campaign, Kambaksh's death sentence was commuted, but he was still sentenced to twenty years in prison. Moreover, the fact that he remains in jail serving such a long sentence is as outrageous as his arrest in the first place. His brother, Yaqub Ibrahimi, is a well-known journalist who has reported on the crimes and brutalities of the warlords, and I believe Kambaksh was targeted by the authorities to silence his brother.

This case shows why we need to keep religion, the state, and the justice system separate. It is an example of religion being invoked to limit freedom of speech and journalistic freedom. Real Muslims do not require political leaders to guide them to Islam.

The democratic parties of Afghanistan have shown great courage in supporting Kambaksh. They held rallies in his defence despite threats of suicide bombings and reprisals. In July 2008, demonstrations were held in fifteen provinces demanding his release. The Afghanistan Solidarity Party staged demonstrations in support of Kambaksh in Kabul and Jalalabad despite the ever-present danger of suicide bombers.

I wrote Kambaksh a letter when he was in prison. I wished him a long life and I expressed my desire that he be released from prison soon. If and when he is set free, I hope that he uses his fame for the benefit of our people, and that he tries to set a good example. Kambaksh has endured a great deal, even though his death sentence has not been carried out. A doctor's report revealed that he was tortured while in custody after his arrest. As of early 2009 he was still being held in prison despite the fact that so-called witnesses against him had not turned up to testify.

The situation for Afghan and foreign journalists has been deteriorating, despite the claims that a 'free press' is one of the great successes of the Western intervention. The attacks on reporters have come from the Taliban, warlords and government officials. Zakia Zaki, a great women's rights activist and reporter was, as I mentioned, gunned down in her home.

In April 2007, an Afghan journalist named Ajmal Naqshbandi was murdered by the Taliban. He was a guide for the Italian reporter Daniele Mastrogiacomo when arrested. The Afghan government released five dangerous Taliban commanders from prison in exchange for Mastrogiacomo but did nothing for Ajmal and the driver Sayed Agha. Both were beheaded by their Taliban captors. Ajmal had been married only six months earlier.

During that time it was learned that Italy had paid the Taliban 2 million euros to release an Italian photographer named Gabriele Torsello, who had been abducted in October 2006. This sparked a huge protest and debate in Afghanistan on why the lives of Afghans have no value to the government, while foreigners are rescued at any expense. I met with Ajmal's mother, father, wife and other family members, who were furious with the government. They asked me to take up their cause and tell the world that as far as they are concerned their son's real killers are Hamid Karzai and Foreign Minister Rangin Dadfar Spanta – the ones who said no to the Taliban's demands.

Even inside the Parliament journalists have been beaten up by MPs at least four times. In August 2007, a Tolo TV crew was attacked by Members of Parliament after the station broadcast some MPs sleeping on the job; 2007 was called the bloodiest year for journalists in Afghanistan.

Women and those critical of the government have been targeted. Nilofar Habibi, a young woman who appears on Herat TV, was stabbed after being ordered never to appear on television again. Shaima Rezayee, a presenter on Tolo TV, was warned by the fundamentalists about her 'unIslamic' programming. She was found shot dead in her apartment at age twenty-four. On 1 June 2007 Shekiba Sanga Amaaj, a newscaster for the private Shamshad TV was also killed in Kabul. And in July 2008, Muhammad Naseer Fayyaz, a political talk show host with Ariana TV, had his show cut off in mid-broadcast and was then arrested by Afghan Intelligence Services after criticising members of the government's cabinet.

For myself, after my suspension especially, television and radio stations became more reluctant to interview me or to report on my case, for fear of repression and reprisals. Kicking me out of Parliament was not enough. My enemies also worked to keep me out of the media. They disliked seeing me on television as much as they disliked hearing me in Parliament. I was invited on a television programme for a debate with Jabar Shelgari – an ally of Sayyaf's. But apparently nobody told Shelgari I would be there. In the middle of the programme, he actually said that if he had known it was Malalai Joya he would not have come. The journalist told me that he had a lot of difficulty finding any of the warlords to come on the programme to face me. First they called Sayyaf; he accepted, but later one of his men called to say, no, he couldn't make it. Later they called Mohaqiq, who accepted, but hours before the recording someone called and said he was not feeling well enough to come. (Again I made him sick!) So when they called Shelgari they didn't tell him that he would be facing me. When he entered the studio and saw me he was amazed, but it was too late to back out.

Many progressive publications, magazines and newspapers, which gave a lot of positive coverage to my initial speech at the Loya Jirga have since been forced to close, either because of censorship or lack of funds. The terrible situation of the media in Afghanistan is just one symptom of the deadly disease affecting everyone in my country. Unfortunately, in the West the media is also a problem, as it rarely presents a real, in-depth picture of the many-sided tragedy of Afghanistan or other conflict zones. One glaring example is that the civilian casualties caused by the US/NATO bombardments are rarely reported by the Western mainstream media.

Since so many of the media outlets are owned by the same business interests that support the governments in these countries, it is natural that they focus on the good news from Afghanistan. As the years go by in our occupied land, there is less and less good news to report. The truth involves a lot of bad news, and yet the truth must still be told. During my tours to Western countries, after hearing my speeches, many people told me that what I said about the conditions of Afghanistan was new to them. Their media does not reflect these realities, and only reports on how well things are progressing.

Fortunately, there were people all over the world who were aware of the real plight of Afghanistan, and they reached out to support my message. Even before my election and then suspension from Parliament, I had the opportunity to travel abroad to tell my story. International support has proven to be very important in helping me to raise my voice, spreading as best I could the message of Afghanistan's tragedy to the corners of the earth.

In Afghanistan, the media are 'free' only if they do not try to criticise warlords and officials. Mentioning any warlord by name will cause problems and even bring death threats. Many journalists have to resort to self-censorship to survive. For example, if you write anything about Ahmad Shah Massoud and mention any of his crimes and dealings, the next day you will be tortured or killed by the Northern Alliance warlords. Although under the US-led occupation they have been trained to talk about democracy and women's rights and deliver nice speeches, they do not believe in any of it and only know the language of the gun when they face their opponents.

Some government ministers even own their own TV stations to broadcast their own propaganda. Rashid Dostum runs his own channel called Aiena TV, which is broadcast in Afghanistan and also through a Turkish satellite in the region. Sheikh Asif Mohseni has his own satellite TV station called 'Tamadoon', Mohaqiq runs a TV station called 'Farda' and there are rumours that Quanooni is involved in the TV station 'Noorin' and Rabbani with the TV station 'Noor'.

———

With such dangerous conditions in Afghanistan many foreign journalists have asked me why I don't seek asylum in another country. But I can never leave when all the poor people of Afghanistan that I love are living in danger and poverty. I am not going to search for a better and safer place, and leave them in a burning hell. I am still based in Kabul, where I will continue to fight for my lawful seat in Parliament.

Some people have urged me to help create a new political party. If at some point we can be sure that such a new party could help to unite progressive-minded Afghans and make us stronger, then I believe we should consider it. Other people have suggested that I run for president. I appreciate that people say this, but I ask that they understand that I am very young and I never even really planned to be a politician. Presidential elections in Afghanistan are even more of a joke than the parliamentary elections. In the competition for the Wolesi Jirga, some democratically minded people can win despite all the frauds and dealings, otherwise everyone would doubt its trustworthiness. Unfortunately, at this moment in our history, the only people that will get to serve as president are those that are selected and backed by the US government and the mafia that holds power in Afghanistan. Changing this situation will require years of work, from those both inside and outside the country.

In these international efforts, I have been greatly honoured to have a Defence Committee to support me and to connect me to the media and the outside world. This committee is made up of volunteers working together online. They are Afghans living inside and outside the country – most of them from the young war generations. They represent no one ethnic group and no political party – they are independent people who have joined together to support me. Because they do not sign their names when they correspond with people outside Afghanistan, sometimes people have assumed they are all women. Friends in Italy, for instance, were writing to them 'Dear sisters …'. After that, members of the Defence Committee asked me to please let these friends know that there are both brothers and sisters doing this work.

The Defence Committee is made up of men and women who, after the Loya Jirga, got in touch with me and explained that they were politically independent and wanted to help to connect my struggle with the outside world. They asked if they could establish a website for me and, after I found out more about them, I agreed. My Defence Committee works with a lot of dedication and heart; their support has been invaluable. When I'm in Afghanistan, they inform me of important news. They keep me up to speed on international media coverage, and sometimes they print out and collate a series of articles and send it to me to read. Day and night, they answer emails from people. This is very helpful because in Afghanistan I do not have frequent Internet access.

When I'm asked about my Defence Committee I am often

speechless, unable to properly express my gratitude and my thanks. As a political independent, a social activist without a party, taking on this struggle alone would have been impossible. They have provided wise advice for me, suggesting for instance that I record as many of my visitors in Farah as possible. This helped to thwart the plot being carried out by the man named Najibullah, for instance.

The Defence Committee is especially helpful when I need translations of my speeches and interviews. When I thank them, they say 'Joya, we are doing it not for you, but for the people of Afghanistan.'

Now I am fortunate to have defence committees in other countries, such as the United States and Germany, as well as informal networks of supporters in many other countries. I feel that my name being attached to these committees is really only symbolic, because we are all working together to make a better future for Afghanistan. I am just one among many who are willing to sacrifice their lives to allow the brightness of liberty to shine in my poor country. There are many worthy causes in Afghanistan, and many Malalais among our people.

Although I am no longer able to stand up in Parliament and raise my voice for justice, my enemies have accidentally given me a gift. Because now my message is being carried further than ever before, and the cause of my people is heard all over the world.

CHAPTER 11

THE VIEW
FROM ABROAD

A real friend is one who takes the hand of his friend

in times of distress and helplessness.

*D*URING THE SIXTEEN MONTHS I was struggling to be heard in
Parliament, *Enemies of Happiness*, Eva Mulvad's documentary about
my election campaign was winning awards, including one of the
highest honours at the Sundance Film Festival and the Silver Wolf
Award at the Amsterdam International Documentary Festival. As
the film gained international attention, it also increased my
visibility on the world stage. In June 2007, just weeks after I was
suspended from Parliament, I was invited to speak at screenings of
the film at the Human Rights Watch film festival in New York City
and the Silverdocs Festival in Maryland. Some have speculated that
this film was a great source of income for me, but I want to make
clear that I only received a modest donation from the production
company. But I was grateful to be able to use the film's popularity
to protest about my illegal banishment from Parliament and to call
attention to the plight of the people of Afghanistan. I had been
taking my message abroad even before I became a parliamentarian;
now I had an even wider audience.

My first opportunity to travel to the West to tell the story of my suffering people came in 2002, when I was a regional director of OPAWC. Soon after we had set up Hamoon Health Centre and the orphanage, I was invited by women's rights groups to speak in Germany. I was only twenty-four years old at the time, so I was very honoured by the invitation. Our German hosts organised a whole series of events over the course of a week, with fifty or a hundred people in attendance each time, at which we bore witness to the crimes committed against women by the Taliban regime.

I made the trip with a group of women from Afghanistan whose stories were a litany of tragedies caused by the successive criminal regimes in our country. There was, for instance, a young woman who was from the Hazara minority. She had been married only three months when, in January 2001, the Taliban attacked her village of Yakaolang and massacred hundreds of people, including her husband. They even savagely murdered groups of elders who came to negotiate with them.

There was another aged mother who had lost seven sons; some were killed by the Russian puppet regime and some by the fundamentalists. Two of her sons were only thirteen and fifteen when they were abducted by agents of Gulbuddin Hekmatyar's Hezb-e-Islami in Peshawar and killed in the party's private prison in Shamshato. This was the camp where Hekmatyar and his men ran their own militia with the full support of the Pakistani intelligence agency, ISI.

I remember clearly that some Germans in the audience cried when we described the conditions of life in Afghanistan. I also met a Russian woman at this conference, who came up to us and said how ashamed she was that her country had caused so many problems. It was very impressive to me. It was on this first trip abroad that I really began to realise the universal humanity that unites everyone who is working for a better world. These Westerners were human just like we Afghans are human. We are all flesh and bone, we all live and die and we all have hopes and dreams for our families and friends. Westerners and Afghans both

have women and young generations that want something better –
all of this unites us in spite of just how different our conditions of
day-to-day life are.

But while I was physically present in Germany, in my mind I
was still very much in Afghanistan. I saw that they had water,
electricity and, most importantly, security. And I would think
about how my country did not have these basic things of life,
and about how every day is a struggle to survive and to stay safe.

Before this trip, I had no idea what to expect of Germany or of
'the West'. My only images of this world had come from the movies.
Even the Western journalists I had met in Pakistan hadn't dressed
like Westerners. So it was in Germany that for the first time I really
saw 'the West'. Here there seemed to be health and education pos-
sibilities, and at least the laws protecting women were enforced,
even if women were still victims of violence and abuse. I was constantly thinking, *When will we finally achieve this in Afghanistan? How
long will it take?* These values will only come when a government
of the people will finally come to power, never from the sworn
enemies of Afghanistan who currently run things.

———

Over the next six years, I was able to visit four continents –
Europe, Asia, Australia and North America. The response to my
speaking trips has made me very hopeful and has helped me to
understand that there are freedom-loving people in all countries. I
have learned a great deal from these exchanges and have been
inspired by this international solidarity. One reason that I believe
these trips have been valuable is that it's important for people
abroad to learn about our culture in Afghanistan. I hope that my
speaking tours have played some part in dispelling the very bad
image of Afghan culture that has been propagated by the fundamentalists and by foreign powers – especially the wrong picture
they have painted about Afghan women. We are not merely passive
victims and we are capable of standing up for our rights.

Many foreigners are surprised when I explain that there are

sixty-eight women in the lower house of the Parliament, 28 per cent of the total, which is in fact a higher percentage than in many Western countries. This is largely a result of a 25 per cent quota mandated by law. Unfortunately, too many of these spots are actually occupied by women from fundamentalist parties and warlord factions who advocate anti-women policies. As I have told many a disappointed audience abroad, the quota system has in fact been abused by the warlords, who intimidate independent women from running for office, ensuring that their stooges are elected instead. This is why some of our female MPs are among the most anti-women of all representatives.

Many women's groups have hosted me abroad, but my trips to various countries have also been sponsored by peace and human rights groups, anti-war movements and progressive political parties. All the messages of support I have received have been invaluable for me to bring back to my people. From these trips, the Afghan people have received moral support, material support – often in the form of generous donations dropped into simple donation boxes passed around at meetings – exchanges of experience and exchanges of culture. This is the helping hand we need from *the people* of NATO and Western countries – the honest and disinterested support that we have never received from *the governments* of the big powers that have occupied and interfered with Afghanistan for so many years. When people work together for the same ideals, their power can be like the power of God – nothing can stop it.

My enemies have tried to discredit me by spreading the lie that my trips abroad are like luxury vacations, and that I am only travelling to have an easy time. However, these people are not speaking about reality, but rather holding up a mirror that reflects their own mindset and priorities. In fact, my trips are often sponsored by groups with very limited financial resources, and are made possible by the dedication and commitment of activists. In some cases, if a group does want to take me out to have an expensive meal, or to buy something for me, I ask them not to and tell them it is better to save the money and donate it to projects that will benefit the Afghan people.

When I speak around the world, I represent all the suffering people in every corner of my country. Some of the funds raised abroad do go to help pay for my security costs within Afghanistan, since the Karzai government cut the funding for my security. But most donations go to fund desperately needed projects like Hamoon Health Centre. Even though after I was elected to Parliament I had to resign my job with OPAWC, I still do everything I can to support their projects. A little money can go a long way, especially when it does not pass through the corrupt hands of many government officials, warlords or even local or foreign NGO officials.

This is a problem that we could call 'NGO-lords', which goes hand in hand with the problem of warlords and drug-lords. Today, foreign 'aid' only disappears into corrupt officials' pockets or is in fact used for programmes that legitimise the NATO war. About this aid, our people can only say, 'Don't show me the palm tree, show me the dates.' Only bitter fruit has grown in recent years.

Most governments give huge donations to NGOs and political groups that they know will follow their orders and work for their strategic plan. In fact by their donations, they want to buy Afghans and make puppets of them. And it's not just the United States and other Western countries. Even the brutal fundamentalist regime in Iran spends a huge amount of money in Afghanistan through its stooges. With this money Iran tries to export its brand of Islam and Taliban-like ideas to Afghanistan.

We have another proverb in Afghanistan that says, 'May Kabul be without gold rather than without snow.' This saying refers to the importance of melt water for farming and drinking water. But today many Afghans may be thinking, *May Kabul be without foreign interference, 'aid' and NGOs, rather than without snow*. Under every stone of Afghanistan today, if you look you will find an NGO, but most are corrupt. They are getting money in the name of reconstruction, but they are putting it in their own pockets. Unbelievably, some staff people for USAID earn as much as 22,000 dollars a month in Afghanistan, which is 367 times more than Afghan teachers, according to Integrity Watch Afghanistan. Far too great a percentage of the total aid money from donor countries returns to the donors and their citizens by way of salaries paid to consultants, subcontractors and expatriates. Many of these consultants make as much as 250,000 dollars per year, or 200 times the average annual salary of an Afghan civil servant.

But I am proud that I have received only small amounts from the peace-loving and kind ordinary people of other countries. Every penny from these supporters has a huge moral value for me and I am thankful for it.

For instance, in April 2008 my Defence Committee announced that money collected from donations during my tour abroad in Germany, Italy and the United States would go towards new public services in Farah. We consulted with tribal elders, and it was decided that the monies should fund the construction of a waiting area for the Civil Hospital in Farah City. With so many poor people travelling long distances to seek medical help, patients often have to spend the night outside on the hospital's porch. I was unable to attend the ceremony where this project was initiated, so I was represented at the ground breaking by one of my supporters. In the past, money raised abroad has supported the work of our Hamoon Health Centre.

In other cases, funds raised from my travels have gone to support worthy projects in other parts of Afghanistan. For instance, donations have been made to provide food and supplies to some of the swelling population of refugees in and around Kabul. On another occasion, we made a contribution to help restore the site of the grave of the beloved singer of the Afghan nation Ustad Awalmir, who died, impoverished, on 4 May 1982. I also paid for reconstruction of another famous Afghan folk singer's grave, that of Ustad Duri Logari. He was a very popular Pashto singer of Afghanistan, but tragically on 21 June 1981 he was killed along with around 200 other people in a bombardment by Russian war planes. His tomb is located in Logar, a neighbouring province of Kabul. I sent some of my supporters to reconstruct it and, in late 2007, his rebuilt tomb was inaugurated by a group of singers from the Afghanistan Artists Union.

In my tours abroad I've given lectures to many universities, and some of them offered me free sponsorship to continue my education there. I am always very grateful but I've had to turn down their generous offers. Despite the importance of higher education and my love of learning, I simply can't take the time to study abroad now and give up my struggle against the enemies of my people.

During my travels I have learned that Afghans are very popular guests at conferences around the world. Sometimes this means that I find myself seated at the same table as my adversaries from back home.

In 2006, I was invited to Spain to attend an international conference on the future of Afghanistan. I was not among entirely friendly company, as I came to the conference as part of a large Afghan delegation that included top government ministers. When I met one of the Spanish organisers of the conference, she explained that the Afghan government had been reluctant for them to issue me a travel visa. But the organisers had insisted because I was to be one of their main speakers.

On the day we arrived in Madrid there was a dinner for conference delegates. I found myself sitting – without any supporters – at a round table with a number of Afghan government ministers and officials. Among them was Abdullah Abdullah, the Foreign Minister at the time and one of the most powerful men in the Northern Alliance. When I spoke I explained the difficult situation I faced in Parliament (I had not yet been banished). I described the threats, attacks and insults hurled at me – and condemned the domination of warlords in the government. Abdullah Abdullah, who was eating his dinner, cut me off.

'Is there really nothing else to talk about?' He was getting visibly angry.

I continued, 'Why are you getting angry? Is it because I am tearing the mask off your brothers? Did they not use rape as a weapon? Did they not kill 65,000 people during the civil war and destroy the country?'

Hanif Atmar, the Minister of Education at the time, also tried to change the subject, 'Malalai, please forget the past, do not be harsh.' Other ministers also urged me not to continue speaking in this way. 'Please, let's eat now and discuss this later. Malalai, do not get angry.'

But I told them I was not angry, I only wanted to continue telling the truth – we weren't in Parliament, after all, where I was never allowed to finish my remarks. I told Atmar, 'How can we forget? If they raped your mother, would you forget? Those mothers who buried their daughters, should they forget and forgive?'

Atmar had no reply. He is now the Minister of Interior, and therefore one of those who works alongside the warlords.

Abdullah Abdullah, for his part, went back to eating, but he was clearly very angry.

After this exchange another Afghan minister warned me to be careful at the conference and not to let anyone know my room number. Imagine: this was a member of the Afghan government warning me about his own people.

I told this minister not to worry about my safety while we were in Spain.

'They will not kill me here,' I said. 'Remember that here they wear their masks of democracy, they are puppets and they don't want to lose all the money they will get here. They will kill me in Afghanistan, not here in the face of their foreign masters.'

At the head table on the day of my speech, I was seated right next to Abdullah Abdullah. When I started to speak, he got up and moved further away from me. He looked very angry.

Atmar later implied that the speech I had given and my

criticisms of the warlords and of government corruption had been responsible for the donor countries not pledging as much money as they might have for Afghanistan. Of course this is beside the point. These Afghan ministers were just putting on a show abroad and denying the crimes being committed against the Afghan people. I was only telling the truth about them.

Since this conference, I have had the chance to return to Spain on trips organised by peace and social justice activists – and I have received very warm support from the people there. On one occasion the government even helped to provide me with armed security for my visit. I did not request this, but the organisers felt it was important to ask the authorities to take this precaution.

Late in 2006, I attended another conference where I had some sharp exchanges with fellow Afghans. This gathering took place in Holland, and brought together 200 or so intellectuals, academics and politicians to debate the future of Afghanistan. At one of the sessions, I debated with the likes of Dr Khalilullah Hashimyan, Dr Rostar Taraki and Habib Mayar, Pashtun national-ists who were justifying their support of the Taliban on the grounds that it represents a 'national liberation movement'. I told them, frankly, I was shocked that they, who had lived in the West for many years, were prettying up political forces who wanted to return medieval values and practices to our country. And I argued that they would do better to support those working to unite Afghans across ethnic lines against our common enemies. Hashimyan, for his part, went so far as to boast that he had kissed the blind eye of the notorious Taliban leader, Mullah Omar. I told him that if this was true then he had contaminated his lips by putting them on this criminal man. This sent him into a rage, and he stormed out of the room. Most of the Afghans present, however, appreciated what I had to say about these so-called intellectuals and their defence of the Taliban.

I am not always able to accept every invitation to travel abroad. In 2006, I was very honoured to receive South Korea's

Gwangju Prize for Human Rights. It is awarded by the May 18th Foundation, commemorating the Gwangju Uprising which took place in 1980. Many Koreans lost their lives when that great democratic uprising was suppressed. But the people of Gwangju inspired others in South Korea, which was a military dictatorship at the time, and in the wider region to struggle for democracy. I believe that today, we still need more Gwangjus. But I could not attend the award ceremony because I had to be elsewhere, so one of my friends went and accepted the award on my behalf. I sent a video message that was shown at the event:

> This award has a very special meaning to me. It links me to a shining history page of the Korean people for liberation, democracy and justice. It links me with the heroic May 18 Gwangju Uprising which is always a source of inspiration to me. By giving me this award, you motivate me to fight with the same determination and steadfastness against enemies of humanity in my ill-fated country, which was demonstrated by the freedom-loving people of Korea in Gwangju. It connects me to the sprit of May 18 victims who bravely fought the criminals to establish democracy.
>
> Afghanistan is still a land of tragedies under US control. We need a May 18 in our land, too, and the great people of Korea set a shining example for all those who care for real democracy and freedom.

In all my travels, I have only on a very few occasions been granted an audience with high-level government ministers in the West. Most often government officials have made no comment about my criticism of their policies in Afghanistan. The few meetings I have had mostly felt like a waste of time. Some ministers listened politely or even offered to help, but I have never been hopeful after this type of discussion. On one occasion I met with Maximum D'Alema, a cabinet minister of the Italian government, and within minutes I could tell that he would not actually follow through to help the Afghan people. Many journalists were waiting outside and they asked me what I thought of the meeting. My answer was brief: 'Hopeless.' They all liked the answer and the next day a big heading on one of the Italian newspapers was 'Joya Hopeless After Meeting With D'Alema'.

Friends in Italy have organised many events for me, and I have been recognised with honorary citizenship and awards from several levels of government and from NGOs in that country. This is a tribute to the many wonderful supporters of the Afghan people in Italy. But I think that, most likely, the minds of ministers like D'Alema will never be changed, certainly not by me, since they seem to take their direction on Afghanistan from the government in Washington, DC.

Despite my strong criticism of the US government, I have had the opportunity to visit the United States on a number of occasions, and have met some wonderful peace-loving people there. Thanks to the work of my friends Sonali Kolhatkar, James Ingalls, Briana Lawrie, along with other activists, I was able to make a speaking tour across the United States in 2006, visiting many cities. And I have returned several times since then. In March 2008, for instance, I got to speak to an anti-war rally of thousands in Los Angeles.

During my tours to the US, I've met with some of the soldiers from 'Iraq Veterans Against the War' (IVAW) who, inspired by the 'Winter Soldier' programme for Vietnam War veterans has set up 'Winter Soldier: Iraq & Afghanistan 2008'. It is a chance for veterans who served in those occupations to give an accurate account of what is really happening day in and day out, on the ground. I've seen some of their testimonies, which are quite horrifying, and I admire their courage in exposing the crimes carried out by the United States in Iraq and Afghanistan.

Kelly Dougherty, Executive Director of IVAW said, 'We believe that the only way this war is going to end is if the American people truly understand what we have done in their name.'

I am sure the majority of US and allied soldiers deployed in Iraq and Afghanistan belong to the most disenfranchised segments of their societies. Either they are there to make a living or they have been fooled by their governments into joining a fraudulent mission. They, too, are the victims of the wrong-headed policies of their governments – and when they die in the field, their governments are their true killers. The high level of suicide and psychological traumas among these soldiers also shows that they are suffering from what they have been forced to do in the so-called 'war on terror'.

I feel that, unlike the US government, the people of that powerful country are kind and caring and have great sympathy for Afghan women. I have been extremely impressed by their expressions of solidarity and support; once they know the truth they really want to help. In Boston, I learned about the story of two amazing women, Susan Retik and Patti Quigley, who lost their husbands in the terrorist attacks of 9/11. These widows have dedicated themselves to supporting *Afghan* war widows. This is an astonishing example of the power of the human spirit, and I was very moved.

But I also found – especially in the United States, more so even than other countries – that the media plays a very negative role, keeping people in the dark about events in other parts of the world and particularly in Afghanistan. I found that most of the facts and realities that I spoke about were brand new to the audiences, who in many cases had a completely different, bright picture of the situation. I have had to tell them they need to look beyond the mainstream media and the pronouncements of their leaders to seek the truth.

Zoya, a spokeswoman for RAWA, has also been telling the truth about Afghanistan to audiences around the world. I had the chance to meet Zoya at a conference in New York City, and we later saw each other again at an event in Italy. Zoya made a strong impression on me. We share many of the same values, and she gave me some good ideas for education projects in Farah. Zoya is a young woman, as are so many of the representatives of RAWA. They all go by pseudonyms, and even when they are abroad they avoid having their picture taken for the sake of their security in Afghanistan and Pakistan. The fact that RAWA must still operate as an underground organisation, even though their only goal is to improve women's rights and participation in society, is surely a sign that true democracy has not yet emerged in Afghanistan.

The world became aware of RAWA in the months after the tragedy of 9/11, when videos that their members had secretly recorded of executions in Kabul's main stadium were played repeatedly in the international media. But today, unfortunately, rarely is RAWA's work spoken about abroad. Yet their perseverance is a good example for people everywhere. They are proof of the saying 'You cannot kill an idea', because they have continued even after Meena, their founder, was murdered in 1987.

Not all of my experiences in the United States are positive memories.

On my 2006 tour, I had a meeting with Charlotte Ponticelli, who was the senior co-ordinator for International Women's Issues in the US Department of State. Walking into her office, the first thing I saw was a picture of Ahmad Shah Massoud and Abdullah Abdullah hanging on the wall, and so I was not too surprised by how our conversation went. As I tried to explain the suffering that the US occupation had wrought in my country, Ponticelli kept cutting me off to justify her government's actions. I pleaded with her to let me finish making my points, 'This isn't the Afghan Parliament. If you say you have democracy here, the least you can do is let me finish speaking.' But she kept interjecting, even stating that the American mothers who had lost sons in Afghanistan would never forgive me if they heard what I was saying. So I showed her a picture of an anti-war veteran's mother whom I had met, and I explained that as time passed, the people of the United States would come to understand that their government had deceived them.

'No power can hide the truth,' I said.

After this rough meeting, some of my American supporters joked that Ponticelli would be having sleepless nights thinking about my criticisms. In reality, I was not surprised that this meeting ended up like this – what else could we expect from a high-ranking official in that administration?

Fortunately, at the vast majority of my public meetings in the United States, my message has been greeted with the very opposite reception to the one I got from the State Department. On one occasion, however, the warlords managed to extend their reach to disrupt an event in Fremont, California. A forum where I was speaking was disrupted by supporters of Rabbani's funda- mentalist Jamiat-e-Islami Party. When I started my remarks they stood up and shouted slogans against me, holding up banners with the words 'Down with Joya!' And 'Joya is an agent of the ISI!'

My supporters were alarmed, and wondered if it was too dangerous for me to stay. They offered to get me out of there, but I refused. Instead, I invited the protesters to bring their placards up from the back row and put them on the stage.

'I'm not afraid of your threats,' I told them. 'Just like I'm not afraid of your bosses in Afghanistan who have guns to try to silence me there.'

Most of the audience were clapping and cheering for me as I continued my speech. Somebody had already called the police, and two officers arrived just as one of the fundamentalists came up to the stage to try to take over the microphone. As soon as he and the others saw the police, they dropped their placards and ran away. It didn't take much to scare them off. After the event was finished the organisers and some of my supporters hugged me and said that now they understood the risk and difficulties which my struggle entailed.

The next day, pro-warlord websites and even *Payam-e- Mujahid*, the central organ of Jamiat-e-Islami in Kabul, published articles against me and wrote lies that I had run away when I was attacked by 'mujahideen'. Later, some other Afghans who were present at this incident wrote articles to disprove their lies.

It is not unusual for those with links to fundamentalist groups or for other Afghans who oppose me to get up at meetings in the West and dispute my claims about the dismal state of affairs in Afghanistan. They argue that the war has improved things and that I am too critical. When I hear this, I say to them, 'Well, if everything is great in Afghanistan why don't you come back with me.' They never have an answer.

In October 2007 I was invited to a conference in Washington, DC, organised by the Center for Strategic and International Studies (CSIS). I thought it would be an important forum for my point of view, but once I arrived I was told that I was not actually scheduled to speak from the stage at all. The conference was full of commentators and analysts who were very much in favour of American foreign policy. I think that maybe they invited me there just to be able to say that an Afghan woman Member of Parliament had attended. When I met people at the conference, they could not understand why I had been invited to attend but not speak. At this gathering, I still managed to find a way to make my message heard. I spoke from the floor microphone for about five minutes during the discussion period. The speaker on the panel, who was from Amnesty International, said that she did not have time to address the points I made. After I did this, the organisers became less friendly, and they did not arrange any interviews with media for me while I was there. But a few of the participants later came and told me that they liked my comments and I should have been one of the main speakers.

But this type of experience has been the exception. For the rest, I am speechless to describe my gratitude and warm solidarity. I am convinced that it does not matter in what part of the world we find ourselves. If we share ideas and we carry out a struggle for justice, then we are united together by strong bonds.

Unfortunately, some of the same countries whose people have been kind to me have governments who provide sanctuary to people who still have many hard questions to answer.

On my trip to the United States in 2006 I spoke at Yale

University, and at that time I pointed out an important example of American hypocrisy in the 'war on terror'. Sayed Rahmatullah Hashemi had been a top Taliban spokesman and representative of the foreign ministry. Somehow, after 9/11, he was granted special status to study at Yale. During my talk, I said it was disgusting, an unforgivable insult, that Hashemi was studying at this prestigious institution. I held up a picture of him as a Taliban – with his beard – next to a picture of him as a Yale student – clean-shaven – and asked the question, 'Is this democracy?' If the war is about 'fighting terrorism', I asked, 'Why isn't this Hashemi in Guantánamo Bay?' One could ask the same question about a number of the Members of Afghan Parliament.

There are other Afghans abroad who I believe should be being questioned about their involvement in our country's bloody past instead of enjoying the hospitality of foreign countries, including:

- The many former Russian puppets, who had key roles in the suppression of Afghan people, and are freely roaming in European counties, the US, Canada and elsewhere. For example, Ghulam Dastagir Panjsheri was a key element of the PDPA (a Russian puppet party) in Afghanistan, but today he lives in Washington, DC, and from there writes pro-warlord articles on fundamentalist websites.
- Some other Afghan intellectuals such as Dr Khalilullah Hashimyan (now in the US), Dr Rostar Taraki (in France), and Eshaq Negargar (in London), who were key lobbyists for the Taliban. They enjoy freedom still all living in the West while trying to portray the medieval Taliban regime as a popular mass movement of Afghanistan.
- The fundamentalist elements of Rabbani's Jamiat-e-Islami, who are very powerful in Canada and especially in Toronto, where they have their own

publications, radio and TV channels. In 2006, when I was in Toronto to deliver a speech to hundreds of Afghans, they mounted a huge propaganda campaign against me. Rabbani supporters also operate in the American state of Virginia, and they maintain pro-fundamentalist websites in other Western countries.

You can find dozens of articles against me on fundamentalist websites where they denounce me and stamp me as being a foreign agent. Some of their claims are truly ridiculous, like the time they said that I was travelling abroad on 14 February because it was Valentine's Day and I wanted to do some love-making on that day! They even posted a fake photo of me with a man on their website.

When I was in Finland, my supporters organised an appointment with some progressive MPs there. One Member of the European Parliament of Finland asked me in the meeting about the name of my party. I told her that my party has no name, but it is a powerful party whose members are the help-less, barefoot and hungry people of my country; in other words, they are the ordinary people of Afghanistan. I added that they are most loyal to me and have never abandoned me. If I am still alive today, it is because of the support of this strong party which is not in power now.

In February 2008, I was able to return once again to Germany to receive the Cinema for Peace Human Rights Award at the Berlin Film Festival for my role in the documentary *Enemies of Happiness*. One excited Afghan told me he thought, at this awards ceremony, that I should come on stage to receive the award wearing a burqa, and then tear it off before giving my speech. I preferred a less dramatic entry. And I do not want to encourage the idea prevalent in the West that the burqa is the only or the most important problem facing Afghan women. Without security or a justice system that protects women from rape, without employment, food and basic services, the issue of the burqa is secondary.

At the festival I had the opportunity to talk briefly with French actress Catherine Deneuve; the world chess champion (1985–2000) and Russian opposition leader Garry Kasparov; Somalian model and a UN special ambassador Waris Dirie; Bob Geldof, the Irish musician, actor and political activist; and many more. Once again, I felt it was important to use my time on stage in Berlin to deliver a hard-hitting message about the true situation in Afghanistan. Here is part of what I told the audience:

> Although the authorities in my country tried every possible way to prevent me being with you here today, I am here and accept this award on behalf of oppressed Afghan women who do not have the opportunity to speak for themselves. But they are brave and fight for their rights. You gave this award to a daughter of a land that was bombed by the US and its allies for seven years in the name of democracy, peace and human rights. But today we are as far from these values and these vital human needs as we were in 2001.
>
> I dedicate this award to my betrayed people who do not have liberation at all … I want to announce to all human rights defenders that the US-occupied Afghanistan is still a burning hell and a brutal joke made against democracy and human rights. Unfortunately today the worst enemies of these values are the current policymakers of my country.

I also explained that this award, like the rest of them, gives me determination to continue speaking up until Afghan war criminals are prosecuted and secular democracy is established. The many honours that I have received really belong to all those who seek freedom and peace in my bleeding Afghanistan. And, as I have explained, my wish is that all the warmth and attention that has been directed towards me at these ceremonies could be redirected and shared with the poor orphans and widows of my country.

In October 2008, I visited the United Kingdom for the first time to receive the Anna Politkovskaya Award, presented by the group Reach All Women in War. I was deeply honoured to receive this award, which links me to the memory of an extraordinary woman who sacrificed her life for telling the truth and fighting for justice. Politkovskaya was a Russian journalist who was murdered in a contract killing after writing a book on the war in Chechnya and the presidency of Vladimir Putin. A final collection of her works, *A Russian Diary: A Journalist's Final Account of Life, Corruption, and Death in Putin's Russia*, was published post-humously. She was a woman who used her profession to denounce the injustices committed in Russia's war against Chechnya, and to criticise government corruption. Her persever-ance, bravery and dedication to justice inspire me.

After I received this award in London, six female Nobel Peace Prize laureates – Shirin Ebadi, Jody Williams, Wangari Maathai, Rigoberta Menchú, Betty Williams and Máiread Corrigan Maguire – issued a joint statement: '... We commend this courage, and call for Joya's reinstatement to Afghanistan's national parliament ... Like our sister Aung San Suu Kyi, Joya is a model for women everywhere seeking to make the world more just.'

The voices of these distinguished women, along with so many others, have so far fallen on deaf ears in the Afghan government.

At the same time, it was clear that the government of President Karzai was paying close attention to the statements I was making during my trips out of the country.

In May 2008, representatives from western Afghanistan's provincial councils gathered in Kabul for a seminar on security issues and women's issues. It was an important meeting, with Hamid Karzai in attendance.

One of the speakers was Belquis Roshan, head of the Provincial Council of Farah Province. She told me that, before she spoke, Ghulam Jelani Popal, the General Director of the Independent Directorate of Local Governance in Afghanistan, had asked her not to give an abrasive or radical speech. Sebghatullah Sanjar, head of policy for Karzai's Presidential Palace, even wanted her to give him a copy of her speech to make sure that it would not be objectionable. She told him not to worry, and that she did not have a written copy of the speech on hand. She would speak freely, but it wouldn't be too radical.

In spite of this pressure, Roshan used this opportunity to condemn Karzai's silence about my expulsion from Parliament. She told the president, 'The people of Farah think that since Malalai Joya criticised you, and your government too, you dealt with this issue as a personal matter.' These words infuriated Karzai and he spent most of the seminar, which was supposed to be on the security problem of the western provinces of Afghanistan, on Malalai Joya's suspension. He said, 'I know Joya. She is a very brave girl. I supported her words in Loya Jirga and have never gone against any of her activities. I didn't even say anything when she insulted great personalities like Ismail Khan.'

He glanced over at Ismail Khan, who was present at the seminar.

'Isn't it like this, Ismail Khan?' he asked. 'How many times has she insulted you?' He continued, 'The Parliament was formed by about six million votes of the people, yet she insulted it. This can be overlooked. But when she goes to foreign countries and says they shouldn't support the Afghan government, this means they should not support the people of Afghanistan. This cannot be tolerated. And for this reason, I am not supporting her any more.

'If she has abused Ismail Khan, she can do the same to me, even face to face,' he continued. 'It would not matter to me if it was treated as an internal matter. But these problems should be solved within Afghanistan. She should not cross the line and talk about it during her foreign trips.'

Later he added, 'If she asks for forgiveness from the people's representatives and kisses Ismail Khan's hands, I might forgive her after that.'

Belquis Roshan replied, 'If it's a question of asking for forgiveness, then Ismail Khan and others like him should ask for forgiveness from the people of Afghanistan! Joya just exposes them.'

'She calls the Parliament a stable, then why is she trying to come back?' said Karzai. 'What is so hard about asking forgiveness?'

Roshan shot back, 'The Parliament has abused Malalai many times but no one said anything in her defence and they were not punished. When she insulted Parliament once, she was suspended. And you, as the president, remained silent.'

In the end, Karzai ignored Roshan's challenge. He suggested that the discussion should continue and Joya should also be present.

Roshan replied, 'Joya is ready to defend her statements, but she will not be asking for forgiveness.'

Later, some of the representatives were saying that Karzai turned the seminar into a forum about Malalai Joya since he didn't have an answer to any of Afghanistan's real problems. Instead he used the opportunity to impress the warlords and keep the criminals around him in power happy by insulting me.

My response to President Karzai is simple: I do not believe that the present corrupt government of Afghanistan represents the people, so I am not insulting them when I criticise Karzai's ministers or a Parliament filled with warlords and their lackeys. I am one of the few legitimately elected representatives in Parliament. The people of Farah sent me there to expose the crimes of the Afghan government, and I am obliged to carry out this mission, even when the government tries to silence me.

My goal abroad has always been the same as when I am inside Afghanistan: to unite people and to build power to destroy the domination of the warlords and the Taliban, and to end the occupation of our country. My wish is that this international solidarity will build strength and unity, and that when people become aware, they will rise like a storm that brings the truth. One voice – or even many isolated voices – is powerless. But when we weave our voices and our efforts together, we can become unbreakable.

This movement we are weaving must come from struggles in every corner of the world: our voice of resistance in Afghanistan, the cries of agony of the children of Palestine, the tears for democracy denied in Burma, the young freedom-loving students of Iran, the struggle of men and women in Turkey from whom I hear inspiring stories of bravery and courage in the face of horrible torture and killings in the Turkish prisons, the endeavours of Venezuela, Chile, Cuba, Bolivia and progressive movements in other American nations, the fight of African people for just and free societies. Our sufferings – and enemies – are the same. And our joy and happiness is the same.

CHAPTER 12

A BIRD WITH ONE WING

*'The mothers and daughters of Afghanistan
were captives in their own homes...
Today women are free.'*

President George W. Bush,
2002 State of the Union address

*I*N JUNE 2008, Laura Bush made her third and last visit to
Afghanistan as First Lady of the United States. As usual, her trip
was brief and heavily guarded, and served mainly to expose her
complete ignorance of the reality of life in Afghanistan.

She defended Hamid Karzai in her statements to the
American media, insisting that he was a 'popular' president. 'It's
really not that fair to blame him for a lot of the things that may or
may not be his fault,' she said. 'He inherited, just by becoming
president, a country that's been totally devastated.'

During her nine-hour stopover, Mrs Bush was flown by
helicopter to visit some of the devastation in the town of Bamyan
where the Taliban had famously demolished two enormous,
ancient statues of Buddha because they were 'un-Islamic'.

'It's more important than ever for the international community to continue to support Afghanistan, certainly for the US to continue to support Afghanistan,' Mrs Bush said as she surveyed the ruins. 'Because we don't want it to be the way it was when the Buddhas were destroyed.'

Of course, Laura Bush did not understand that the situation in Afghanistan is actually worse than it was when the Taliban blasted those statues – and that the special 'support' of the US was one of the main causes of our misery. Like so many other Western dignitaries, the former First Lady did not recognise that the devastation in our country was not caused by the Taliban alone – but by years of foreign interference. The Taliban is not the problem, it is a symptom of the disease of corruption, violence and feudalism that has plagued my country since the United States, Pakistan and Iran started funnelling arms and money to fundamentalist terrorist groups and warlords. Instead of ridding Afghanistan of these criminals, Karzai has embraced them. The people hate the warlords, and so they have come to hate Karzai. He says he champions the rights of Afghan women – which was supposedly one of Laura Bush's main causes – but he supported as Chief Justice of the Supreme Court a hard-line fundamentalist who revived some of the Taliban's oppressive policies against women.

And for this reason, Afghanistan remains like a bird with one wing – women – clipped. As long as the subjugation of women persists, our society will not be able to take off and move forward. Not only are women still denied their rights but, in a cruel irony, the cause of women has been used to justify and perpetuate a brutal occupation.

A few weeks after the US invasion in 2001, Laura Bush had made an official White House radio address: 'I hope Americans will join our family in working to ensure that dignity and opportunity will be secured for all the women and children of Afghanistan.' The First Lady's words of concern for Afghan women showed much more nuance and understanding than the crude rhetoric of her husband. And yet her sentiments have proved meaningless, more dust in the eyes of the world, considering the brutal policy they have helped to justify. Just as the Bush administration's lies about 'weapons of mass destruction' were used to rationalise its invasion and occupation of Iraq, the cause of 'liberating women' was added to the list of reasons for the United States to invade and remain in Afghanistan.

In 2005, Mrs Bush made a six-hour stop in Afghanistan, staying just long enough to proclaim how pleased she was with our progress. At a teacher training institute in Kabul, she cluelessly announced, 'Tyranny has been replaced by a young democracy and the power of freedom is on display across Afghanistan.'

In a way, she was partly right. 'The power of freedom' was – and remains – available for the warlords, drug-lords and Taliban to brutalise people, particularly women. Women are 'free' to beg in the streets under the cover of the burqa; they are 'free' to resort to prostitution to feed their families; they are 'free' to sell their children instead of watching them starve to death; they are 'free' to commit self-immolation as the only way out of the cycle of humiliation, destitution and despair.

During her drive-by visit to Kabul, Mrs Bush and other US officials met a group of so-called 'representatives' of women's progress in Afghanistan. In fact, whenever Western officials, including President and Mrs Bush, make their brief stops in my country, they usually meet a group of pro-government women such as Masouda Jalal, Fouzia Kofi, Noorzia Atmar, Husn Bano Ghazanfar, Shamim Jawad, Sima Samar, Qadria Yazdanparast, Azieta Rafat, Suraya Parlika, Fatima Gailani, Siddiqua Balkhi, Sharifa Zarmati and others. I believe that these women don't represent Afghan women, and they fail to touch the depth of their problems. They don't stand up in public for those women who have been victims of violence and brutal domination, women who have no rights in the real Afghanistan beyond their guarded compounds. But when these 'representatives' are allowed to speak for all Afghan women and are displayed as symbols of our 'progress' I believe they then become part of the problem.

———

Western journalists rarely challenge the fables that are spun for them. Because of the laziness and complicity within the mainstream media, the United States and its allies have been able to perpetuate the myth that Afghanistan has always been an ungovernable state, and that the oppression of women is embedded in Afghan culture. The brutality of the Taliban, the myth goes, was only an extreme expression of an old problem. And that only foreign occupation could save Afghanistan from itself.

I want you to know that this is a lie. We are not a helpless country, we have been able to manage our own affairs, and women's rights have not always been in such a terrible state. It is the policies of the big powers intervening and backing the most extreme elements in Afghanistan that have rolled back the rights of women.

Afghanistan's first modern ruler, King Amanullah Khan, who won independence from the British in 1919, was a freedom-loving and democratic leader. He believed that Pashtuns, Tajiks, Hindus, Uzbeks, Hazaras and people from other different tribes are simply Afghan. He strengthened national unity so that there was no racial, linguistic or religious discrimination. He also advanced a modern constitution that incorporated equal rights and individual freedoms.

His wife, Queen Soraya, played a vital role in regard to his policy towards women. She made trips to European countries on behalf of women, without wearing a scarf and in modern clothes. In 1920, she gave a public speech – a first for an Afghan queen – describing the benefits of women's rights. After that many women volunteered to help her, and a number of organisations were established for the benefit of women.

The nation's first women's magazine, called *Irshadul Naswan,* was published on 17 March 1921. Women workers were accepted by factories. The first women's hospital was established in Kabul, and for the first time women served as representatives in the Loya Jirga of 1928. Amanullah Khan in that Jirga suggested abolishing polygamy and forced marriage. The legal age for marriage was established at eighteen. The king encouraged the building of roads, factories, and railway lines. He built libraries, cinemas and theatres. Wageless labour, forced labour and slavery were abolished.

During the time of Amanullah Khan, education became compulsory for every Afghan. The first girls' school was established in 1924. A group of girls was sent to Turkey for higher education, without having to wear the hijab, or Islamic covering, or be accompanied by a male relative, or Mahram. Later on, hundreds of girls went to school in foreign countries such as Germany, Russia and France.

Unfortunately, some of the king's reform measures went too far, too fast. For example, he announced that no Afghan man could go out without a modern-style hat and trousers, and if they failed to do so they were fined. It was the same case for women who went out wearing a burqa. He also changed the religious holiday from Friday to Sunday. The fundamentalists were in an uproar, and Amanullah Khan's enemies used this to their advantage.

The British were still angry at the loss of their colony and afraid of having a modern, independent country next to India, which was still under its control. Britain maintained a network of its own puppets in Afghanistan among reactionary religious scholars and rival aristocrats. Through these people, the British quietly sowed rebellion against Amanullah Khan and his reforms. As a majority of the Afghans were uneducated and deeply influenced by religious beliefs, this was successful and the king lost the support of the people. He went into exile and, in 1929, was forced to give up the throne.

His era of reform is remembered fondly by all Afghans who believe in democracy and constitutional rule. And, incidentally, this was why it was such an insult when, in December 2008,

Hamid Karzai presented George W. Bush with the medal of King Amanullah during the American president's last trip to Afghanistan. Only one day earlier an Iraqi journalist said goodbye to Bush by throwing a shoe at him – a much more suitable honour!

Amanullah Khan's overthrow is considered a disaster in the history of Afghanistan. Immediately after he was exiled, a strongman named Habibullah Kalakani became emir. He was a dark-minded and ignorant man backed by the British. His first official act was to close all the schools. Only months later, Kalakani's forces were overcome by Mohammad Nadir Shah, a Pashtun aristocrat, who invaded from India with British help. Nadir Shah lured Kalakani to a peace conference and then had him executed. The brutal Nadir Shah immediately repealed most of Amanullah's reforms – he even brought back the women who had been sent to Turkey for their higher education and made them stay at home. Nadir Shah was assassinated in 1933, and was succeeded by his son, Zahir Shah, who was only nineteen at his coronation.

King Zahir served as a passive figurehead for most of his rule. His paternal uncles, who were the real power-holders, presided over a reign of terror for much of the next three decades. Non-Pashtun ethnic groups were particularly oppressed during this time. But constitutionalists continued to struggle against the repressive monarchy, and they eventually forced the government to accept some reforms in order to keep the people from open rebellion. By the middle of the twentieth century, King Zahir started to assert his authority and began experimenting with a limited democracy, if only to satisfy the people and put an end to mass movements. Zahir freed more than 500 political prisoners and brought in other reforms. University students were allowed to form unions, and political parties that were banned in previous years were given some freedom to regroup. But the government wouldn't tolerate too much opposition, and some were rounded up, jailed and killed.

During these turbulent years, however, women's rights were gradually restored.

By the 1950s, women in Afghanistan were encouraged to work in many professions. By the end of the decade they were staging demonstrations and asking for their rights. The government even passed laws to ban the wearing of the burqa and to legalise the wearing of skirts and short sleeves. Here, for example, is how the *New York Times* reported on the condition of Afghan women half a century ago, on 8 November 1959: 'Afghanistan's Women Lift the Veil' read the headline. 'A new world of freedom, spiritual as well as sartorial, has been opened to the women of this Moslem nation after centuries of seclusion.'

The freedoms achieved by women were not the result of some invasion from the West, but from the development of our own society, our own political process and the struggle of democratically minded people of Afghanistan who risked death for their beliefs. What is true of women in Afghanistan has been true throughout history. The great Indian writer Arundhati Roy made this point in a speech she delivered in the United States several years ago:

> It's being made out that the whole point of the war was to topple the Taliban regime and liberate Afghan women from their burqas. We are being asked to believe that the US Marines are actually on a feminist mission. (If so, will their next stop be America's military ally Saudi Arabia?) Think of it this way: in India there are some pretty reprehensible social practices against 'untouchables', against Christians and Muslims, against women. Pakistan and Bangladesh have even worse ways of dealing with minority communities and women. Should they be bombed? Should Delhi, Islamabad and Dhaka be destroyed? Is it possible to bomb bigotry out of India? Can we bomb our way to a feminist paradise? Is that how women won the vote in

the US? Or how slavery was abolished? Can we win redress for the genocide of the millions of Native Americans upon whose corpses the United States was founded by bombing Santa Fe?

Although Zahir Shah tried to establish a constitutional monarchy, the people lost faith in him and took to the streets in demonstrations. In 1973, while King Zahir was out of country for medical treatment, he was overthrown by his pro-Soviet cousin, Daoud Khan. Afghanistan's 'constitutional era' was over, replaced by a nominal republic, and, in 1978, Russian invaders.

It was the women of Afghanistan who offered the first show of resistance against the Russian puppet regime by staging a demonstration in Kabul. The police reacted with violence, and women such as Nahid Sahid and Wajeha were killed on the spot. It was during this era that RAWA – the Revolutionary Association of the Women of Afghanistan – was established by Meena and some other women intellectuals in Kabul.

As recently as the 1970s, the extremists who now have so much power to implement anti-women policies – with their misinterpretations of Islam to justify them – were marginal figures. The notorious warlord Gulbuddin Hekmatyar, for example, was a totally discredited force in those days, known for having led attacks on unveiled women at the University of Kabul which included burning these women with acid. It was the United States, Pakistan and Iran arming these forces during the 1980s – Hekmatyar was one of their favourites during this period – that helped unleash the religious fascism that has plagued Afghanistan for the past three decades.

It is hard to fathom the pivotal role the United States played in nourishing a violent, fundamentalist mentality in generations of young Afghans. But starting in the 1980s the US government spent more than 50 million dollars to publish textbooks through the University of Nebraska that promoted a fanatic, militaristic agenda. The *Washington Post* called it the 'Jihad Schoolbook

Scandal' in a March 2002 article, describing the books as 'filled with talk of jihad' and warlike images. It taught children to count using 'illustrations of tanks, missiles and landmines'. The books were shipped into Soviet-occupied Afghanistan to fuel a jihad against the Russians, but, according to the *Post*, they made up the core curriculum in the Afghan school system long after the Soviets were defeated. 'Even the Taliban used the American-produced books, though the radical movement scratched out human faces in keeping with its strict fundamentalist code.' And after the Taliban was gone, USAID continued to send the textbooks into Afghanistan, where fundamentalists still use them to teach a violent brand of Islam.

These fundamentalist groups gained prominence and support, as I have said, partly because of the aggressive and criminal invasion of our country by a great power that claimed to be 'bringing women's rights' to Afghanistan. All sectors of Afghan society fought against the Soviet invasion and the people's resistance was hon-ourable and legitimate. Unfortunately, some of the mujahideen factions – the criminal mujahideen that I speak of – then turned their weapons and their violence against the Afghan people – espe-cially women. Some of these groups even burned down girls' schools, much as the Taliban has done in more recent years.

It is important to remember that when the Taliban first swept into power in 1996, many Afghans – at first – welcomed this development because at least it put an end to the vicious killings that had taken up to 80,000 lives in Kabul alone during the civil war of 1992 to 1996. Even the then so-called president Burhanuddin Rabbani called the Taliban 'angels of peace' and Ahmad Shah Massoud, then the Defence Minister, went to meet the Taliban leaders and told them that they shared the same way of thinking.

It is not widely known in the West, but Benazir Bhutto, who was prime minister of Pakistan during this time, played a key role in funding the Taliban and promoting its domination of Afghanistan. Many Afghans, in fact, referred to Bhutto as 'the mother of the Taliban'. Her goal was to exploit trade routes through Afghanistan while undermining India's influence in the country. Once again, Afghanistan was used as a pawn in a regional chess match we had no way of winning.

I was a teenager growing up in the refugee camps of Pakistan when Bhutto was prime minister. I was too young to understand the politics of the time, but I do remember being happy and hopeful that a woman was in power. Of course, I realise that it's a person's ideas and character that matter, not gender, but I do think that seeing women in leadership positions can give young girls hope. I know that millions of Pakistanis were looking to vote for Benazir Bhutto when she returned from exile in 2007. Despite the corruption during her past tenure, her recent candidacy offered hope for an end to military rule, and for democracy and secularism.

Bhutto's assassination was a terrorist act and I condemn it absolutely. This is true even though I had many disagreements with her politically. No political disagreement should ever be solved through this type of violence, and I would never condone the use of assassination even against the worst enemies of Afghanistan. Democracy – real democracy – and courts of justice should decide the fate of political leaders. Still, in spite of the outrage we feel over her murder, I must acknowledge that many progressive Afghans remember well the role that Bhutto played in the destruction of our country, and the rise of the medieval-minded Taliban.

The Taliban's denial of women's rights, including enforcing the use of the burqa, is common knowledge. These facts were well publicised in the United States, especially after 9/11 and in the run-up to the war in 2001. Because the Taliban regime had been so repressive, many of our people – even those who detest the very idea of foreign troops on Afghan soil – were hopeful that this incursion represented a chance for democracy. They hoped the United States had learned from its past mistakes. Some took Laura Bush at her word when she said the purpose of the

American invasion was to restore women's rights, or took at face value the words of then-US Secretary of State Colin Powell, in November 2001: 'The rights of women in Afghanistan will not be negotiable.' Perhaps Powell had meant to say that women's rights would not be negotia*ted*. It was obvious from the very first days that the United States had compromised the rights of Afghan women by supporting some of the worst enemies of women that our country had ever seen.

It is important to remember that the Taliban has never been the only force in Afghanistan that represses women. A number of the laws against women were actually first implemented during the civil war, and then maintained and enforced by the Taliban. For instance, the Ministry for the Promotion of Virtue and Prevention of Vice, which would become infamous under the Taliban, was actually first set up in the civil war era. Not only are many of these laws still on the books but, what's more, many of the warlords that introduced these restrictions are still in power in the current NATO-backed government.

The crimes of the warlords during the 1990s are well documented in the book *Bleeding Afghanistan*, by Sonali Kolhatkar and James Ingalls, who are great supporters of mine and who work to raise money for Afghan women in the United States. In their book, they point out the US government's lack of concern for the impact of their policy of encouraging extremists: 'If Afghanistan ever deserved the label "failed state", it was most appropriate in the years 1992–1996, when U.S. eyes were averted while U.S. weapons were eliminating the buildings, institutions, and people required for the survival of the State of Afghanistan.' If today Afghanistan is failing as a state it is because the warlords who have failed our country before were once again put in power even though they had earned the well-deserved hatred of our people.

Those same warlords not only control Parliament and many of Karzai's cabinet posts – they also run the judiciary system. At the Loya Jirga in 2003, for instance, Abdul Rab al-Rasul Sayyaf and other warlords used their influence to put a fundamentalist named Fazl Hadi Shinwari into the key position of chief justice of the Supreme Court and Abdul Malik Kamawi as his deputy. In fact all nine justices of the Supreme Court are dark-minded mullahs. They and Shinwari are among the main reasons that women's rights have improved so little since the fall of the Taliban.

According to Pakistani journalist Ahmed Rashid, in his book *Descent into Chaos*, Shinwari was in fact 'controlled by Sayyaf. European ambassadors privately told me that the US had struck a deal with Sayyaf in which he would later have the power to nominate judges to the Supreme Court if he gave concessions now on other fronts. Sayyaf emerged more powerful from the 2003 Loya Jirga. To the Americans, he was a fundamentalist, but he was "our fundamentalist."' Shinwari, Sayyaf and other fundamentalists insisted at the Loya Jirga that the new constitution name the country the Islamic Republic of Afghanistan, and they have misused Islam through the courts to deny women's and human rights.

Shinwari used his position to impose his extremist views on the nation. He shut down a television station for its alleged immoral programming. He told a reporter from America's National Public Radio that anyone who didn't follow Islamic law should be beheaded. In an interview with the *Christian Science Monitor* in 2006, Shinwari revealed that women did not belong in the high court. '... A woman cannot be a judge over the general country, and she cannot sit in this chair,' said Shinwari. 'If a woman becomes a top judge, then what would happen when she has a menstruation cycle once a month, and she cannot go to the mosque? Also, a woman judge cannot give an execution order, according to Islamic law.' The article pointed out that not only was Shinwari head of Afghanistan's Council of Islamic Scholars, he was a long-time member of Sayyaf's militia group, the Ittihad-i-Islami.

Karzai tried to reappoint Shinwari as Chief Justice in 2006, but in a rare show of independence, Parliament blocked him, saying he was unqualified for the job. Now one of Karzai's former legal advisers, Abdul Salam Azimi, serves as Chief Justice. Azimi, who is also from Farah, has had long-term connections with the United States, and in fact was the head of the USAID-sponsored education programme in Peshawar that distributed the scandalous pro-jihad schoolbooks. Since Azimi became chief justice there has been no change in the make-up of the Supreme Court, which is still dominated by the mullahs.

Even after his departure, Shinwari had a lasting influence on the judicial system because he made sure that many of the other judges were also strict fundamentalists. And so the courts have systemically prevented rapists from serving any meaningful sentences for their crimes. Men still have impunity to abuse and even kill their wives and other women and girls. The law is only really used as a tool with which to limit women's rights. Commanders of the Northern Alliance and other warlords and their militias still abduct and rape women and girls – they reign with terror in their areas.

Karzai's justice department is no better. His choice for Attorney General was Jabar Sabet, who once belonged to Hekmatyar's party. To show the level of justice in Afghanistan: consider that the journalist Kambaksh was given a death sentence – later commuted to twenty years in prison – just for downloading an article that was termed un-Islamic by the court. While a lesser penalty was meted out to Assadullah Sarwari, a former head of the secret police, who ended up with a seventeen-year sentence for torturing and killing thousands of political opponents in the late 1970s. Kambaksh, who harmed no one, still sits in prison, but during the same time President Karzai ordered three men released who had been sentenced to seventeen years for gang-raping and killing a woman.

It does not seem that the legislature will deliver any higher degree of justice than the courts. In September 2008, the Wolesi Jirga prepared a draft law which, when approved, will ban obscene movies, female dances and high-volume music at parties. According to the proposed law, those behind professional dancing events and those co-ordinating such programmes will face up to a year in jail. It will also be illegal for hotels to allow males and females from different families to get together. Organisers of sports events involving male and female participants will also be punished. The new bill forbids wearing shorts and skin-tight outfits. It also proposes different penalties for the practices that lead to a delay in marriage, while allowing girls to be given away to settle disputes as well as condoning forced marriages.

Another myth about Afghanistan is that women and girls are now all free to go to school. It is true that in Kabul and in some other cities some girls are now able to go to school and certain jobs are available to women, but this is the situation of a fortunate minority. The conditions of schools outside Kabul are deplorable and in remote areas there are neither teachers nor any buildings available to house these so-called schools. In many villages girls learn their lessons while sitting in the dirt.

When Laura Bush made her last visit to Afghanistan she boasted that 6 million children are enrolled in school, a figure that is always trumpeted as an Afghan success story. But according to the UN, more than 5 million children are still not getting any education at all. In early December 2008, an Afghanistan Independent Human Rights Commission (AIHRC) survey showed that only 5 per cent of girls and 11 per cent of boys could pursue their education all the way to the twelfth grade.

According to the Ministry of Labour, Social Affairs, Martyrs and Disabled (MoLSAMD), more than 6 million children in the country face problems such as smuggling, abduction, child labour and lack of education. Due to severe poverty, many children have to leave school to work at hard labour to help their parents make a living. A study released by the AIHRC revealed that 60 per cent of families surveyed stated that almost half their children were involved in some kind of labour. This could be anything from working in brick factories and markets, to car washes and workshops.

Radhika Coomaraswamy, the UN's special representative for

Children in Armed Conflict said, 'I can't think of any country in the world where children suffer more than in Afghanistan … In all our meetings with children it takes a lot of time to make them smile. That to me shows that there is not happiness in their hearts.'

Abduction and sexual violence against children has become an epidemic in recent years. Many such cases have been reported in Takhar Province, a warlord stronghold. In 2007 Halim, the father of two children, aged six and seven, came to meet me in Kabul with a terrible tale.

He had openly accused local commanders in Takhar of being criminals. This heartbroken father described how his children were abducted by some of their gunmen in order to silence him. The children were brutally murdered and their dead bodies stuffed in a sack and thrown in a river, where local villagers discovered them. These kinds of crimes have resulted in many large protests against the warlords by the people of Takhar, but the central government does nothing at all to control their lawlessness. Halim said he had seen President Karzai and told him his story. 'I showed him pictures of my sons, and he cried but told me to forget it,' Halim said. 'He said, "You are young, have more babies."'

Going to school is becoming more and more dangerous for girls, with renewed attacks against teachers and students. In November 2008, eight girls were splashed with acid while on their way to school, in an attack by men on a motorcycle in Kandahar. Incidents like this are multiplying, and girls' attendance at school is declining. It was heartening to see one of the girls who was badly injured tell reporters that she was not afraid of such acts, and would finish her studies even if this would cause her to lose her life.

After many years of teaching in underground classrooms during the Taliban, it is painful for me to know that girls and women still have to be afraid to get an education.

Not only is it dangerous for women to go to school, in many

regions of the country women cannot even leave the house unless accompanied by a male relative, or Mahram. And women continue to wear the burqa, even in Kabul. To all intents and purposes, the position of women is the same now as it was under the Taliban. In some respects, the situation is worse, with higher rates of suicide and abduction, and total impunity in cases of rape.

The statistics are shocking: a United Nations Development Fund for Women (UNIFEM) survey found that violence affects 80 per cent of Afghan women at some time in their lives. Much of this abuse is domestic, and in our country studies indicate that between 60 and 80 per cent of marriages remain forced, with young girls being traded and sold like commodities. Women in my country also suffer from the highest rates of depression in the world.

According to the United Nations Population Fund (UNFPA), 25 per cent of Afghan women face sexual violence. Some specific examples will suffice to illustrate the brutal treatment of women in Afghanistan today. These are disturbing stories, but they are the reality and, sadly, they represent only the tip of the iceberg of women's oppression.

In May 2007 in Takhar Province, an eight-year-old girl named Bibi Fatima was abducted, raped by several men and then murdered. In this all too rare instance, authorities responded quickly and arrested five individuals. The case was reported on Ariana TV and the news was translated into English for RAWA's website, which has documented many of the horrific cases of violence against women.

In the Gulran district of Herat Province, Fatima, a twenty-two-year-old woman, checked herself into hospital with multiple wounds. She reported that her husband had carried out serial assaults against her, in addition to killing their newborn baby. He had pulled her hair out with his bare hands, and burned her with boiling hot water. Fatima is not the only woman to suffer mutilation at her husband's hands. Also in Herat, a woman named Nafisa reported that her opium-addicted husband broke her nose and cut off her ear with a knife.

Recently Bashir Chaabi, one of the warlords of Takhar, was assigned to be governor of the northern Sar-e-Pul Province. Under his rule there have been many reports of young girls being gang-raped there. In these cases, few of the victims have the courage to raise their voices and make it public because rape is regarded as a shame to the family. But a fourteen-year-old girl named Bashira and her father decided to speak out. Bashira was gang-raped while going to pick up supplies from an aid distribution centre. One of the accused is the son of a Member of Parliament. This MP intervened to help make sure his son escaped from facing real justice for his crime. So while I have been kicked out of Parliament for demanding the prosecution of war criminals, other MPs use their positions of power so that friends and family can avoid prosecution for their crimes against women.

I met Bashira and her father in Kabul in the presence of British journalist Glyn Strong, who later made a short documentary about the case. Bashira was so distraught after the rape that she tried to burn herself to death. Her hands still bore the scars when I met her. Her lovely young face was creased with worry as I held her against me and listened to her agonising story. Everyone was weeping as she and her father described the assault and the horrors that followed. Her father said that his daughter's rapists tried to bribe him to drop the case, and when he refused, they had him beaten so badly he spent two weeks in hospital. But despite his complaints, the authorities and the courts turned a blind eye to his plea for justice.

When Glyn Strong asked Bashira why she came to see me, she said, while crying bitterly, 'Because she speaks the truth.' This poor girl and her father could find no one to stand up for them.

Because Bashira and her father are from the Hazara ethnic group, he hoped to get help from Mohammad Mohaqiq, the most powerful Hazara warlord in Afghanistan. He hoped this MP would criticise Dostum's commander for covering up his son's crimes. But when he arrived at Mohaqiq's luxury house in Kabul, where he lives with three wives, and announced that they wanted to meet him, Mohaqiq's secretary turned him away. When Bashira's father left the house his heart was full of hatred.

Later, he told me that this act was enough to show him the real nature of these people. The warlords are all the same, no matter what ethnic group. Bashira's father was now seething with anger that no one would listen to his cry for justice. He even said in an interview with a local TV channel that if justice was not done, then he would become a suicide bomber and get revenge by himself.

Six months after Bashira's attack, while her case was still being discussed in the Afghan media, two other young girls named Anisa and Samia were gang-raped by warlords in the same province of Sar-e-Pul. Bashira tearfully told me that if the government had punished her rapists, then the men who raped these two other innocents wouldn't have thought they could get away with it.

After a few months I managed to get in contact with Anisa's family and I met her in a supporter's house in Kabul. She couldn't tell me the full story; she was so traumatised she broke down at the beginning. I learned that her mother was raped in front of her, and then Anisa was raped by five men.

These suffering young women came to me just to share their sorrows. But because I have been deprived of my parliamentary rights, I am not in a position to do much for them except to listen, and then tell the world what is happening in our country. It was painful to hear their stories but I was happy to meet them to discuss their pains and try to give them hope. Both of them had dropped out of school after this violence occurred, and I tried to get them to return to their education.

Unfortunately, both the law and some traditions work against women's rights in the case of rape. Many times a woman who has been raped will be seen as damaged and unable to marry. Sometimes her own family members will even kill her to remove the shame.

Sadly, there are thousands of Bashiras and Anisas in

Afghanistan. Many women who are raped or are forced into marriage lose all hope. In recent years, literally hundreds of women have committed suicide to escape abusive relationships, many of them by burning themselves to death.

In Laghman Province, twenty-five-year-old Puktana immolated herself in front of the local courthouse as a protest against this intolerable state of affairs – the *injustice* system in Afghanistan today. Keeping in mind that the real figures may be much higher, in the first half of 2007 a shocking 250 suicides were reported. Integrated Regional Information Networks (IRIN) humanitarian news documented these cases, but I am afraid they have received too little attention in the Western media. This terrible phenomenon is a result of the total failure of the courts and legal system in Afghanistan. Husbands can abandon their wives with ease, yet it is extremely difficult for a woman to legally obtain a divorce.

Samiya was an eighteen-year-old girl living in the Farkhar district of Takhar Province. When she was forced into a marriage with a sixty-year-old man who already had other wives, she hanged herself from a tree in her family's front yard. Also in Takhar, a twenty-two-year-old woman named Bibi Gul poured petrol all over her body and killed herself by immolation in her family's animal stable. She too was a victim of domestic abuse.

I can remember many cases where women and girls came to me to unburden their sorrows; I would try to comfort and help them, and to urge them not to choose suicide, but to choose to be part of the collective struggle to achieve justice for women in Afghanistan. The extent of the misery of Afghan women was captured in a UNIFEM study that found 65 per cent of the 50,000 widows in Kabul felt that suicide was the only option to get rid of their desolation.

There are an estimated 1.5 million widows in Afghanistan, most of them living in terrible poverty. Some have even resorted to prostitution in order to survive. Although prostitution is nothing new in my country – and it even existed during the

Taliban regime – it is now much more widespread. According to the *South China Morning Post*: 'Afghan women's rights groups believe the number of sex workers in the country is increasing at a greater rate than before because the country has reached an unprecedented level of economic hardship and lawlessness.'

Despite all the violence, corruption and poverty, leaders in the West still insist that Afghanistan is much better off than it was before the invasion. Soon after he left his position in charge of the Pentagon, Donald Rumsfeld bragged about his role in leading the war in my country: 'In Afghanistan, 28 million people are free. They have their own president, they have their own Parliament ... [Things have] improved a lot on the streets.'

In Afghanistan there is a saying: 'Every anguish passes except the anguish of hunger.' According to the United Nations Food and Agriculture Organisation (FAO), 70 per cent of Afghans – 18 million people – live on less than 2 US dollars a day and suffer from acute food insecurity. As the winter of 2008–2009 set in, there were reports of potential widespread starvation.

Afghanistan, like other developing countries, has been feeling the disastrous outcome of globalisation in the years following the US occupation. The reliance on privatisation and the unchecked market economy has had a terrible impact on the poorest people, and it has widened the gap between the rich and the poor. Remember, with the worldwide increase in the price of staple foods, it is the poor in places like Afghanistan who suffer the most. And women and children suffer most of all.

In Herat, it was reported that a mother had to sell her baby for 10 dollars. Mothers, especially widows, often have to make the painful decision to leave a child at an orphanage or, worse, to sell one baby to try to feed herself and her other children.

In the winter of 2007 more than 1,000 people are estimated to have died due to exposure, because of poverty and poor housing. With the grinding poverty and lack of health facilities, diseases such as tuberculosis also thrive and claim too many lives. Electricity is scarce and the service unreliable, and many people do not even have fuel for heating their homes or cooking. Over 37,000 children work and beg in the streets of Kabul alone, some 80 per cent of them boys, 36 per cent of whom are aged eight to ten years old. There are at least 200,000 children in Afghanistan living with permanent disability (physical, sensory and/or mental impairment), according to a 2005 survey by Handicap International.

Statistics put the rate of unemployment around 60 per cent, but in reality it may be closer to 90 per cent. Although some women in Kabul and a few other cities have access to education and jobs, life for women in rural areas is worse than ever. Infant and maternal mortality rates are amongst the highest in the world. Every twenty-eight minutes an Afghan woman dies during childbirth. Badakhshan Province has the highest maternal mortality rate in the world – 6,500 deaths out of 100,000 live births, 123 times higher than in the United States.

If the United States and its allies were serious about liberating Afghanistan's women, then it would not be protecting and promoting the warlords and fundamentalists who cause us such grief. And more importantly women's rights can't be donated from abroad or forced at gunpoint. Equality is a value that should and will be achieved through the struggle of Afghan women and men. The fact is that women's rights were merely the pretext, and not the real motivation, for the war. My situation itself speaks to the ongoing plight of women in Afghanistan. The support that my own cause has garnered is evidence that things must not always remain the same. I have been backed and welcomed by the suppressed people of Afghanistan in every corner of the country. That they see me as their voice is a source of inspiration and honour to me. Many people from faraway provinces come to meet me in Kabul and share their problems and feelings and announce their support for our common cause.

To fight for women's rights in a besieged and benighted country like Afghanistan is to accept a big risk, with many challenges. It is like trying to swim against a strong current. But it is a proud struggle. It is a dream of mine that one day a democratically minded woman will take the reins of power. By shining a light on the real state of women's rights in Afghanistan today, we can teach even the most dark-minded misogynists that women are capable of changing the world when they act together.

Wherever I have travelled, I have met wonderful activists working for women's rights. It is very meaningful to me that women who face so many struggles in their own country take time to support the women of Afghanistan. This solidarity is a living example that as long as one of us is not free, none of us is free.

CHAPTER 13

THE ENDLESS WAR

O N 3 NOVEMBER 2008, a day before the US presidential elections, an American warplane dropped a missile on the village of Wech Baghtu, near Kandahar. The bomb was meant for Taliban fighters, but it landed in the middle of a wedding party that Abdul Jalil was hosting for his niece. Thirty-seven civilians died that afternoon, twenty-three of them children. The bride was hospitalised with shrapnel wounds.

According to Human Rights Watch, civilian deaths from US and NATO air strikes nearly tripled from 2006 to 2007. The United Nations reported that more than 2,000 civilians were killed in the conflict in Afghanistan in 2008, a 40 per cent increase over the number of casualties the previous year.

During this time, the Taliban and fundamentalist warlords have gained control of 70 per cent of Afghanistan, opium production is at an all-time high, the security situation has deteriorated everywhere, and we have watched our faint hopes of real peace and democracy crushed once again. Despite the presence of forces from over forty countries, the Taliban and al-Qaeda continue to become stronger day by day. In early 2009, Hamid Karzai assured the Taliban leader, Mullah Omar, that if he joined in talks with the government, his security would be guaranteed. Omar's answer was simple: 'Thanks, we don't need your security. We are already feeling very secure in Afghanistan.'

Now the American President George W. Bush has been

replaced by Barack Obama, who seems intent on following – and even expanding – the same failed policies that produced such devastating results. Obama pledged to send another 30,000 American troops to Afghanistan, and we are expecting even more civilian casualties along with more bitter resentment and protests against the brutal occupation.

In the past thirty years every kind of atrocity has been committed in Afghanistan in the name of socialism, religion, freedom, democracy and liberation. Now these acts are justified by a so-called 'war on terror'.

There are many kinds of terror in this world. I have already written about the terror against women, and the terror of poverty in my country. But those who get their news from the corporate media may not realise that allied attacks on supposed al-Qaeda and Taliban targets are also killing, maiming and terrorising innocent Afghans. We live every day of our lives in the terror of an endless war.

Death comes all too easily, and in too many different ways, in our 'liberated' country. As I have already written, countless Afghans have died in recent years because of the continuing systemic denial of women's rights. Then there are the deaths of innocent bystanders, killed in suicide bombings by the Taliban and others. This too is a terror against the Afghan people, a threat that must be coped with around the clock. Whenever we leave our homes – to go to school, to the bazaar or to a demonstration – we never know if we are leaving for the last time. On 8 July 2008, a powerful suicide bomb blast in Kabul killed close to 200 people. I know a two-year-old child who lost her mother and a family who lost five members in this one explosion.

Then there is the terror that comes from the skies. In 2007 and 2008 the United States dropped far more bombs on Afghanistan than on Iraq. The missile strike on the wedding in Wech Baghtu was only one of many such massacres. For example, on 6 July 2008, US forces bombed a wedding party in Nengarhar Province, killing forty-seven civilians including the

bride. In another tragic incident, twenty-seven civilians perished
in air strikes on the remote village of Nouristan. In both of these
cases, American military officials refused to even apologise. In the
first case they initially claimed they had killed 'militants' when in
fact they had killed members of a wedding party.

Then, in August 2008, an American bombing in the
Shindand district of Herat killed dozens of civilians. US officials
at first denied the massacre; after months of delay they finally put
the number of killed at only thirty. But locals reported that close
to ninety civilians had perished, a figure that was confirmed by
the UN, which also reported that sixty of the dead were children.
And when hundreds protested about the bombing in the city of
Azizabad, their demonstration was fired upon by Afghan
National Army forces. Almost every day there are new reports of
civilian deaths.

All told, according to Professor Marc W. Herold of the
University of New Hampshire, at least 7,000 civilians have been
killed by US/NATO forces since the invasion of Afghanistan.
Herold documented the civilian toll of the war in an important
study, released in October 2008, entitled 'The Matrix of Death:
(Im)Precision of U.S. Bombing and the (Under)Valuation of an
Afghan Life'. According to Herold, his estimate is undoubtedly a
low figure, 'because [it] exclude[s] the thousands who later die from
injuries incurred in a US/NATO attack, those killed in incidents
which went un-reported, those who die from lack of vital resources
in refugee camps, etc.' The majority of the Afghan victims, according to this study, were killed in so-called 'Close Air Support (CAS)'
strikes called in by NATO forces on the ground. And the number
of CAS bombings has increased sharply over the years, 'from 176
in 2005, to 1,770 in 2006, and 2,926 in 2007'.

Herold sums up the predictable impact of these bombings in
Afghanistan: 'In effect, the US/NATO forces are relying upon air
power in lieu of ground forces and in so doing causing high
levels of civilian casualties which, in turn, push locals towards
the resistance. This is particularly important in Afghanistan,

where the culture of revenge has long stalked Americans there. US/NATO aerial attacks turn friends into enemies.'

Espingul, a young boy from Garoch village, whose five family members were among thirty-five civilians killed by US bombs in Laghman Province in mid-January 2009, told an Al Jazeera reporter, 'I am requesting Hamid Karzai to kick out Americans from Afghanistan otherwise I will put a bomb in my body and blow myself up. I was serving the government, what they did to me is unfair. We don't want the Americans to build up bridges and roads for us, we ask them to just leave.'

Professor Herold, as a friend of peace himself, has established the online Afghan Victims Memorial Project, which lists the names of the Afghan casualties of war. There can never be lasting peace if the lives of Afghans are not valued as much as the lives of Western soldiers. Every death is a tragedy, but too often the Afghan victims of this war are merely nameless 'collateral damage' reported in the media as having been killed by 'mistake'. I met Herold while I was on a tour of the USA, and I had the opportunity to express heartfelt thanks to him on behalf of the Afghan people, for doing such an extraordinary job in documenting and remembering the innocent civilians killed by US/NATO weapons in the past seven years.

Along with the terror from the sky, there is terror in the ground.

The fields and roadsides of Afghanistan are still riddled with unexploded landmines from as far back as the Soviet occupation – like the kind that cost my father his leg. There are an estimated 10 million landmines in Afghanistan, making it the most mined country in the world. The most recent war has added other components to this lethal landscape in the form of cluster bombs and depleted-uranium shells.

Anti-personnel cluster bomblets used against the Taliban during the invasion look like little yellow toys when they lie, unexploded, in the streets and fields. In 2002 the Red Cross had to warn Afghan children not to play with them – so many were losing their eyes and their limbs. More than a hundred countries reached agreement in May 2008 to ban cluster bombs, but the United States has still refused to sign the agreement. If they continue to use these cruel, deadly bombs against civilians, it is no less than a war crime.

Another hidden danger lies in the invisible radiation in the shrapnel of depleted-uranium shell-casings. Depleted uranium is a highly toxic and extremely dense metal that is used in 'bunker-busting' bombs and other penetrating missiles. The use of DU weapons has not only harmed children but also contaminated plant and animal life in my war-ravaged and impoverished country. A large number of health specialists in Afghanistan as well as international observers regard the increased number of birth defects in Afghanistan to be the direct result of the thousands of US/NATO bombs dropped.

So when will this violence finally end? How many more civilians -- brides and grooms, women and children – have to be killed? In June 2007, the new ambassador to Afghanistan from the United Kingdom said, 'It's not a three-year sprint, it's a thirty-year marathon – we should be thinking in terms of decades.' The only way this war needs to last decades is if its real purpose is for the United States and its allies to establish permanent bases to serve their strategic aims. To our people, the idea that the US with all its military technology and power could not have already defeated these small medieval-minded groups – if that was their real war aim – is like a bad joke. Instead it looks like they are playing a game of cat and mouse, in order to justify keeping their military in Afghanistan.

The so-called war on terror is in fact an extremely dishonest policy. The whole world saw this when Bush and his friends made up outrageous lies to justify invading Iraq. But their purpose was to get control of Iraq's resources – oil. The war killed hundreds of thousands of Iraqis and created millions of refugees. On top of that, everyone acknowledges that the war has also increased the regional influence of the theocratic regime in Iran, whose leaders have the same mentality as the Taliban. The United States has, in addition, created another fertile breeding ground for terrorists.

The theory behind the 'war on terror' is that it will make America safe from the kind of terrorists that carried out the deplorable attacks of 9/11. But this is not at all what is happening.

Just as Afghan and Iraqi populations have become less secure in recent years, so too the Western world is becoming less and less secure *because* of this policy. More and more Afghans have lost all hope that the foreign troops will bring any benefits. In June 2008, a survey conducted by the Senlis Council found that six out of ten Afghans wanted the troops to leave. The survey was called, 'Iraq: Angry Hearts and Angry Minds', and it found similar attitudes about the 'war on terror' in Somalia as well as both Iraq and Afghanistan. This poll reflects a major shift in attitude about foreign troops from years past, and it illustrates the failure of American policy to 'win hearts and minds'.

And it isn't accurate to say that Iraq is a 'bad war' but that Afghanistan is a 'good war' as some have argued. The US-led war has pushed Afghanistan from the frying pan into the fire. Once again, the United States is using my country for its own strategic interests. They would like to stay in Afghanistan for ever, so they can keep military bases and a presence in the region. Central Asia is a key strategic region, and the United States wants to have a permanent military presence there to counteract China's influence in particular. The superpower would prefer to keep the situation unstable so they can stay indefinitely and use and occupy our country as part of a big chess game.

Central Asia is also very rich in oil and natural gas resources. One of the reasons that NATO wants to stay in Afghanistan is to ensure the West has better access to these riches. For instance, it was recently announced that a pipeline is to be built from the Caspian Sea, through Turkmenistan, Afghanistan and then on to Pakistan and India. The West does not want these resources flowing through Iran or Russia.

Afghanistan has many other untapped natural resources.

There are, for example, massive deposits of copper and other metals in eastern Afghanistan. In northern Afghanistan, we have natural gas deposits and iron. Recently, China successfully bid billions of dollars for the right to exploit our copper deposits, which are estimated to be worth 88 billion dollars. With the current government we have in place – the most corrupt in the history of Afghanistan – these resources will be looted while the money will go to only a few people. If we could establish a real democratic government without foreign interference, these mining and energy resources could be developed for the benefit of all Afghans. If the system was not corrupt and we could control our own resources, then our country could stand on its own two feet. The tragic situation of Africa today shows what becomes of those whose wealth is looted by powerful countries. For example, Sierra Leone has the largest reserves of diamonds in the world, but is one of the poorest countries.

The people of many other countries have suffered too because of these wrong-headed policies, and the United States is not the only government justifying aggressive actions against other countries with the excuse of 'fighting terrorism'. The language of the 'war on terror' has been used by repressive governments all over the world as an excuse to justify their own aggressive policies and to crack down on civil liberties. China has used it to legitimise its actions in Tibet and its moves against minority communities in its remote provinces, and of course there was the destruction that Russia rained down on the people of Chechnya. In 2006, Israel bombarded Lebanon, killing over 1,000 civilians, and, needless to say, the more recent massacres of Palestinians were also carried out in the name of 'fighting terrorism'.

The 'war on terror' today serves as an excuse for war and intervention. As in the past when many democratic governments were overthrown and replaced with dictatorships in the name of 'fighting communism', so it is today with the language of 'fighting terrorism'. It was in the name of 'fighting communism' in Chile that the CIA overthrew the elected government of Salvador

Allende on 11 September 1973 and installed the fascist dictator Augusto Pinochet. Under directions from the White House, Allende was murdered and, in what is now remembered as 'the first 9/11' tens of thousands of innocent students and democratically minded people were rounded up, tortured and killed.

In the wonderful documentary film *War on Democracy*, John Pilger, the great film-maker and journalist, opened our eyes to many other such atrocities in countries around the world which have been directed or supported by the United States.

Other recent world events prove that 'exporting democracy' is just a hoax behind US foreign policy. In 2002, the United States backed a failed coup against the elected government of Venezuela; in 2004, France (along with the United States and Canada) overthrew the democratic government of Haiti. Meanwhile, some of the closest allies of the United States are anything but democratic. In the Middle East, for instance, two key pillars of US influence in the region are the dictatorship in Egypt and the fundamentalist monarchy in Saudi Arabia. When we analyse this record, it should not be too surprising to see the type of anti-democratic figures that the United States is propping up in positions of power in Afghanistan.

It is bad enough that war criminals wear the mask of democracy and sit in our Parliament where they are free to pass an amnesty bill to ensure that they will never be brought to justice for their past crimes. But what is perhaps more disgusting is that, due to the silence of almost all the Western governments, these criminals have won immunity at the international level, as well. They should all have been taken to The Hague to stand trial at the World Court long ago. In a just world, they would spend the rest of their days behind prison bars. In other countries, taking criminals to court is an *important issue*, but in Afghanistan it is a *key issue*. If these people can finally be brought to justice, everything will begin to get better. The people of our country feel very strongly about this, to the point where they not only want them to meet their fate in court, but they want even their bones to be condemned. The people want these men to pay for their crimes even after their deaths.

I know that in some other parts of the world, including within the United States, there are efforts underway to bring charges of war crimes against George W. Bush, Dick Cheney and other key members of that administration. Ultimately, I would hope that the American people are able to hold their own leaders accountable.

In Afghanistan and in the 'war on terror' the United States has put some small fish in jail, but only to deceive people. They must target the big fish, the sharks. And in my opinion the biggest sharks of all are bin Laden and Bush.

Although the US/NATO forces say they are staying in Afghanistan to hunt down both bin Laden and a resurgent Taliban, they might consider beginning their search in Kabul. As I have said, this new Afghan government is not only a photocopy of the Taliban, but some of the prominent figures from that former regime have been recycled and repackaged and now hold positions of power.

Arsala Rahmani, a former official in the Taliban government, was appointed to head a religious commission in the upper house of Parliament. Wakil Ahmad Muttawakil, a former Taliban Foreign Minister, was arrested after the 2001 war but today lives freely and is reportedly looked after by the Karzai government. Once, this Mullah Muttawakil, when questioned in a television interview about why the Kabul stadium was used as a venue of execution, responded by asking that the international community build the Taliban a better place to kill people. Today he is a pro-American media commentator. Mullah Raketi, known by the nickname 'Commander Rocket', is a former Taliban now sitting as an MP from Zabul Province. Mullah Abdul Salam Zaeef, Taliban ambassador to Pakistan and the Taliban spokesperson following 9/11, is also freely roaming in Kabul. All of this goes to show that the United States is not so much interested in destroying the Taliban, as in cultivating 'our Taliban', the 'good Taliban' or any other 'good' fundamentalists who will serve their interests.

In March 2008, the Afghan media reported, and it was acknowledged by the local authorities, that NATO helicopters dropped three large containers full of food, arms and ammunitions to a Taliban commander in Arghandab district of Zabul Province. NATO called it an error, but it has raised many questions among Afghan people about possible hidden contacts with the Taliban. People in Farah have seen similar contacts between US Provincial Reconstruction Teams and Taliban commanders.

In fact in October 2008, high-ranking US officials began to suggest that it was time to negotiate with the Taliban. 'If there are people who are willing to reconcile (with the government), then that would be a positive step in some of these areas that have actually been spiralling downward,' General David Petraeus, who is now responsible for American operations in Afghanistan, said at a forum hosted by the Heritage Foundation, a neoconservative think tank. 'The key there is making sure that all of that is done in complete co-ordination, with complete support of the Afghan government.'

Saudi King Abdullah had already hosted a meeting between representatives of the Taliban and the Afghan government, according to Reuters, 'fanning speculation about a potential dialogue'.

It is incredible to me that these criminals and misogynistic killers could be considered part of a 'settlement' of the 'Afghan conflict'. Although, frankly, it is impossible to tell the difference between those who call themselves Taliban and those who hold all the power in Kabul today. They dress up like democrats, only to hide their Taliban mentality. And because of them, after more than eight years of intervention by the United States and NATO, women's rights have not been brought to Afghanistan, and we have achieved neither democracy nor justice. It seems clear that the American government simply wants any gang in Afghanistan that will obey its directions accurately and act according to US policies, and these fundamentalist bands of the Northern Alliance have proved all along that they are ready to sacrifice Afghanistan's national interests for their lust for power and money.

Today, without funding from the United States and its allies, the whole machinery of the Karzai government could not function. For example, the Afghan National Army is not really a national army right now. It is not a volunteer army. Recruits are paid, and unfortunately most of the ANA forces are controlled by different North Alliance commanders and warlords.

With a situation like this, of course our country cannot stand on its own feet and will remain dependent on foreign troops. It's the policy of the American government to keep us in this situation. If things were to continue on this course, I believe the foreign powers could even lead us toward the break-up of our country along ethnic lines. They have inflamed ethnic and religious differences in Afghan society in recent years, creating conflicts that are not only a disaster for our country, but threaten to destabilise the whole region. Some politicians now talk about federalism as a solution to governing Afghanistan. In a war-ridden country like Afghanistan, federalism will result in nothing more than Balkanisation – with warlords ruling each fragment of the shattered state. And it is painful to some of us that outside Afghanistan, Latif Pedram has actually been given some human rights awards for his dangerous ideology. As Afghans, we must fight against the disintegration of our national unity. We do not want to lose our Afghanistan.

Meanwhile, it is reported that more than 15 billion dollars has poured into Afghanistan since 2001 through direct aid and fraudulent NGOs. Instead of helping us, these billions have bought us nothing but grief and corruption.

The Global Corruption Report 2008 released by Transparency International has ranked Afghanistan 172nd in a list of 180 countries. Afghanistan has been given 1.8 points out of a total score of 10, reflecting that corruption has gained ground during the post-Taliban era. According to the UN, 'A staggering $100–$250 million is paid in bribes every year in Afghanistan. This is equivalent to half the national development budget for 2006.'

According to an article in the *Sunday Telegraph*, 29 January 2007: 'Defence officials in the United States and Britain estimate that up to half of all aid in Afghanistan is failing to reach the right people. A Pentagon official said thousands of cars and trucks intended for use by the Afghan police had been sold instead.'

Endemic corruption combined with the vacuum of leadership in Kabul has made Afghanistan fertile ground for the trafficking of narcotics. The country is capable of growing food to feed its own people, but most of our best agricultural land is planted with poppy seed because it's a cash crop for export. The IMF says opium production has risen by more than 4,000 per cent since 2001. Of the total world supply of opium, the raw material for heroin, 93 per cent comes from Afghanistan today, with a total of 8,200 tons estimated to have been produced in 2008. The opium boom has made the traffickers and warlords rich, but life is even more miserable for ordinary Afghans. When the small farmers' poppy crops fail, they are often forced to pay back loans by selling their daughters – known as 'opium brides' – into marriage to the warlords and opium-lords. Women are treated like just another cash crop. And the proliferation of drugs in the country has also caused a growing problem of addiction among Afghans.

And now the Taliban – which once officially banned poppy production as un-Islamic – is benefiting from the opium trade. The money they make cultivating the once-forbidden crop – an estimated 500 million dollars in 2008 alone – is reportedly helping finance their terrorist activities and insurgent attacks. Once again, the United States government's cynical policies have come back to haunt it.

Opium is the Cold War's gift to Afghanistan. Along with supporting the mujahideen during the anti-Russian resistance, the CIA started to promote the cultivation of poppies in Afghanistan and Pakistan border areas. There are allegations that in 1981 President Reagan approved a covert programme to weaken Soviet soldiers fighting in Afghanistan by addicting them to illegal drugs. There have been reports of CIA agents directly involved in the heroin trade, and abundant evidence of CIA-supported mujahideen rebels trafficking in drugs, often receiving weapons and sending opium back along the same supply lines. Gulbuddin Hekmatyar, who is one of the biggest drug-lords in the region, is said to be using his old CIA-generated trafficking network to fund the current insurgency. In 2006, Pervez Musharraf, then prime minister of Pakistan, accused Hekmatyar of using his influence and drug money to protect the United States' arch enemy Osama bin Laden.

In recent years Afghanistan has also become the world's major producer of cannabis. The government has proudly announced that some provinces are poppy-free, but they never mention the fact that the producers just switched to a crop from which marijuana and hashish are derived. For instance, the former warlord Atta Mohammad, governor of Balkh Province, was praised for wiping out opium poppies and promised a reward of millions of dollars in development aid, but it was largely kept secret that Balkh is now producing a large quantity of another illegal crop: cannabis.

The NATO-led International Security Assistance Force has been mostly indifferent to the drugs issue in Afghanistan, arguing it is the duty of the Afghan government to tackle the problem. The British forces stationed in Helmand Province, which produces two-thirds of Afghanistan's opium crop, even broad-casted radio messages to farmers assuring them that they will not destroy their fields.

Michel Chossudovsky of the Canadian organisation Centre for Research on Globalisation, says that 'drug trafficking consti-tutes the third biggest global commodity in cash terms after oil and the arms trade ... The IMF estimated global money laundering to be between $590 billion and $1.5 trillion a year, representing 2–5 per cent of global GDP ... The Afghan trade ...

constitutes a large share of the worldwide annual turnover of narcotics, which was estimated by the United Nations to be in the order of $400–500 billion.' But the latest figures suggest that Afghan farmers barely earn 1 billion dollars each year from poppy production. According to Chossudovsky, 'The proceeds of this lucrative multibillion dollar contraband are deposited in Western banks. Almost the totality of revenues accrue to corporate interests and criminal syndicates outside Afghanistan.'

Hamid Karzai's administration is filled with warlords who are implicated in the drugs trade. During her confirmation hearing, the new US Secretary of State, Hillary Clinton, called Afghanistan a 'narco-state' with a government 'plagued by limited capacity and widespread corruption'.

As if this was not bad enough, in January 2007 Karzai appointed Izzatullah Wasifi as Afghanistan's anti-corruption chief. The problem with the president's pick? Wasifi is a convicted drug trafficker who spent almost four years in a Nevada state prison after being arrested for trying to sell heroin to an undercover police officer. But then he was an old friend of the Karzai family. He had also formerly been the governor of Farah and was removed after the people protested against him. As we Afghans say, 'Karzai assigned a rabbit to take care of the carrot!' When an ex-drug-runner is in charge of the country's anti-corruption efforts, you can see that it is no exaggeration when I say that today Afghanistan has the most corrupt government in the world.

The people of Afghanistan can see very clearly that the warlords are supported and protected by the United States and other foreign troops. They could not continue their fascist agenda for even one day without the backing of the United States and NATO.

As I have repeated in speeches around the world, today the Afghan people are tragically sandwiched between two enemies – the anti-American terrorists such as the Taliban, and the pro-American terrorists that came back to power with the Northern Alliance. This was not an inevitable outcome. Former US Defense

Secretary Donald Rumsfeld, who is so proud of what he accomplished in Afghanistan, made the decision to follow the 'warlord strategy' of paying and arming extremists to control regions of the country in alliance with the United States.

Even Senator Joseph Biden, now US vice president, foresaw the foolishness of this course. Biden is quoted in Ahmed Rashid's book *Descent into Chaos*: 'America has replaced the Taliban with the warlords. Warlords are still on the U.S. payroll but that hasn't brought a cessation of violence. Not only is the U.S. failing to rein in the warlords, we are actually making them the centerpiece of our strategy.'

The windfall profits that these warlords have reaped from drug trafficking, bribery, theft and direct payoffs from the US government are being invested in huge private armies. These warlord militias are thinly disguised as 'private security contractors'. Their commanders are often former combatants who should be disarmed. By October 2008, up to 20,000 Afghans had reportedly applied for permits to carry weapons for these 'security companies'. The warlords use these private troops to intimidate their enemies and to terrorise ordinary Afghans.

According to *Pajhwok Afghan News*, in his testimony before a parliamentary commission, crime investigations chief General Alishah Paktiawal said both foreign mercenaries and local employees of the security agencies have been involved in criminal activity. He said the companies possessed 11,000 different arms and had 700 offices and branches in the central capital. 'Most of the companies don't allow us to monitor their working.'

Various of the Northern Alliance commanders run some of these security companies. Their guards are accused of robberies and other crimes but no action has been taken against them. They are so powerful that one group attacked and beat the Attorney General, Jabar Sabet, but no one could arrest and punish them for it.

In the current Afghan regime, the Northern Alliance figures have joined hands with former Russian puppets such as former Interior Minister Sayed Mohammad Gulbazoy, monarchists such as Mustafa Zahir the grandson of Zahir Shah, and some so-called intellectuals who have spent most of their lives abroad and even hold second nationalities. They live in luxury while the rest of the country languishes in poverty.

The Shirpur neighbourhood of Kabul has become a symbol of the corruption and power of these 'untouchable' warlords and government officials. Shirpur was army land until 2003 when it was parcelled out to ex-ministers, former militia commanders, ministers – all but four cabinet ministers were sold plots at nominal prices – and high-ranking government officials. In a drive headed by Kabul's then police chief, Basir Salangi, the houses of poor people were bulldozed so that the elites could build mansions. Even the UN tried to intervene to prevent this action, but it was fruitless.

According to the *Chicago Tribune* of 16 March 2008:

> The homes in the fancy Shirpur neighborhood are a child's fantasy of mirrored columns, rainbow-colored tiles, green glass, imposing arches and high gates. They also are evidence of what has gone wrong with Afghanistan, almost seven years after the Taliban was chased from power into the mountains. Instead of calling the fancy neighborhood in Kabul 'Shirpur,' which means 'child of a lion,' Afghans now call it 'Shirchoor,' which means 'looted by lions.' English speakers describe the architecture style as 'narco-tecture.'

But Shirpur is not the only piece of land taken by the warlords. Land-grabbing has become a big problem and another sign of corruption in Afghanistan. The Afghan Urban Development Minister says land is being appropriated illegally by powerful individuals at a rate of two square kilometres (0.8 square miles) a day. He called this syndicate a 'land-mafia'.

As I write these words in early 2009, Barack Obama has just taken office as president. It is possible that he will take a hard look at the corruption, bloodshed and instability that US policy has created in Afghanistan and change its direction. But the early signs are worrisome.

Judging from what Obama said during his campaign and in the months after his election, it could well be that people in Afghanistan will soon say that Obama is even worse than Bush. He and his foreign policy advisers do not appear to have learned from the past seven years – the course they are pursuing will only push the region into a wider war and more destruction.

During Obama's campaign visit to Berlin, CNN's Candy Crowley asked whether he believed the United States needed to apologise for anything over the past seven and a half years in terms of foreign policy. Obama responded, 'No, I don't believe in the US apologising. As I said I think the war in Iraq was a mistake ...'

Obama's response seemed to echo the answer of Zbigniew Brzezinski, President Jimmy Carter's National Security Adviser, the man behind the policies that helped push Afghanistan to its current state of devastation. Some years ago, when Brzezinski was asked if he regretted having supported Islamic fundamentalism, having given arms and advice to future terrorists as part of US proxy efforts against the Soviets in Afghanistan, he said: 'What is most important to the history of the world? The Taliban or the collapse of the Soviet empire? Some stirred-up Moslems or the liberation of Central Europe and the end of the Cold War?'

For successive US governments, their own military, regional, economic and strategic interests have been considered before everything else, and they have been ready to sacrifice millions of Afghans to meet these interests. Their nice words about 'human rights', 'justice', 'freedom', 'liberation', 'democracy', and so on are nothing more than lies. They put no value on the lives of Afghan people. And in this Obama appears no different from the previous rulers of his country.

Rather than talking about pulling troops out, the new Obama administration is talking about adding as many as 30,000 more troops in 2009. That will bring the total number of foreign troops to about 70,000, not including the so-called private contractors in Afghanistan. The Soviet Union had far more troops than this in Afghanistan in the 1980s, and perhaps NATO leaders should heed the words of some of their Russian predecessors.

Colonel General Boris Gromov, who commanded the Soviet forces when they withdrew in 1989, has said, 'I believed and believe that the war was a huge and in many respects irreparable political mistake of the leadership of the Soviet Union at the time.' Of course it was not just a mistake, but also a crime that created millions of refugees and martyrs in our country. The United States is not the only superpower that prefers not to apologise.

Either Obama does not want to acknowledge or he is not aware of the main problem in Afghanistan and thus he will continue the wrong policies of past administrations. He did not even try to change the Defense Secretary Robert Gates, who has been behind the failed US war in Afghanistan and Iraq. If Obama wants to do anything positive in Afghanistan or if he has genuine concern for the plight of the Afghan people, he must first criticise strongly the past mistakes of the US government. He must criticise the fact that the United States helped to turn Afghanistan into a safe haven for fundamentalist terrorists, and now helps prop up a corrupt regime and a powerful drug-mafia.

If I ever do have the chance to meet President Obama, I will try to convey to him these points and tell him very clearly that American governments have betrayed the Afghan people enough. I would ask that he please stop this pattern, and to put an end to the ongoing crimes against my sorrowful people.

Day by day the Afghan people become more frustrated by the foreign troops and by the 'warlord strategy' of the United States. Unfortunately, in the weeks after his inauguration, there was still no evidence that Obama understands the source of the problem in Afghanistan. One of his first official acts was to authorise an air strike in the tribal region of Pakistan. Bombing raids across the border in Pakistan will only further inflame the people against the US, and will do nothing to change the situation in Afghanistan.

I have to say I did not pay much attention to the race leading up to the most recent US election. Both candidates offered only more of the same in foreign policy, especially regarding Afghanistan. If we look at the historical record, the policies of US governments have been very consistent for decades. War-making has been the policy of every president. Backing Israel and its oppression of the Palestinians is the policy of every president. Obama even went so far as to say during his campaign: 'Israel's security is sacrosanct. It is non-negotiable ... any agreement with the Palestinian people must preserve Israel's identity as a Jewish state, with secure, recognised and defensible borders. Jerusalem will remain the capital of Israel, and it must remain undivided ... let there be no doubt: I will always keep the threat of military action on the table to defend our security and our ally Israel.'

Intervening against countries where governments take action against American corporate interests is the policy of every president. It is after all militarism – imperialism – that has given the United States a dominant position in the world, and without war their empire will have no future. The foreign policy of the United States, in reality, is already made, and the job of the president is simply to implement it. I believe only the people in the United States and other countries, once they understand their responsibility, can change this situation. In my heart I really believe that ordinary people can change this bleak reality.

Please understand that this is how the new president of the United States looks from where the Afghan people are sitting. I know that his election has great symbolic value in terms of the struggle of African-Americans for equal rights, and this struggle is one that I admire and respect. But what is important for the world is not whether the president is black or white, but rather his ideas and his actions. You cannot eat symbolism, and for us Obama will only become a symbol of an unjust policy of war and domination if he continues down the path set out.

The new leadership of the United States should learn from

the failure of past policies. Even many officials within the military and intelligence communities of both the US and UK are starting to admit that the war in Afghanistan is going very badly. The UK's Brigadier Mark Carleton-Smith, Britain's senior military commander in Afghanistan, made international headlines when he admitted that the war cannot be won, and that the public should not expect a clear 'military victory'. In early 2008, US National Intelligence Director Michael McConnell told the Senate Armed Services Committee that 70 per cent of Afghanistan was lawless. The Afghan government still has control of only 30 per cent of the country, and where the Taliban and local warlords hold power there is no rule of law.

It seems the terrible results of the cycle of violence unleashed by the war and occupation of Afghanistan are now becoming so obvious that even the Western media have begun to report on the situation. In 2007, a *New York Times* feature wondered 'How a "Good War" in Afghanistan Went Bad'. Since Obama was elected president, the same paper has run front page stories about the rampant corruption in Afghanistan. And only days after Obama took office, a front page headline read: 'Obama's War: Fearing Another Quagmire in Afghanistan'. There was talk that the Obama administration may look for ways to press Mr Karzai to crack down on corruption and drug trafficking. It may even finally withdraw US support for Karzai himself.

There were presidential elections scheduled for 2009, and as the date approached, Karzai began to criticise publicly Western strategies in Afghanistan and to accuse them of failing to fulfil their promises to the Afghan people. But everyone was saying this change in tone was just part of Karzai's election campaign and not genuine concern for Afghanistan's miserable people. Even some people like Ali Ahmad Jalali, Karzai's former Interior Minister, and Ashraf Ghani Ahmadzai, former Finance Minister, who had key roles in creating Karzai's corrupt administration, were positioning themselves as critics of his regime. They tried to convince the Afghan people that they were patriots so that they could stand in the next presidential election. But many Afghans simply laughed at them and said that they would probably just be the next pawns in America's chess game in Afghanistan.

Over the last thirty years, we have lost almost everything, and I think in many ways that the only positive thing we have gained is our people's political consciousness. Today we live under the shadow of the gun, and with the most corrupt and unpopular government in the world. The struggle to build a genuine democracy in Afghanistan is one that will take many decades.

I believe that it is unlikely that I will live to see that final outcome, but I trust that there are many among our young people who will take up the fight. It will be up to the courageous and valiant youth of Afghanistan to complete what we have only just begun. It is a struggle of generations, but I share the optimism that Martin Luther King Jr. often expressed: 'The arc of history is long, but it bends toward justice.'

From my travels in the United States and beyond, I know that there are many of you who are determined to change Obama's mind and to work for peace. The young people I have met give me great hope that future generations can enjoy a world where the 'war on terror' will be only a distant memory, or a cautionary tale told in history textbooks.

If the current policy in Afghanistan is failing, what alternative course is there? Despite every tragedy that has befallen our country in recent decades, I believe that, given the opportunity, the Afghan people are capable of charting a path towards peace and independence.

CHAPTER 14

THE LONG ROAD
AHEAD FOR
AFGHANISTAN

O NE IMPORTANT THING I have learned from my travels is that there are countless people of all nationalities who want to help Afghanistan, kind-hearted women and men who will act once they know the truth. I hope that reading about Afghanistan's plight has motivated you to want to extend a much needed helping hand to our people.

It is my hope, then, that in the preceding chapters I have helped expose some of the common lies and myths about Afghanistan. There are also a number of policy changes that I feel are urgently needed. So I will spell out some of the things that the outside world can do to actually help Afghanistan. Foreign governments involved in our country must be pressured by their people to adopt some of these measures if they are to act as true friends of the Afghan people.

END THE WAR

The very first thing that the international community must do is to reject the United States-led war. The citizens of Australia, Germany, Italy, France, the Netherlands, Canada and all the other countries with troops on the ground have an important role to play. Right now, it must be said, their soldiers are seen by Afghans as no different from American troops – as an occupying force, not as liberators or peace-makers of any kind. These countries need to find the courage to act independently of the current policies of the government of the United States. It is not in any country's interest to blindly follow in the steps of the US. And, furthermore, by changing their direction in Afghanistan smaller nations can send a big message to the superpower.

This means strongly condemning the tactics of night-raids, torture and aerial bombardment that only lead to an escalation of violence all around. This includes the new US government policy to expand the war with air strikes in Pakistan. I have outlined the impact of these bombings in Afghanistan, and taking the war across the border will only further destabilise Pakistan, leading to the loss of more innocent lives. A couple of years ago, Canadian Major General Andrew Leslie was quoted as saying, 'Every time you kill an angry young man overseas, you're creating fifteen more who will come after you.' Even by the maths of the military leaders, then, the policy of frequent air strikes is self-destructive and counter-productive.

The war in Afghanistan has fostered terrorism, when the stated goal was to fight against it. The biggest beneficiaries of the conflict have been the extremist groups who take advantage of the legitimate grievances against NATO. Rather than destroying these fundamentalist forces, the bombing and occupation of the country has added fuel to their fire and swollen their ranks. Just as it was during the 1980s, the occupation of Afghanistan has also served as a rallying point for so-called foreign fighters, who have flocked to our country again in recent years. According to the British journalist Robert Fisk, '... Fighters are now joining the Taliban's ranks from Kashmir, Uzbekistan, Chechnya and even Turkey. More than 300 Turkish fighters are now believed to be in Afghanistan, many of them holding European passports.' And some Afghans, grief-stricken after losing a relative in an air strike, are joining the Taliban because they see it as a way to carry out revenge.

Now that the United States is less intent on pursuing its 'war on terror' in Iraq, it has turned its attention to Afghanistan. But how can you fight 'terror'? Who is terror? It's not a person or a country, it's an emotion. And terrorism isn't a person or a country, either. It's a tactic. How can you wage war against a tactic?

In this hoax of a 'war on terror', which groups are labelled 'terrorist' depends on how useful they are to the goals of the United States. The US calls the Taliban terrorists, but not the warlords who murder and rape innocents to impose their will on the people. And are not the night raids that US Special Forces carry out in Afghan villages acts of terror? These violent home invasions are supposed to round up al-Qaeda and Taliban sympathisers, but the soldiers often end up killing innocent civilians. Again, the result is a terrorised and angry population with an urge to seek vengeance. Education is a much more effective weapon for defeating terrorism and fundamentalism, in all its forms, than an endless war.

President Obama would be wise to look into an exit strategy for Afghanistan, rather than following a policy of escalation that will only create more terrorists and more hatred of the United States, while bringing only more misery and devastation to my country.

SEND REAL HUMANITARIAN AID

The Americans alone spend 100 million dollars a day in Afghanistan for the war, while total international aid for reconstruction comes to only 7 million dollars a day, the vast majority of which falls into corrupt hands, never reaching those who need it. Afghanistan needs real humanitarian aid and help with reconstruction. The Congressional Budget Office says that the United States will spend 2.4 trillion dollars over the next ten years on the 'war on terror'. If they instead spent this money properly and honestly, not only could Iraq and Afghanistan be made into heaven on earth but, also, world poverty could be eliminated. As it stands, huge sums of taxpayers' money are being poured into a counter-productive war, while urgently needed social spending at home is neglected. I have seen the poor and the homeless on the streets of wealthy Western cities. The homeless are humans too – I do not understand how their governments can ignore their suffering. The money needed to alleviate their pain never reaches them, just like the money that has poured into Afghanistan has never reached the poor who so desperately need it.

In June 2008, foreign donor countries held a summit in Paris to discuss aid to Afghanistan. Unfortunately, they again failed to take seriously pleas like this one from Brad Adams, Asia director at Human Rights Watch:

> The Paris conference will take place at a time when the Afghan government is increasingly unpopular because of abuses, corruption and lack of security. If the donors just offer more of the same and ignore the need for systemic reform, including a commitment to take on warlords and address impunity, then the situation in Afghanistan is likely to deteriorate.

The Afghan government presented a 'poverty reduction plan' to this gathering – for the drafting of which they received at least 15 million dollars of donor funds – but even the World Bank called it a 'very poor quality draft'. Alluding to the corruption which is rife in Kabul, one Western observer called this 'the world's most expensive poverty reduction plan'. Another 21 billion dollars was pledged at this gathering in Paris, but many reports have documented either the shortfall of funds or their misallocation.

As I have written, too often corrupt Western NGOs have become the problem instead of the solution. The misuse of aid money in Afghanistan is truly criminal, because of the urgent needs that continue to go unmet. After thirty years of war, our country is in desperate need of infrastructure investment, for instance. The only 'reconstruction' projects that have taken place are some highways – and those are not even up to standard. Meanwhile, investment in power generation and agriculture has been woefully inadequate, with more dams needed and irrigation projects terribly underfunded. Building up Afghanistan's infrastructure is not only key to our progress as a modern nation, but it will also generate jobs for millions of unemployed Afghans, many of whom have to leave the country to find work. Right now Afghanistan is still an agricultural economy, but the nearly complete neglect of this sector has left millions with the 'choice' of growing poppies or facing starvation.

There must a renewed effort to ensure that aid money to Afghanistan does not end up in the pockets of those shipping the heroin that is sold on the streets of London, New York and Tokyo. Everyone in the West should think about the fact that the heroin that is killing people on the streets of their cities originates in our war-torn land.

Afghanistan needs intervention that will save lives, not intervention that ends lives or destroys people's means to eke out a livelihood. There are many great, small projects run by democratically minded Afghans, but the money from Western governments almost never reaches them.

A reliable mechanism to monitor and report on the distribution of all aid money is desperately needed, and there must be prosecution when misappropriation and embezzlement of funds is discovered.

PUT AN END TO THE RULE OF THE WARLORDS

Governments must demand and help implement real disarmament in Afghanistan. The United Nations' mandated disarmament programme, supposedly part of the ISAF mission, was never implemented. It was never even taken seriously. Today, warlords and drug-lords control huge swathes of Afghanistan, and there won't be any meaningful solution to our problems while that continues. Many warlords still control private armies and militias that are much better organised and more powerful than the Afghan National Army. This is the only reason the impunity in the regions they control is able to continue. My enemies have little true footing among the people of Afghanistan and this is their greatest weakness. The day they are disarmed, the people who have been victims of their brutal actions for decades will find justice.

The warlords and the Islamic fundamentalism they wield is like a cancer in the body of the Afghan nation, injected by neighbouring countries and foreign powers. This cancer needs to be cut out for Afghanistan to survive and prosper. As long as these warlords and thugs remain part of the government – while retaining the ability to terrorise with their private militias those who oppose them – there will be no solution to Afghanistan's crisis.

Instead of backing and shielding these warlords, and leaving some of them armed to the teeth, the international community should support a proper investigation into their conduct during the wars and, where relevant, their prosecution for war crimes. Then they can have their day in court before the people of Afghanistan, and they should also be targeted for investigation and trial by the International Criminal Court. This includes those criminals who are currently enjoying exile in other countries, including in the West – their immunity must end, as well.

WITHDRAW ALL FOREIGN TROOPS

Finally, and as soon as possible, all troops should begin to leave Afghanistan. By this, I mean the withdrawal of US and NATO troops and also the removal of the thousands of private soldiers – mercenaries – working in the country. On behalf of all the freedom-loving people of my country, I offer my condolences and share the pain of all those families who have lost their loved ones in our country. By raising our voices together – Afghans, Americans and all those living in countries with troops in Afghanistan – we can help prevent the loss of more innocent life. In my travels to the United States, I was moved and inspired by the peace activists who have raised the slogan 'Not in Our Name' in opposition to their government's destructive policies and warmongering.

Some people say that when these troops withdraw a civil war will break out. Often this prospect is raised by people who ignore the vicious conflict and humanitarian disaster that is already occurring in Afghanistan. The longer the foreign troops stay in Afghanistan doing what they are doing today, the worse the eventual civil war will be for the Afghan people. The terrible civil war that followed the Soviet withdrawal certainly could never justify, after the fact, the destruction and death caused by that decade-long occupation.

But the danger of civil war is true to a point, and so it is important that other measures be taken along with the withdrawal of the troops. In addition to the much-needed disar-mament of warlords and their militias, the international community must support and empower the democratically minded individuals and parties who are able to fight the influence of extremism and bring real democracy to our country. Only by disempowering the warlords and all fundamentalist groups can we really prevent the further Talibanisation of Afghanistan.

The United Nations must act to ensure that countries like China, Iran, India, Pakistan, Uzbekistan, Turkey, Russia and others cease their influence and practice of peddling arms and weapons to warlords. Both Russia and China, especially, are competing with the United States for control of the energy resources of the whole region. All of these countries are meddling in Afghanistan, with Pakistan and Iran playing a particularly nefarious role with their backing of fundamentalist forces. If this type of intervention were curtailed, the chance of a civil war would be minimised.

However, we know the US administration does not want to see the policies that I have described implemented. The entire situation would be improved if Afghans were finally able to decide about their own problems. We are right now under the 'protection' of armed forces from forty-three countries, yet we are still living with war, brutality, poverty and crime.

If the United States and its NATO allies leave, the warlords will lose power because they have no base among our people. At least with withdrawal of foreign troops, we would have our independence. Today, we neither have freedom nor independence, justice or security. All Afghans must work for national unity, and not allow extremists from all our diverse ethnic groups to whip up sectarian divisions. And we must resist any efforts to balkanise and split up our country.

I feel confident that if foreign countries stop meddling in Afghanistan and if we are left free from occupation, then a strong progressive and democratic force will emerge. I am hopeful that in other parts of the world today, such as Latin America, there are now governments and movements that are bringing progressive change and acting independently of the interests of the United States government.

We see this change happening in a democratic way in countries such as Bolivia, Ecuador and Venezuela. These countries are increasingly working together, and working to help and empower the poorest people in their societies. More and more, the countries of Latin America do not follow the lead of the United States only. They are trading more with each other and rescuing their cultures and economies from foreign domination. And they are teaching their people to read and write – without basic literacy it is very difficult for democracy to have a chance. Progressive Afghans are very interested in learning from the experiences of other peoples like this who are struggling for justice and for real independence.

I should add that I think the leaders of these countries should be careful with some of the allies they have made. When Hugo Chávez, the president of Venezuela, met with Mahmoud Ahmedinejad, his counterpart from Iran, he called him a 'revolutionary' and embraced him. I think this ranks as one of Chávez's biggest mistakes, and one that is sometimes also made by anti-war groups in the West who see Iran's reactionary regime as 'anti-imperialist'. Chávez's action sends a bad message to the women and people of Iran, who are struggling for their rights against this repressive, anti-women government. Iran's fundamentalist government has played a very negative role in Afghanistan, backing warlords like Ismail Khan, Khalili, Mohaqiq and others, while working to destabilise the country by stoking religious and ethnic strife.

In the past few years, every effort has been made to block the emergence of progressive political forces in my country. Funds were blocked, and no effort was spared to marginalise these groups. No political party or organisation that is critical of the government and the warlords is able to operate openly in Afghanistan. The suppression of my voice and my expulsion from Parliament is but one symptom of this larger disease.

WHAT CAN YOU DO?

I hope, now that you have learned something of the troubles that plague Afghanistan, you are thinking about a question I have been asked many times by audience members around the world: What can I do, *personally*, as a concerned citizen, to help make this situation better?

We Afghans need your help and support to break the fetters of slavery in our land. First and most importantly, *stay informed about the reality of Afghanistan today*.

It is said that in time of war the first casualty is truth. Governments can only continue unjust policies as long as their people remain deaf and blind, unaware of the truth. You can help to break the propaganda of silence that is carried out today by the mainstream media. Tune out Fox News and tune into honest media sources. An excellent source of aggregated news reports about the real conditions in Afghanistan is the RAWA website (http://www.rawa.org/temp/runews/). Look for other good sources of news about the war online. And if your own local and national newspapers are not providing enough in-depth coverage of the war and the reality in Afghanistan, write letters to the editor and suggest articles for them to run. If you are already well informed about Afghanistan, share what you know with friends and family by whatever means you have – email, Facebook, discussion forums or blogs.

Get involved with groups that are working honestly to support women and men in Afghanistan, and give financial support. When there is no corruption and you can donate to a real grassroots project, a little money goes a long way. Progressive-minded Afghans working on humanitarian projects are desperately short of funds. It's not just our orphanage in Farah City that has had to close down in recent years. Seek out and support groups that are raising money for organisations in Afghanistan which are working for people's needs. Your donations will be warmly welcomed, by destitute women and children across Afghanistan.

All over Afghanistan, we are in desperate need of schools and money for training teachers and for salaries. I know that young people abroad, who benefit from more access to education, are anxious to help change this situation. Schools could take on fundraising projects, and in the process their students could learn about the reality of Afghanistan.

I must also say that some Afghans living in the West are

wealthy and live extremely comfortable lives. They should try to live more modestly and contribute to the process of rebuilding Afghanistan. There are so many projects and organisations that desperately need their financial support.

Monitor, criticise and work to improve your own government's foreign policy. Challenge your own political leaders. Write letters and emails to your elected representatives. Make appointments with them and explain your concerns. You can have a much more powerful impact if you meet and speak with politicians directly. Explain that real aid goes a lot further than bombs to promote peace and development around the world. If your country is a member of NATO and has troops in Afghanistan, tell your politicians that they must stop blindly following the United States. If they do not listen, you can join peace groups that are trying to change these wrong-headed policies.

Please understand that for us in Afghanistan, seeing that people all over the world are willing to stand publicly in solidarity with us in our hour of need has great moral value. Demonstrations for peace in the West in fact undermine the message of the fundamentalists that the people of North America and Europe are the enemy of the people in Muslim countries. The demonstrations against the Iraq War – on 15 February 2003, when millions of people in dozens of countries joined the largest protests in human history – did not stop the war from happening but they showed people in Arab and Muslim countries that there were a great many peace-loving people who opposed Bush's war. This outpouring for peace helped to remind our people of the distinction between the people and the governments of the West. Never underestimate the importance of the message your actions can send both to your own government and to the people of Afghanistan. Peace movements pose a threat to the war-makers, fundamentalists and terrorists. In Afghanistan, demonstrating in public is very risky, but people still go out into the streets to make their voices heard. If you live in a country where there are less severe obstacles to public protest, it is important that you use your democratic right to organise meetings, rallies and demonstrations. All of our human rights have been won through struggle, and all of them can be lost through neglect.

Wherever you are, *take part in the political process and organise for social justice*. You will always face obstacles and challenges when you work to make democracy real and expose corruption and injustice. But nothing worth fighting for is easy. A great way to help the people of Afghanistan is to fight to have a fair-minded, progressive government in your own country.

Expressing these hopes I have shared with you for the future of Afghanistan has put my life in danger and has got me kicked out of Parliament. And continuing to express these ideals may well get me killed. But I remain confident about the future.

With your help and participation, I know the suffering of the Afghan people can end. My dream is to see an Afghanistan where women are considered human beings, and where one day a woman could even take the reins of power; where there are no more warlords, Taliban or terrorists of any kind; and where we are free to decide our own future.

Above all, my dream is the establishment of a powerful, progressive movement within Afghanistan that would challenge the fundamentalists, fight for equality and freedom, and force this latest foreign occupation of our country to be replaced by genuine democracy.

There is a long road ahead for Afghanistan but, with your help, I know that our people are capable of walking it, forging a path towards a future of peace, prosperity and equality. Your support is essential. In the words of Albert Pike, 'What we have done for ourselves alone dies with us; what we have done for others and the world remains and is immortal.'

CONCLUSION

A River is Made Drop by Drop

I WAS DRIVING THROUGH KABUL not long ago when a friend and I decided to stop for some ice cream. It has always been my favourite, ever since we lived as refugees in Iran and my father used to slip me a little money to get myself a treat.

I was travelling without my bodyguards and, as usual, I was wearing the burqa so that I would not be recognised while I was out and about. Once we had ordered and sat down, I thought it would be safe for me to uncover myself for a few minutes while I enjoyed my ice cream. I was recognised almost right away.

'You are Malalai Joya Jan, right?' said one of the other customers.

Normally I am encouraged when people greet me and express their support and sympathies. But it can be very dangerous. You never know who will make a phone call. So my friend and I had to eat up our ice cream very quickly and leave. It's the reality of my life that I can no longer go out in public just to enjoy a moment with a friend.

There are other painful realities to deal with, including long periods of time when I am unable to see my husband and my family. Regrettably, in recent years, it has been very difficult for me even to travel to my home province of Farah. So I have rarely been able to visit the people who elected me and who shared my hopes for our suffering country and who placed their trust in me. I continue to fight to return to Parliament to denounce the tyrants on their behalf. I still receive death threats and my supporters have uncovered and thwarted even more assassination plots.

But I would never want to take back any of the speeches I have made, nor any of the statements I have issued denouncing the corrupt and violent men and women who use and abuse their power to keep Afghanistan in their grip. I am truly honoured to have been vilified and threatened by the savage men who have condemned our country to such misery. I feel proud that even though I have no private army, no money and no world powers behind me, these brutal despots are afraid of me and scheme to eliminate me. But it is not really *me* these men fear – they fear the wrath of our people who know the crimes they have committed. They know they cannot evade justice indefinitely, and the Afghan people have already decided the verdict.

Each day I am more convinced that I had no choice but to speak the words I did at the Loya Jirga in 2003. When I began my life as an activist, I was motivated by a simple desire to serve the poor and suffering people I grew up with in the refugee camps of Pakistan, and to share the gift of education with other Afghan women and girls. I never thought I would become a politician, and I certainly never thought I would end up travelling through-out the world to spread my message. The awards and recognition I have received have only made me feel a greater sense of respon-sibility to speak out about the plight of the Afghan people.

I hope that my life story, above all, shows the importance of education, especially for girls. Among my best memories are the times when I was able to convince Afghan parents to let their girls attend school. Sometimes the children came to me to ask for my help, and then I worked to convince their parents to let them learn. There are still far too many Afghan girls unable to attend school – whether because of family attitudes, insecurity, their economic sit-uation or the insufficient supply of facilities and teachers.

I must make clear that only fate and history have made my name known. Among our people there are thousands of Malalais who could have stood in my place. I also know that there are women and girls all around the world who are willing and able to take a stand for their rights, no matter what the odds against them or the hardships they face.

The hundreds of Afghan women who set themselves ablaze are not only committing suicide to escape their misery – they are crying out for justice. These heart-rending cases of self-immolation are acts of defiance as well as despair, and these women are not just victims but symbols of resistance; they are the first stage of larger protests against injustice. What a better day it will be when such women are given an education and have the chance to develop a political consciousness. Only then will they be able to direct their anger away from themselves and toward the root causes of their suffering.

Every single day democracy-loving people inside Afghanistan take great risks. Self-organised protest rallies erupt in different parts of Afghanistan almost daily, either in response to the killings of civilians by US/NATO forces or against the corruption and crimes of the warlords and Taliban. These women and men inspire me to continue speaking out.

Today we Afghans remain trapped, between two enemies: the Taliban on one side and US/NATO forces and their warlord hirelings on the other. We are feeling the squeeze and it is costing us in blood and tears. But the situation is not hopeless. I believe in the power of the people, and I know that there are millions of women and men standing and waiting – eager to play their role in history. Afghans have lost all patience with the corruption and violence that surrounds them, and they are just one spark away from an uprising that will once more demonstrate their power and show their thirst for freedom and justice.

As far as the prospects for Afghanistan's future, which today look so bleak, I take hope from the words of Martin Luther King Jr., who said that no injustice could last for ever: 'I believe that unarmed truth and unconditional love will have the final word in reality. That is why right, temporarily defeated, is stronger than evil triumphant.'

The unjust and criminal occupation of Afghanistan and its puppet regime cannot last for ever.

The use, abuse and destabilisation of Afghanistan by great powers and neighbouring countries cannot last for ever.

The domination of our country by warlords, Taliban and their so-called intellectual lobbyists cannot last for ever.

The impunity of war criminals – whether sitting in the Parliament in Kabul or at the ranch in Texas – cannot last for ever.

The subjugation of women as second-class citizens cannot last for ever.

The unpunished rape, abduction, murder and mistreatment of women and girls cannot last for ever.

The government and NGO corruption and embezzlement, the drug-running profiteering, all of which deny Afghans basic services like health care and education, cannot last for ever.

The terrorising of honest journalists and the silencing of dissenting voices through violence and intimidation cannot last for ever.

The suppression of the democratic and progressive people and parties in Afghanistan cannot, and must not, last for ever.

With the help of peace-loving people around the world, I know that the Afghan women and men are ready to do their part and end this cycle of misery and build a better future. The 'war on terror' is a dead end for the people in the Middle East, in Central Asia and in the West. Only a great, united movement of people can put an end to this foolish policy. I hope President Obama in particular will be made to understand that more troops, more bombs and an expanded war will solve nothing. Might does not make right, and war does not make peace. In Afghanistan we know this lesson well.

Our fight for independence has gone on for centuries, and it will continue because it is a just and dignified struggle. As Afghans, we must strive to minimise sectarian divisions, and maintain national unity in the face of our common enemies. Our history teaches that if you betray our people and try to occupy our country by force of arms, you will meet our resistance and you will fail. This lesson was learned by the British Empire; it was learned by the Soviet Union, and today unfortunately it is being learned the hard way by the NATO countries.

It will be a long struggle. *A river is made drop by drop.* But if we can unite for justice and democracy, our people will be like a flood that no one can stop.

I am young and I value my life; I don't want to be killed. But I don't fear death; I fear remaining silent in the face of injustice. I fear becoming indifferent to the fate of my people, which is a path that too many Afghan intellectuals have followed. Some who used to speak out for the people's interests have given up their principles and chosen silence in exchange for money or high posts in the Karzai regime. But I have chosen to follow the glorious paths of Sarwar Joya, Abdul Rahman Mehmoodi, Ghulam Nabi Khan Charkhi, Meena, Abdul Khaliq, Nahid Sahid, Abdul Rahman Loudin, Mohammad Wali Khan Darwazi and hundreds of other such heroes in our history who stood by their people to the end and preferred to be killed rather than be silenced.

I say to those who would eliminate my voice: I am ready, whenever and wherever you may strike.

You can kill me, but you can never kill my spirit.

As I often say, there are many others to follow me. Afghans are more than just a handful of warlords, Taliban, drug-lords and lackeys. I have a country full of people who know what I know and believe what I believe: that we Afghans can govern ourselves without foreign interference. That democracy is possible here but can never be imposed at gunpoint. That the blood of millions of freedom-loving martyrs runs through our veins, and their memories live on in every corner of our country. That Afghan women have been at the forefront of our struggle throughout our proud history. Like Malalai of Maiwand, they inspire us to pick up the flag and carry on the struggle for justice and freedom. It is a battle we will never surrender.

Our enemies can cut down the flower, but nothing can stop the coming of the spring.

I have many hopes and dreams for my country and for my life. I want to spend happy times with my husband, my dear friends and my family – Father, Mother, my sisters and brothers, aunts and uncles, nieces and nephews. I want to attend their weddings, hold their children and honour them in their old age. I want to stand next to my people for ever. I want to live to see them strong and free.

But if I should die, and you choose to carry on my work, you are welcome to visit my grave. Pour some water on it and shout three times. I want to hear your voice.

INDEX